PROOF

HOW TO ANALYSE EVIDENCE IN PREPARATION FOR TRIAL

Thomson Reuters (Professional) Australia Limited
100 Harris Street Pyrmont NSW 2009
Tel: (02) 8587 7000 Fax: (02) 8587 7100
LTA.Service@thomsonreuters.com
www.thomsonreuters.com.au
For all customer inquiries please ring 1300 304 195
(for calls within Australia only)

INTERNATIONAL AGENTS & DISTRIBUTORS

NORTH AMERICA
Thomson Reuters
Eagan
United States of America

ASIA PACIFIC
Thomson Reuters
Sydney
Australia

LATIN AMERICA
Thomson Reuters
São Paulo
Brazil

EUROPE
Thomson Reuters
London
United Kingdom

PROOF

HOW TO ANALYSE EVIDENCE IN PREPARATION FOR TRIAL

Third edition

ANDREW PALMER

Barrister at Law
Associate Professor, Melbourne Law School

LAWBOOK CO. 2015

Published in Sydney by

Thomson Reuters (Professional) Australia Limited ABN 64 058 914 668
    100 Harris Street, Pyrmont, NSW

First edition................. 2003

Second edition...............2010

National Library of Australia
    Cataloguing-in-Publication entry

Palmer, Andrew, 1963–author.
    Proof : how to analyse evidence in preparation for trial /
    Andrew Palmer.

    3rd ed.

    978 0 455 233697 (pbk.)

    Includes bibliographical references and index.

    Evidence (Law)–Australia.

    347.9406

Project Editor: Sandra Bassam
Product Developer: Natasha Naude
Publisher: Robert Wilson

Typeset in 9.5 pt on 12 point ITC Legacy Sans, by
Midland Typesetters, Australia
Printed by Ligare Pty Ltd, Riverwood, NSW

This book has been printed on paper certified by
the Programme for the Endorsement of Forest
Certification (PEFC). PEFC is committed to
sustainable forest management through third party
forest certification of responsibly managed forests.
For more info: www.pefc.org

PEFC/21-31-17

For Carlos and Jerome

Preface

What does this book do?

This is a book about how to do things with evidence. It presents a method, or set of methods, for analysing and organising the factual information in a brief or file as part of a litigator's preparation for trial. In writing this book, now in its third edition, I have drawn inspiration from many sources, including the extensive literature on the analysis of evidence, my own experience as a practising barrister, the many things I have learnt from the barristers and solicitors with whom I have worked, and my teaching of various versions of the methods in the evidence and proof courses at Melbourne Law School.

It should be understood from the outset, however, that in describing this method, I am not seeking to argue that this is how lawyers *should* prepare for trial; nor am I claiming that this is how experienced and competent lawyers *do* prepare for trial. The only claims that are being made are that the methodology described in this book provides a systematic method of trial preparation; that it can be applied and adopted by any lawyer; and that it requires neither brilliance nor experience to do so. In essence, then, this text expounds a theory of how lawyers *might* prepare for trial. Like the theory of evidence marshalling propounded by Schum and Tillers (1991, p 696), this theory is neither normative nor descriptive, but falls into a third category:

> A theory that does not say how people ought to perform some task or how they actually do perform it, can say how people *might* perform it. This sounds like an heuristic theory; it sounds like a theory designed to facilitate the thinking involved in some form of behavior having an intellectual ingredient. Indeed, that is exactly the sort of theory we are developing – a theory. Our theory of evidence marshalling is simply an heuristic theory about how people might organize thought and evidence when performing discovery-related tasks.

Who is this book for?

This book is aimed at litigators – both barristers and solicitors, as well as non-lawyer litigators, such as police prosecutors – who are looking to improve or enhance their methods of preparing matters for trial. The methods in it are equally applicable whether you are appearing in a criminal or in a civil trial, or before an administrative tribunal, and whether you are acting for the prosecution, the accused, the plaintiff or the defendant. If you are an experienced litigator, content with your current methods of trial preparation, then this book probably has little to offer you. But if you have not yet developed an approach to preparation with which you are entirely happy, then it is hoped that this book will help you to do so.

The book is also aimed at a particular group of "inexperienced litigators", namely students of evidence and advocacy. At the University of Melbourne (where I teach), for example, the law of evidence has for many years now been taught in a proof in litigation context, where students are first taught to analyse evidence for the purposes of proving a case, before being introduced to issues of admissibility. Reflecting this shift, the subject is now called "Evidence and Proof", rather than just "Evidence". The reasons for the change are discussed in the "Note to Evidence teachers" at [10.10] in the Notes section at the end of the book.

In advocacy courses, students will usually be required to develop a theory of the case, but even the best advocacy texts often deal with case theory very briefly. As most texts emphasise, however, the development of a case theory is an essential component of effective advocacy. *Proof* is also therefore intended to provide a useful addition to advocacy courses, supplementing and complementing whatever other texts are currently used.

Finally, the book is aimed at scholars in, and teachers of, evidence and the law of evidence. As is explained in Chapter 1, the body of the text has been written in a style that tends to downplay the place this work has in the overall body of evidence scholarship. Nevertheless, the book does contain significant departures from previous work on the subject, and these departures are discussed in the Notes section at the end of the book.

Although I live, teach, practise and write in Australia (and Victoria, in particular), this text is not very jurisdiction-specific. Because its primary concern is not the *law of* evidence, but evidence per se, the methods it expounds are equally applicable in any jurisdiction where legal proceedings are adversarial in nature. The most jurisdiction-specific part of the book is Chapter 8, "Analysing for admissibility". Even this chapter, however, is written in fairly broad terms, being concerned more with the means of, for example, identifying hearsay, than with detailed analysis of the rule itself, or its exceptions; for that reason no tables of cases or statutes have been included.

Acknowledgments

The Notes and Bibliography sections at the end of the book contain detailed references to the sources for many of the insights, terminology, concepts and methods relied on in the body of the text. The most important of those sources are the works of Professors William Twining, Terence Anderson, David Schum, Peter Tillers, and John Henry Wigmore. For readers interested in more detail and depth, the works of these authors provide the best starting point.

The first edition of *Proof* was a long time in gestation, and I benefited enormously from the many conversations, discussions and interactions I had with, and comments I received from, the colleagues, friends and students acknowledged in the Preface to that edition. Since then I have continued to receive helpful feedback from students, colleagues and friends, and have continued to learn from the barristers and solicitors with whom I have been fortunate enough to work. As always, however, my greatest support and my most insightful interlocutor has been my wife Madeleine. Thank you Madeleine.

ANDREW PALMER

Melbourne
19 November 2014

Acknowledgments

Extracts from the material below have been reproduced in this book:

Austhink Software: http://austhink.com
- bCisive (used to prepare the charts appearing in Chapters 6, 7 and 8 and in the Appendix)

Canberra Times: www.canberratimes.com.au
- R Campbell, "Unravelling a Web of Hatred: The Case Against David Harold Eastman" (4 November 1995)

Incorported Council of Law and Reporting for England and Wales: www.lawreports.co.uk
- Weekly Law Reports (WLR)

Lawbook Co. (part of Thomson Reuters (Professional) Australia Limited): www.thomsonreuters.com.au
- Commonwealth Law Reports (CLR)

Penn State University Press (for Pennsylvania State University Press, University Park, Pennsylvania): www.psupress.org
- D Walton, "Appeal to Expert Opinion: Arguments from Authority" (1997)

John Wiley & Sons, New York: www.wiley.com
- Charles Sanders Pierce, quoted in D Schum, "Evidential Foundations of Probabilistic Reasoning" (1994)

Table of Contents

Part C: Final Preparations

List of Figures

Introduction

1

Aims

[1.10] It is often said that preparation is the key to successful advocacy. This is a book about preparation. Its aim is to describe a series of methods that can be used to organise and analyse evidence in order to ensure that we are as well prepared for trial as we possibly can be. Of course, being prepared is no guarantee of success. However, it does maximise our chances of success: a bad case that we have prepared thoroughly may still be a bad case, but it will be a better prepared and better presented bad case, and we will know what its weaknesses are. Moreover, in the event that we do not succeed, the fact that we have prepared properly should leave us with an easy conscience and, hopefully, a client content that we did all that we could to achieve the best possible outcome for them.

Litigation is a contest between adversaries. Sometimes that contest turns on questions of law. If we are involved in litigation of that type, then the methods contained in this book will be of little use. Most litigation, however, revolves around factual controversies, disputes about what happened. The methods for analysing and organising evidence contained in this book are designed to ensure that we are as well prepared as possible for such factual disputes. If there is an overriding aim to these methods, it is to provide us with a systematic means of answering the two questions that must always be asked during the preparation of any matter for trial:

1. What do we have to prove in order to succeed?
2. How are we going to prove that?

While the focus is on preparation for trial, application of the methods should be useful even if our matter ultimately settles: in any case, it is a common experience that the less well prepared we are for trial, the more likely the case is to run.

Although this text is written from the standpoint of preparation for trial, the approach within it can also be applied to the analysis of decided cases, as, for example, when we want to criticise or defend (whether in an appellate court or in an academic journal) the way in which a trial court dealt with evidence.

Instead of constructing a case to present to a court, we can use the methods described in the book to:

- explain the way in which the court said that it reasoned about the evidence;
- demonstrate that the court must have, or should have, reasoned about the evidence in a particular way; or
- show that the court would not, if it had followed the correct approach, have reached the conclusions that it did.

Overview of the method

[1.20] The methods set out in the book can be summarised as follows:

- *Part A: First Steps*
  Part A contains three chapters dealing with some early-stage methods of analysis:
  — *Chapter 2: Preliminaries.* This is where we define our objectives, organise our paperwork, and work out what we need to do.
  — *Chapter 3: Chronologies.* We put all the information in chronological order. Creating a chronological "inventory" of information ensures that we do not overlook anything, and it is also an essential platform for investigation, and for the development of a theory of the case.
  — *Chapter 4: Investigation.* This chapter examines investigative thinking, and several ways of marshalling information in order to facilitate it.

- *Part B: Theory and Proof*
  Part B contains the core of the book: three chapters dealing with the development of a theory of a case, and methods for proving it.
  — *Chapter 5: Developing a case theory.* Chapter 5 examines two aspects of the theory of the case: the legal case and the factual theory. It explores the attributes of a good factual theory, and explains how to go about matching the factual theory to the legal case.
  — *Chapter 6: Proving the theory.* In this chapter we match the evidence to the factual theory by identifying the arguments we will use in our closing address to persuade the court to accept our case, and thereby create a blueprint for the conduct of the trial. We create a "case map" of these arguments in one of three forms: prose, a chart or an outline.
  — *Chapter 7: Arguing from and about evidence.* This chapter explains how to construct detailed arguments from and about evidence, including arguments

about: witnesses and other sources of evidence, relevance, inferences, negative and missing evidence, and probative value and the standard of proof.

- *Part C: Final Preparations*
  - *Chapter 8: Analysing for admissibility.* This chapter contains a general approach to questions of admissibility. It also discusses three rules that prohibit particular uses of evidence.
  - *Chapter 9: Pulling it all together for trial.* In this chapter we pull together the threads of the analysis in a form that can be used at trial, plan the examination of witnesses, and compile the "Trial Book".

The order in which the chapters are presented loosely corresponds to the order in which the methods might be applied during the life of a litigation matter, although of course trial preparation seldom proceeds in a completely linear fashion; a chronology, for example, may have to be repeatedly updated, and the theory of the case is likely to constantly evolve and be refined until the point at which the closing address is actually delivered.

In any event, the methods do not have to be applied in their totality, or in a particular sequence, in order to be useful. You can, in other words, either treat the various methods suggested in the book as a single, integrated methodology to be applied in total; or you can treat them as a series of ideas and suggestions that you apply according to the particular needs of the litigation in which you are involved, the time and resources available to you and your client, and your personal preferences. In any case, the test you should apply in determining which methods to use is the same test that you would apply in deciding whether or not to use a particular tool to assist you to complete a task: you would use the tool if it helped you in the task, and you would use something else if it did not.

References

[1.30] In order to make the text accessible and user-friendly, I have tried, as much as possible, to separate out the discussion of method from the discussion of the literature on which the method builds, and to which it relates and responds. That discussion has been placed in a separate Notes section at the end of the book. Together with the Bibliography at the end of the book, the Notes are intended to enable interested readers to trace the intellectual history of the ideas on which the text is based, and to find sources and further reading material.

Examples of the application of the methods

[1.40] The methods described in this text are intended to be applied to the masses of complex evidence found in real cases and in real briefs of evidence; but it is not practicable to reproduce a complete brief of evidence within the pages of this book. For that reason, the sample analysis contained in the Appendix is based on descriptions of the evidence in a decided case. The analysis is not complete – it does not include a chronology, for example – nor does it map the details of all of the evidence, inferences and arguments to which it refers. More complete and detailed analyses, based on briefs of evidence in real cases, can be accessed by clicking on the "**sample analyses**" link at the following website:

www.evidence.com.au

The sample analyses reproduced there take the form of "Advices on Evidence", and were prepared by graduate and undergraduate students at Melbourne Law School for their assessment in the subjects Evidence and Proof and Proof in Litigation. Several analyses are provided for each brief of evidence, and the differences between them confirm the obvious point that there is no such thing as a single right way of analysing and constructing arguments from a particular body of evidence.

First Steps

Part

A

Preliminaries

2

This chapter outlines some steps that we need to take before we can begin our analysis of the file or brief.

Define our objectives

[2.10] Litigation is hazardous, and before embarking on it we must be clear about what our objectives are. As lawyers, our objectives are defined by our clients. At a very early stage in the proceedings, then, we must identify what our client wants to achieve as an outcome of the prospective litigation. Clients are not always able to articulate and prioritise their objectives. It is part of our job as lawyers to help them to do this. Part of this involves making sure that they are fully informed about the costs and perils of litigation; and that they have a realistic idea of what is possible to achieve through litigation and what is not possible to achieve. We must also remember that not all of a client's objectives will be legal, in the sense

7

of there being remedies that a court can order: there may be human or business relationships involved, and all sorts of emotions being played out. With these points in mind we can get our client to think about the following questions:

- What is the best possible outcome?
- What is an acceptable outcome?
- What is not an acceptable outcome?
- What is the worst possible outcome?
- What risks are they prepared to take in the pursuit of the best possible outcome?
- What are they prepared to give up in order to achieve a particular outcome?

Once we believe that we have a sense of our client's objectives and priorities it is important to check our understanding with our client. In order to avoid any future disagreements about decisions made and actions taken, it is a good idea to communicate our understanding of this aspect of our client's instructions to them in writing. This gives them an opportunity to change or clarify their instructions; and it provides us with protection in the event that things do not work out to our client's satisfaction.

With our client's objectives identified, we can now choose actions to match those objectives. In choosing actions, we should bear the following questions in mind:

- Is litigation really necessary? (Of course, if our client is the defendant, we may not have much choice in the matter.)
- If litigation is necessary, what remedies will best provide our client with what he or she wants? In which causes of action are those remedies available? For example, in a contractual dispute, does the client want monetary compensation for breach of contract, or does the client want the contract to be performed?
- Are the client's interests best served by an early settlement or plea? If so, how can this be best achieved?

With a general idea of where we are going, we can now start the analysis necessary to achieve our client's goals.

Organise the documents

[2.20] This book is largely concerned with methods for organising *information*. Often that information is contained in documents, because whatever else it is, a legal file or brief is also (usually) a mass of paper. This book is not concerned with methods for organising *documents*. It does, however, subscribe to the following principle: in order to do our job as litigators, we have to know what paper we have, and we have to know where we can find any particular piece of paper. This means that we should adopt some method of organising our documents to ensure that we can meet both of the following goals:

- knowing what documents we have; and
- being able to quickly retrieve any document when we need it.

Provided it is capable of meeting these objectives, it does not matter what system we use. That said, a system capable of meeting these objectives will typically have the following features:

- Documents will be divided into logical categories.
- Within those categories, they will be placed in chronological or reverse chronological order.
- It will be possible to easily add new documents and, on occasion, new categories of documents.
- The steps necessary to locate and retrieve a document will be kept to a minimum. For example, where the number of documents is small, it is quicker to find and access a tagged document (one step), than to have to consult a document index and then locate the document (two steps).

Electronic document management

[2.30] In some litigation, the sheer volume of documents involved makes it impossible for the lawyers to handle them "manually". In such litigation it will usually be necessary to adopt some form of electronic document management. A variety of software exists, designed to perform tasks such as the following:

- convert paper documents into electronic form;
- allow all the members of a litigation team (and sometimes, ultimately, the court) to access the documents;
- classify documents, or segments of documents, according to their relevance to the issues in the litigation;
- search the documents, either for specific text, or according to their classification;
- search and classify particular kinds of documents, such as emails; and
- create links and cross-references between different documents.

There are also several companies whose business is to assist in the document management aspect of litigation.

An inventory of possible categories

[2.40] Without being prescriptive, lawyers preparing a brief typically organise their papers into some combination of the following categories; exactly which combination of categories lawyers use will depend on the nature of the proceedings, and their own preferences:

- Instructions to counsel.
- Correspondence between the solicitors for the parties, including:
  - correspondence dealing with particular issues such as lateness of discovery, or offers of compromise.
- Court documents, including sub-categories such as:
  - the pleadings;
  - notices to admit and of dispute;
  - court orders;
  - orders for discovery, affidavits of documents, and discovered documents.
- Documents reflecting other court procedures such as:
  - bail;
  - offers of compromise;
  - security for costs.
- Witness statements.
- Reports by investigators.
- Expert reports, including medical reports.
- Advice from counsel.
- Letters of advice from the solicitor to the client.
- Documentary evidence, possibly organised into categories such as:
  - invoices;
  - documents discovered by the opponent;
  - photographs.
- Relevant legal authorities.
- In criminal cases, additionally or alternatively, documents such as the:
  - charge sheet;
  - presentment;
  - police brief;
  - depositions;
  - prosecution case statements and defence responses;
  - victim impact statements;
  - prior criminal history.

Remember, though, it does not matter what system you adopt provided that it is capable of meeting the two key aims of ensuring that you:

1. know what documents you have; and
2. can quickly find and retrieve any document when you need it.

Read the material

[2.50] An essential preliminary to any proper analysis of the information contained in a legal file or brief is familiarity with its contents. This can only be gained through the close, and usually repeated, reading of that material. The details are often all important, and these are seldom noticed the first time we read the material. On our first read, then, we might simply mark or tag passages or documents of interest, and make the odd note to ourselves. Subsequent readings could be combined with the preparation of a chronology, the subject of the next chapter.

Work out what needs to be done

[2.60] Now that you have defined your objectives, organised the paperwork and read the material, you must decide what steps you need to take in order to prepare the matter for trial (or for whatever other outcome you are working towards). That is, which of the various methods contained in this book, or others, will we apply? We will decide this in light of the time available to us, the amount of money our client is prepared to spend on paying us to be prepared, our client's objectives, our opinion as to the methods that are best suited to the problems or issues to which the litigation gives rise, and our experience in applying these methods in the past. As well as the methods covered in this text, we will also need to consider doing a whole host of things that are not covered, such as:

- ensuring that all directions of the court, and other compulsory procedural deadlines have been complied with, including deadlines for discovery, the service of expert reports and so on;
- deciding whether or not to take any of the many optional procedural steps open to us, such as the serving of an offer of compromise, or a notice to admit;
- arranging conferences with all relevant witnesses; and
- creating a timetable for performing the tasks required of us, including an analysis of the file in accordance with the methods expounded in this text.

Which methods when?

[2.70] As has been explained, this book contains a series of methods for analysing, organising and using information and evidence in litigation. The methods have been placed in some sort of rough sequence, but they do not constitute a step-by-step procedure. Exactly which combination of methods we use, and the order in which we use them, will therefore depend on the nature of the litigation we are involved in, the issues it presents, and the stage of the litigation we have reached. Trial preparation, moreover, seldom proceeds in a completely linear fashion, and we may, for example, find ourselves constantly returning to some tasks, such as the preparation of our chronology. What follows is, therefore, only a loose guide to the methods that might be useful at particular points during the life of a litigation matter.

All stages, all litigation

[2.80] Whatever litigation we are involved in, and whatever stage of that litigation we are at, we should always start with those preliminaries described in this chapter that, above all, require us to define our objectives.

Investigation and the gathering of evidence

[2.90] This may be required at any point from the moment our client first enters our office until the close of evidence at the trial itself. One of the primary purposes of the methods set out in Chapters 3 and 4 is to help us to work out what evidence to look for, and where to look for it. This book does not, however, discuss any actual methods of evidence gathering, such as client or witness interviewing, discovery, the drafting of interrogatories or the use of private investigators. These are well covered in other texts. Before we can use any of these methods, however, we need to have some idea of what we are looking for, and we need to know what questions to ask. The methods in Chapters 3 and 4 will help you with this.

As far as the specific procedures are concerned, interrogatories can be used as a genuine attempt to find out the unknown, in which case they can be drafted prior to the finalising of a case theory; but interrogatories can also be an attempt to secure admissions in relation to facts that form part of a settled theory of the case. Other procedures – such as a notice to admit – will generally only be used at a point when there is a reasonably coherent theory of the case.

Drafting of pleadings

[2.100] Pleadings are allegations of fact which, if successfully proved, entitle our client to the remedy or remedies sought. A pleading, such as a statement of claim, must contain allegations satisfying all of the elements of a cause of action. Pleadings do not, however, contain evidence – that is, we plead the fact, not the evidence by which it will be proved.

The function of particulars, as Gleeson CJ observed in *Goldsmith v Sandilands* (2002) 190 ALR 370; [2002] HCA 31 at [2]:

> ... is not to expand the issues defined by the pleadings, but "to fill in the picture of the plaintiff's cause of action with information sufficiently detailed to put the defendant on his guard as to the cause he has to meet and to enable him to prepare for trial".

The allegations of fact in the pleadings correspond to the "facts in issue" discussed at [5.190]-[5.200].

Although they reflect a case theory, pleadings are typically issued well before the analysis required to select and refine a case theory for presentation at trial has been completed. Indeed, pleadings must necessarily be issued before all evidence has been gathered; this is because the issuing of proceedings is a prerequisite to the use of some of the most important evidence gathering techniques such as discovery, interrogatories and notices to admit. That said, it is usually a good idea to carry out some factual investigation before issuing pleadings – otherwise the case may be put on the wrong foot, or expenses may be incurred in prosecuting an action that has no realistic chance of success.

In any case, a consequence of the fact that pleadings must usually be prepared before a complete evidential analysis can be carried out is that pleadings will usually include a number of alternative (and possibly even inconsistent) legal theories of the case (causes of action), and a number of ways in which these theories could be factually proven. That is, allegations are pleaded widely enough to cover any of the possible theories of the case that might ultimately be relied on at trial: the net is cast wide in the hope that something will be caught in it.

Although counsel may not have evidence available to support the facts pleaded at the time that pleadings are drafted, it is generally unethical to plead factual allegations that are not based on the client's instructions or that are not reasonably believed to exist. This is particularly true where the pleading alleges criminality, fraud or serious misconduct; in such cases, ethical conduct usually requires that the lawyer already has evidence capable of substantiating the allegation.

The most important marshalling methods to carry out in preparation for the drafting of pleadings are the preparation of a chronology, and marshalling according to legal rules. These are described in Chapters 3 and 4. It is not necessary to have actually finalised a theory of the case: that will come later.

Interlocutory proceedings

[2.110] Any interlocutory application is aided by a chronology covering the steps relevant to the application. Preparation of such a chronology – described in Chapter 3 as a mini-chronology – will ensure that we are able to identify in advance all the facts that favour the outcome we are seeking, or which militate against it. With these facts identified, we are unlikely to be taken by surprise by any submission of our opponent, or question from the bench.

Criminal proceedings

[2.120] Criminal proceedings are different from civil proceedings because of the absence of pleadings and of most of the pre-trial procedures available in civil proceedings. The charges themselves are in some ways equivalent to the statement of claim in civil proceedings, except that charges are often laid at a more advanced stage of the investigative process than is typical for a statement of claim. The involvement of lawyers usually only begins after the charges have been laid, so the parameters of the trial have already been determined to some degree by the police or other agency responsible for the laying of charges.

In some jurisdictions, the prosecution is required to file a statement of its case at some point prior to trial; and the defence may in turn be required to file some response to it. In Victoria, for example, the *Criminal Procedure Act 2009* requires the prosecution to file a summary of its opening, outlining the manner in which the prosecution will put its case against the accused as well as the acts, facts, matters and circumstances being relied on to support a finding of guilt; it should also identify the witnesses whose evidence, in the opinion of the prosecutor, ought to be admitted as evidence without further proof. Such a statement must clearly be based on a reasonably well developed theory of the case. The defence response to the prosecution summary must identify the acts, facts, matters and circumstances with which issue is taken and the basis on which such issue is taken. Again, this can only be done if defence counsel has a case theory in mind.

Advice on evidence

[2.130] An advice on evidence is a document that sets out the analysis we have carried out as part of our preparation for trial. Depending on circumstances, therefore, the advice on evidence might do some combination of the following:

- Summarise and/or analyse the evidence.
- Use the evidence to construct a narrative.
- State the theory or theories of the case being relied on, both in terms of the legal case and the factual theory.
- Identify the opponent's likely theory or theories of the case.
- Identify all of the facts in issue, and in particular those that are likely to be the subject of genuine controversy between the parties.
- Explain how the factual theory will satisfy the elements of the legal case.
- Identify the evidence to be used to prove the factual theory.
- List the witnesses who will need to be called, and the real evidence that will need to be tendered.
- Analyse the strengths and weaknesses of the opposing cases.
- Identify any steps that need to be taken, or further evidence that needs to be obtained.
- Indicate how the trial will be conducted in order to advance the theory of the case.
- Discuss the admissibility of any potentially inadmissible items of evidence likely to be relied on by either side.
- Indicate, in light of the above, the prospects of success.

As aids to its understanding, the advice might also include:

- A chronology or the output of one or more of the other marshalling methods described in Chapter 4.
- A case map in one of the forms described in Chapter 6.

Preparation for trial

[2.140] Trial preparation requires the development of a theory of the case. Case theory is discussed in Chapters 5 and 6. In order to develop such a theory, however, we will first need to have carried out some of the evidence marshalling methods described in Chapters 3 and 4; at the very least, we ought to have prepared a chronology, as described in Chapter 3. In some cases, more detailed analysis of the evidence is helpful, as described in Chapter 7. A theory of the case developed in accordance with the methods set out in those chapters will enable us to:

- determine whether our opponent's case is so strong, or ours so weak, that our client would be well-advised to settle the matter or, in criminal proceedings, to drop some or all of the charges, or to plead guilty;
- draft our opening and closing addresses;
- defeat a no-case submission (or realise that we will be unable to do so);
- identify the evidence we need to adduce from each of our witnesses;
- identify aims for the cross-examination of our opponent's witness; and
- identify the witnesses through whom all of our exhibits will be tendered.

Another aspect of our preparation for trial is the identification of evidence in relation to which issues of admissibility may arise. The application of the law of evidence is discussed in Chapter 8. It is often easier to apply the law of evidence if that evidence has first been mapped in some detail, as discussed in Chapter 7. Finally, Chapter 9 contains some suggestions about how to pull together the threads of our analysis for trial.

Conduct of a trial

[2.150] The methods discussed in this book stop at the point at which we walk into court. That said, most of what we do at trial is dictated by our pre-trial preparation, from the preliminary steps described in this chapter to the final preparations discussed in Chapter 9. Through our theory of the case we will have identified our aims for the trial and our aims with each witness. How to go about achieving those aims, however, is not the province of this work. Witness examination and trial advocacy are well covered in a number of other works. Before we can make meaningful use of the techniques described in those works, however, we need to know what we are using them for. That comes from our pre-trial preparation, which is the subject of this work. Useful texts on advocacy and witness examination are mentioned in the Notes to the final chapter.

Summary

[2.160] The preliminary steps identified in this chapter include:

- defining our objectives;

- organising the documents;
- reading the material; and
- working out what further steps we need to take in order to prepare the matter for trial.

Chronologies

3

Introduction

[3.10] No matter how well organised our documents are, they can not provide us with a single overview of all the information available to us. There is simply too much information contained in the average file or brief for us to be able to store and analyse it all in our head. Because of this, there is a risk that we will overlook something. One of the first steps we need to take, therefore, is to create an inventory of all that information. The inventory needs to be organised in a way that makes it easy to understand exactly what evidence we have and what evidence we do not have.

Generally, the best form of inventory is one where the information is placed in chronological order. A chronological inventory of information – or "chronology" – is ideal for many reasons:

- it is easy to access or retrieve the information;
- as new information comes to light it can easily be added to the chronology;
- a chronology tends to highlight any gaps in the information available to us;
- a chronology tends to highlight conflicts and inconsistencies in the information,

and therefore enables us to identify likely areas of dispute or agreement between the parties; and

• it ensures that we do not overlook evidence, or the juxtaposition of evidence, that may support or undermine our or our opponent's case.

A chronology is also an important precursor to the development of a **theory of the case**. This is because the information in a brief or file tends to be split between a variety of witness statements and other sources, each telling its own story. But at trial we are attempting to tell a single story (albeit one that must be sourced from many different witnesses and documents). First, we need to bring all of those separate stories together in one master document: the chronology. Then, because a chronology is organised according to the same reference point as a standard narrative – namely, order of occurrence – it will tend to suggest possible narratives. This is not to say that a chronology is a substitute for a theory of the case. A chronology is merely a sequence of events, whereas a theory of the case is a narrative based on a sequence of *causally related* events. In a chronology, event B may occur after event A; in a theory of the case, event B may not only occur after event A, it may occur *because* of event A. In other words, a chronology is the *what*, the *when* and the *where* of the evidence; a theory of the case also includes the *how* and the *why*. Putting the events into chronological order helps us to perceive the possible relationships between those events, to turn a sequence of events into a narrative. The mere juxtaposition of events may reveal or suggest connections that might otherwise have remained hidden.

Chronologies are not the only method of marshalling information that can produce these or related benefits. Several other methods are discussed in the next chapter. In particular, we may need to supplement our chronological inventory with a separate inventory of information about our sources of evidence: see the discussion under "Marshalling according to sources" at [4.70]. Nevertheless, chronologies are the most important of the methods: whatever other method we may use, we should usually prepare a chronology.

Other uses of a chronology

[3.20] Aside from its role in the general preparation of a case for trial, a chronology can be used for several other purposes:

• A chronology can be used as a basis for the interview of a client or witness. The witness (or client) may have made an earlier statement. If a chronology has been prepared then any subsequent interview with the witness can be based on the chronology. This will enable us to fill in any gaps in the information provided by the witness, ask the witness about any areas of dispute or inconsistency, and easily see whether the witness is now departing from their previous version of events. If the witness has not made a statement already, then we will also be able to see whether the witness's version of events corroborates or conflicts with the versions of events told by other witnesses, and to see whether the witness can help us to fill in any of the gaps we have identified in our information.

- Subsequent to any interview, we might provide a copy of the chronology to our client, to give them an opportunity to correct any mistakes, or to fill in any gaps.

- A chronology can be used in court to ensure that we have all the evidence at our fingertips. This is helpful even in interlocutory applications, or when making a plea in mitigation of sentence. A chronology will enable us to instantly answer questions about when events of interest occurred. If the court wants to know when a particular letter was sent, a demand was made, an interlocutory step was taken, bail was posted, a prior offence was committed, or a guilty plea was first entered, we will be able to answer immediately, without having to rustle through our paperwork trying to find the relevant document. This will obviously suggest to both the court and our opponent that we are well prepared and fully in command of the evidence. This can only enhance the authoritativeness of our courtroom presentation.

- A chronology can be used as the basis for, or can be appended to, an affidavit.

- A chronology can also be provided to the court as part of our submissions or supporting material. Not only may the provision of a chronology be helpful to the court – for which the court may be appropriately grateful – it will avoid any confusion about the sequence of events, and assist the court to understand any evidence that we may adduce. Moreover, a well selected and phrased sequence of events may itself suggest to the court the theory of the case for which we are contending – that is, the court may perceive the same relationships between events that we did in developing our theory of the case. However, much of the point of providing a chronology will be defeated if our opponent successfully objects to it. We may be seen by the court as having attempted to mislead it, and if this happens then our standing with the court will be damaged. *We must therefore be careful to ensure that any chronology provided to a court is uncontentious.* In general it should only contain undisputed facts; and those facts should be described in a manner to which our opponent could not reasonably object. If disputed "facts" are to be included, then they should be clearly indicated as such.

Preparation and updating

[3.30] The sooner we start preparing the chronology the more benefit we will get from it. To state the obvious, we will be unable to use a chronology to support and direct our interviews with witnesses if we have not prepared one. Nor will we be able to embark on the development of an adequate theory of the case until we have prepared our chronology. Just as the chronology should be started early, so must it be constantly (or at least regularly) updated as further information becomes available. An incomplete or out-of-date chronology is simply misleading. So, when we first become involved in a matter, if there is not already a chronology in existence, we should start one; and if there is already a chronology, we should ensure that it is kept up to date.

Use all available information

[3.40] In preparing a chronology we take information organised according to its source – that is, in witness statements or other documents – and reorganise it into one master document. The process of preparing a chronology requires us, then, to systematically read all the source material available to us, extract the information contained in that source material, and enter it into our master document. This is a slow and laborious process, and the preparation of a chronology is, undeniably time-consuming.

When preparing the chronology we should err on the side of inclusiveness. The significance of particular events may not become apparent until we have developed our theory of the case; if we leave them out of the chronology they may be lost to us forever. Of course, this also means that we may be including lots of information that subsequently – in light of our theory of the case – proves to have no bearing on the issues. But we will not know that at this stage: so put everything in!

Nor should we exclude an event from the chronology on the basis that the evidence to prove that event, or the event itself, is likely to be ruled inadmissible. Leave questions of admissibility for later. Just because an event, or the evidence to prove that event, is inadmissible, does not mean that the event can not form a part of, or need not be accounted for by, our theory of the case. Further thought may suggest a means of getting the evidence admitted; or further investigation may uncover a permissible way of proving the event.

Not only should we err on the side of inclusiveness in terms of the events that we enter into the chronology, we should also err on the side of inclusiveness in terms of the way in which we describe those facts. If we merely state that A sent a letter to B on a particular date, without saying something about the contents of the letter, then we are going to end up having to go back and look at the letter again. This defeats one of the main benefits of a chronology: it becomes a master document that relieves us of the need to refer constantly to the source material to find out what happened.

Ultimately, the fact that everything has been included may become an obstacle to certain uses of the chronology, and we may need to edit it down for particular purposes: see "Mini-chronologies" at [3.110]. Other methods of analysis based on the chronology are described in Chapter 4, in particular marshalling according to scenarios and clues.

Before, during, after

[3.50] In a typical chronology, the events can be divided into three main timeframes:

1. events that occurred before the event in question;
2. the event in question itself and the immediately surrounding events; and
3. events that occurred after the event in question.

These three timeframes correspond to the three temporal categories of evidence discussed in "Marshalling for 'clues'" at [4.110]. Distinguishing between these timeframes in our chronology will help us to perceive relationships between pieces of information of the type discussed in Chapter 4.

Cross-reference the source material

[3.60] Although one of the aims of the chronology is to avoid having to go back to the source material to find out what happened, it is absolutely essential that our chronology records the source of every single piece of information it contains. Ultimately, we are going to have to prove the events contained in the chronology by means of evidence, and we need to know which witness or document is going to be used to prove what fact. There are few things more time-wasting than having to go back through all of the source material again to rediscover the identity of the witness who was the source of a particular entry in our chronology.

Moreover, our cross-reference to the source material should be as precise as possible, enabling us to instantly find the correct passage in the correct document. If our documents are organised according to numbered tabs, we might include the tab number of the document in question. If the document has many pages, we should record the page and/or paragraph number where the particular fact was stated. If the source is a police record of interview, we should include the number of the question to which the answer was given. This will save us time in the long run.

If there are multiple sources for particular facts, we should record all the sources. Multiple sources equate to corroboration, and strong corroboration may mean that this is a fact that will be difficult for us or our opponent to challenge. It also means that we may have some choice about which witness we will use to prove a particular fact.

Record conflicts and inconsistencies in the evidence

[3.70] The chronology is not just a list of the evidence that supports our case, cross-referenced to the witnesses or documents that will be used to provide that evidence. It needs to record all the information available to us. This means that our chronology must also include:

- facts that do not support our case, whether sourced from our witnesses and documents or from those of our opponent;
- inconsistencies in the description of an event between different witnesses and documents; and
- outright conflicts over whether or not an event occurred.

Recording all this information in the chronology will help us to identify those factual issues that are likely to be the subject of dispute in the litigation. Obviously, it is those factual issues to which we will then devote the greatest attention. Reviewing the chronology may also reveal other oddities or inconsistencies. A strange order of events might, for example, lead us to question whether the dates and times we have been given for particular events are accurate.

Identify gaps in the information

[3.80] Once all the information available to us is entered into the chronology, it may become apparent that we do not have all the evidence. For example, our chronology records that a meeting took place, but we have no information about the way in which the appointment for the meeting was made, or about any events that may have occurred as part of the follow-up to the meeting. Or we may simply realise that we do not have an exact date or time for the meeting. In any case, the gaps revealed by our chronology provide leads for further investigation. Investigation is discussed in Chapter 4.

Until the gaps are filled, however, we should not enter in our chronology "facts" for which we have no source; or, perhaps more accurately, we should clearly indicate their status as gaps. For example, if we know that a meeting took place in December 2014, but do not know the exact date, we could show the date in our chronology as ? Dec 14, or ??/12/14, rather than guessing the date on which it might have occurred. Krehel calls this "fuzzy dating". Unfortunately, dates in this format can not be electronically sorted, so an alternative is to assign a complete date, indicating in some way, however, to ourselves and other users of the chronology that the date is only a guess – for example, by italicising it.

Similarly, we may want to make a note somewhere in the chronology to remind us that we have no information about the lead-in or follow-up to the meeting. Then, when we interview a witness who may be able to provide us with this information, we will know what questions to ask.

Identify weaknesses in our case

[3.90] Just as we can use the chronology to identify gaps in our information, so we can use it to identify weaknesses in our evidence and case. These weaknesses can take many forms. For example:

- our source for an important fact may be unreliable or inadmissible; this will alert us to the need to look for an additional or alternative method of proving that fact;
- where there is a conflict of evidence – that is, two or more witnesses or documents assert contradictory versions of an event – we may take the view that the weight of evidence actually favours our opponent's version of the event. Again, we may attempt to remedy this by finding further evidence to support our case; but ultimately we may be forced to concede that the particular factual issue is likely to be decided against us, and we will have to adapt our theory of the case accordingly.

Event chronologies and procedural chronologies

[3.100] Most litigation revolves around the occurrence or non-occurrence of specific past events. We might call these the "events in question". Around the events in question there are a host of facts that either support or undermine one or other of the party's case theory about those events. Distinct from the events in question is the litigation to which they have given rise. Litigation also involves a whole host of facts, such as the serving of documents, the making of demands and so on. Sometimes it is useful to distinguish in a chronology between these two types of facts; indeed, sometimes it is useful to have separate chronologies for each (although there is often an overlap between the two types of fact, which may make this impractical).

The chronology that contains the events relevant to the events in question might be called the **event chronology**. It details in chronological order all of the actions, responses, statements and so on that seem to be relevant to the event in question – that is, that possibly shed some light on whether or not, or how, or why, the event in question occurred.

The chronology of the events arising from the litigation, on the other hand, might be called a **procedural chronology**, or in criminal cases, an **investigative chronology**. This chronology would detail the procedural or investigative steps taken: when letters of demand were first made, court documents filed, and so on. The chronology might be used not only to record steps that have been taken in the past, but also to record steps that need to be taken in the future. This would provide a way of ensuring that deadlines are met (or that missed deadlines on our opponent's part are noticed). A procedural chronology is also an invaluable aid to the making of submissions arising out of the procedural steps taken. For example, it immediately provides counsel with all the information necessary to inform a judge of the dates when certain demands were made of the opposing party, exactly what the course of correspondence was, and so on.

In a criminal context, this chronology is even more important. This is because the conduct of the investigation may have implications for the admissibility of evidence. In a criminal context, then, the investigative chronology should detail all the actions taken by the investigators, including the times at which police officers were contacted and arrived, and the accused was spoken to, cautioned, fingerprinted, arrested, fed and so on. The chronology may reveal unacceptable departures from proper procedure that can be used as the basis for the defence to seek the exclusion of prosecution evidence.

Sometimes, however, a procedural step can also shed light on the events in question. For example, the date on which a witness statement was signed may suggest a connection to some other fact of interest. Moreover, it is often difficult to decide which chronology a particular fact should be placed in. For example, does a record of interview in a criminal case belong in an event chronology or an investigative chronology or both? The timing of the record of interview, and details about how it was conducted, would normally form part of an investigative chronology. On the other hand, the events that the accused describes in the record of interview would usually form part of an event chronology. In addition, the fact that the accused gave a particular version of events at a particular time may be an event in itself, and may shed light on the way in which the accused's story changed over time. Because of this overlap – which is not unusual – it is sometimes simpler to have only one combined chronology.

Mini-chronologies

[3.110] The very comprehensiveness of a chronology can sometimes be an obstacle to the perception of connection between events. For that reason, it is often useful to prepare what might be called mini-chronologies, which only include part of the total available information.

In a complex case, for example, it may be helpful to create separate chronologies to track such things as the continuity of exhibits or the integrity of the crime scene. The creation of such chronologies may expose gaps in the continuity of an exhibit, or compromises in the integrity of a crime scene. Similarly, in preparing for an interlocutory application, we may only need a chronology of the events relevant to that application.

It can also sometimes be helpful to use a mini-chronology to track the movements of one or more of the actors involved in the events in question. For example, we might create a chronology that shows the positions, movements or actions of all of the significant actors at significant moments in time.

Structure of the chronology

[3.120] In light of all the above, it can be seen that when setting up the document or database for our software, we need to include columns or fields that will enable us to record the following categories of information:

- The **date** of the event. Some of the dates may be vague, some will be certain, some may be unknown. If we want to be able to **electronically sort** our chronology, however, we will need to assign a complete date to every event, even if the date we assign is based on guesswork. If this happens, it is important to distinguish that date so that its uncertainty is obvious by, for example, italicising it.
- The **time** or **sequence** of the event. In some cases, the precise time at which an event occurred is of crucial importance, and an additional column or field to record the time may be necessary. We should choose a format for the time which enables us to electronically sort our chronology first by date and then by time. In other cases, we may not know the exact time at which the events on a particular day occurred, but we may be able to work out the sequence in which they occurred; in such cases, if we want to be able to electronically sort the chronology by date and then by sequence, we can assign a number to the event.
- A **description** of the event.
- The **source** or sources of evidence for the event. This may require more than one column: for example, a column for the name of the witness, and a column for the page and paragraph number of their statement; or a column for the title of the document, and a column for the number of the tab in our brief where the document is located.
- A column or columns in which we can note other **matters of interest**, such as:
  - whether the event is **disputed** (we should also include a cross-reference to the witnesses or documents that dispute the fact);
  - any **inconsistencies** in the description of the event, or its timing, as between different witnesses or documents;
  - any **gaps** in our knowledge about the event, or about related events; and
  - anything else that we may wish to note, such as our thoughts on the reliability or admissibility of the source of evidence for a fact, or the need for further evidence.

Our chronology can, thus, be used to record our early analysis of, and thoughts about, the evidence.

A chronology is one tool among many

[3.130] Despite all its benefits, a chronology is not a panacea. Putting events into chronological order is not the only way of organising the information available to us, nor is it the best way for every purpose. The next chapter discusses a number of other ways in which we can organise information to stimulate our thinking about the case. These other methods are intended to complement the creation of a chronology, rather than to replace it.

Summary

[3.140] A chronology is an indispensable aid in most litigation. In order to get the greatest benefit from a chronology, we should:

- start preparing a chronology as early as possible;
- keep updating it;
- put all the available information in the chronology;
- cross-reference the chronology to the source material;
- use the chronology to record conflicts and inconsistencies in the evidence;
- use the chronology to identify gaps in the information; and
- use the chronology to identify weaknesses in our case.

Investigation

4

Introduction

[4.10] Sometimes we need more information or evidence. This chapter deals with a number of methods for marshalling information that can be used to facilitate the search for further evidence. One of the most important of these methods – the preparation of a chronology – was discussed in the previous chapter. Application of these methods will have many of the same benefits as the preparation of a chronology, including acting as a precursor to the development of a theory of the case, as well as enabling us to identify gaps in the information, inconsistencies and conflicts, likely areas of dispute, and so on.

Our focus in this chapter, however, is on the way we can use these methods to identify lines of inquiry that can be followed in order to find evidence that may support or eliminate any possible theories of the case. Before dealing with the specific methods, the chapter begins with a discussion of the kind of thinking the methods are intended to facilitate – that is, investigative thinking. It should be emphasised at the outset, however, that this chapter is primarily about investigative *thinking*, rather than investigative *doing* – that is, it does not purport to describe techniques for carrying out an investigation. Rather, its focus is on the thinking we need to do before we can usefully apply such techniques.

What should also be emphasised, however, is the enormous importance of thorough and diligent factual investigation to the successful outcome of a case. Some litigation seems to proceed almost to the point of trial before anyone gives proper attention to the fundamental question of how the allegations in the pleadings are going to be proved. Typically, the focus of the litigator's attention will have been on the need to comply with the procedural rules and orders of the court, rather than on the evidential issues. Unfortunately, litigation conducted in this way – with a focus on procedure and a disregard of proof – will often have to be settled on disadvantageous terms after enormous sums of the parties' money have been expended in the prosecution or defence of a case, which an early evidential analysis might have showed had no realistic prospects of success.

Of course, complying with the rules and orders of the court is an important part of a litigator's job; but it is only one part of that job. For example, serving an expert report within the time stipulated by the rules or orders of the court will be of little benefit unless the report contains persuasive evidence in support of the case; and an expert report is unlikely to contain such evidence unless we have given real thought – before instructing the expert – to the issues in the case and the means of proving them. If the evidential issues are not properly examined until just before trial, then it will usually be too late to rectify any problems – too late to amend the pleadings in light of the evidence, too late to obtain additional expert reports, too late to withdraw on favourable terms. Ultimately, the party that wins the case will usually be the one that has done the best job with the evidence, rather than the one that has been most diligent in complying with the procedural rules.

INVESTIGATIVE THINKING

[4.20] Investigative thinking involves the identification of possible theories or hypotheses, and the search for evidence that will support or eliminate those theories. There are, then, two parts to investigative thinking, and the two parts are sometimes referred to by logicians as "abduction" and "retroduction". Although these labels may be unfamiliar, the way of thinking they describe will probably not be. Abduction is the creative process by which we identify possible theories of the case; retroduction is the process by which we seek evidence to support or eliminate those theories.

Imaginative reasoning to identify theories

[4.30] As lawyers, we are always circumscribed to some degree in the case theory we can adopt by our client's instructions. That is to say, in cases where our client has instructed us with their version of events, the case theory we put forward at trial must be consistent with that version of events. Of course some clients – such as prosecuting authorities or large corporations – are incapable of instructing us in this way; and even if the client is capable of giving us a version of events, we may choose not to ask them for it. However, if we do have such instructions, we can not get our client to change his or her testimony simply because we have been able to invent a better version of events than the one they have brought to us. That said, a client's knowledge of the events that are the subject of the litigation will seldom be complete, and it is an unusual case in which the client will arrive with a version of events that covers every item of evidence and that we can simply adopt as our case theory.

More commonly, the client will only know part of what happened, and may know nothing at all about the reasons it happened. For example, a client may come to us reporting that he or she was injured when a roller door in a car park collapsed on their car. This bald factual account does not constitute a theory of the case. How then do we go about developing one? The process that we intuitively rely on in these situations is a form of imaginative reasoning referred to by logicians as "abduction". Abduction is the process of "adopting a hypothesis for the sake of its explanation of known facts".

According to the American philosopher, Charles Sanders Peirce (quoted in Schum, 1994, p 461):

> Long before I first classed abduction as a form of inference it was recognized by logicians that the operation of adopting an explanatory hypothesis – which is just what abduction is – was subject to certain conditions. Namely, the hypothesis cannot be admitted, even as a hypothesis, unless it be supposed that it would account for the facts or some of them. The form of the inference, therefore, is this:
>
> > The surprising fact, C, is observed;
> > But if A were true, C would be a matter of course,
> > Hence, there is reason to suspect that A is true.

In our example, the "surprising fact" is the collapse of the roller door. However, if certain other facts were true, this fact would not be so surprising. For example, if the roller door had been faulty for some time, or had not been properly maintained, or had been badly designed, then its collapse would not be a "surprising fact" but almost "a matter of course". Hence there is reason to suspect that one of these possibilities may be true. Notice that in our example the process of abduction produces several distinct possibilities. The word "possibilities" is used because at this stage they are just that: further investigation will be required before we select one of these possibilities as our theory of the case.

It is important to note, however, that while abductive reasoning requires creativity and imagination, there are a number of things we can to do to stimulate our creativity: these are discussed in the second part of this chapter, under the heading "Marshalling information to facilitate investigation" at [4.60]-[4.130]. An even more important point, though, is that the possibilities we have identified can be used to guide our search for further evidence. Once we have identified one or more possibilities, we can look for evidence that will either confirm or eliminate those possibilities. This process of abduction, followed by the search for evidence, will be an ongoing one as some possibilities are eliminated, and others refined or fleshed out. Eventually, the process should produce both a theory of the case and the evidence to support it.

Identifying tests to confirm or eliminate possibilities

[4.40] Abduction or imaginative reasoning is only the first half of our process; with a possible explanation for the evidence identified, we can now use the possible explanation to guide our search for further evidence. We do so by thinking of the possibility as a hypothesis, and then devising "tests" that will confirm or eliminate that hypothesis. This form of reasoning is called "retroduction". It works like this. We have identified as an explanation for the evidence we currently have available to us the possibility "A". We now ask ourselves the following question: if A was true, what other facts would we also expect to be true? We then look for evidence of those facts. If we find that evidence, this tends to confirm A; if we do not, or if we find evidence that is inconsistent with A being true, then we may eliminate possibility A.

Conversely, we may set out to eliminate possibility A by instead asking ourselves the following question: what facts would indicate that A was not true? We can then look for evidence of those facts; if we find that evidence, we can eliminate A; if we do not, we may take this as some confirmation of A's truth. We use retroduction, then, to guide our search for evidence: it tells us what evidence to look for and, in many cases, where to look for it.

For example, there might be a dispute about whether or not a particular meeting took place. We might ask ourselves, if the meeting did take place, what else might we expect to have happened? We might conclude that if there had been a meeting, first it must have been arranged; second, presumably the details of the meeting would have been entered into people's diaries; similarly, after the meeting, there might have been some communication between the parties in relation to the substance of the meeting. If we can prove that these other events occurred, then this will tend to support the fact that the meeting took place; if we can prove that they did not occur, then this will tend to show that the meeting did not take place.

We can use this analysis at all stages of the litigation. In the interviewing of witnesses, this process may direct our questioning as we seek to confirm or eliminate details the relevance of which the witness may not have perceived. It may also guide the drafting of interrogatories, or the instructions we give to investigators or expert witnesses. As the evidence comes in we may discard some of our possible theories of the case while refining and focusing on others.

At trial, we can use the kinds of questions identified through retroduction as a guide to our examination and cross-examination of witnesses. If our witness is testifying to fact A – for example, that the meeting took place – then we may seek to lead evidence from this or other witnesses (including our opponent's) to show that all of the facts that would tend to be associated with fact A also existed. This will make the story more plausible.

Conversely, if it is our case that A is *not* true, then we may seek to lead evidence both in the examination of our witnesses and the cross-examination of our opponent's witnesses, to show that the things that we would have expected to occur if fact A were true did not occur. This will provide the foundation for an inference that fact A did not occur either. For example, if our opponent's witness is testifying that the meeting did take place, we may be able to cross-examine that witness to show that he or she had not done any of the things that we would have expected had there really been a meeting.

To conclude, then, the investigative process involves three distinct stages:

1. **Adduction**: the imagining of a hypothesis or working theory of the case that provides an explanation for the evidence currently available to us.
2. **Retroduction**: the identification of "tests" that might confirm or disprove the hypothesis – that is, identifying the additional evidence we would expect to find if the hypothesis were true, or the evidence that would tend to disprove the hypothesis.
3. **Investigation**: the carrying out of the above "tests" through the application of appropriate investigative techniques.

During the course of an investigation, these three steps are likely to be repeated several times as possible theories are progressively refined, modified or eliminated.

An example: Sherlock Holmes

[4.50] The fictional master of abductive and retroductive reasoning (although he never called it that) was Sherlock Holmes. In *Silver Blaze*, Holmes is employed to find a race horse that has gone missing following the apparent murder of its trainer:

> "It's this way, Watson," said [Holmes] at last. "We may leave the question of who killed John Straker for the instant and confine ourselves to finding out what has become of the horse. Now, supposing that he broke away during or after the tragedy, where could he have gone to? The horse is a very gregarious creature. If left to himself his instincts would have been either to return to King's Pyland [its owner's stable]

or go over to Mapleton [a rival's stable]. Why should he run wild upon the moor? He would surely have been seen by now. And why should the gypsies kidnap him? These people always clear out when they hear of trouble, for they do not wish to be pestered by the police. They could not hope to sell such a horse. They would run a great risk and gain nothing by taking him. Surely that is clear."

"Where is he, then?"

"I have already said that he must have gone to King's Pyland or to Mapleton. He is not at King's Pyland. Therefore he is at Mapleton. Let us take that as a working hypothesis and see what it leads us to. This part of the moor, as the inspector remarked, is very hard and dry. But it falls away towards Mapleton, and, you can see from here that there is a long hollow over yonder, which must have been very wet on Monday night. If our supposition is correct, then the horse must have crossed that, and there is the point where we should look for his tracks."

We had been walking briskly during this conversation, and a few more minutes brought us to the hollow in question. At Holmes's request I walked down to the bank to the right, and he to the left, but I had not taken fifty paces before I heard him give a shout and saw him waving his hand to me. The track of a horse was plainly outlined in the soft earth in front of him, and the shoe which he took from his pocket exactly fitted the impression.

"See the value of imagination," said Holmes. "It is the one quality which [Inspector] Gregory lacks. We imagined what might have happened, acted upon the supposition, and find ourselves justified. Let us proceed."

In this passage, Holmes takes each of the three investigative steps identified in the previous section:

1. **Abduction**: he uses his imagination to identify a working hypothesis: that Silver Blaze might have gone to the stable at Mapleton. This hypothesis is capable of explaining the evidence currently available to Holmes, and is consistent with his beliefs about the nature and behaviour of horses.
2. **Retroduction**: he identifies a test for this hypothesis, namely that there will be hoof prints on any soft ground over which the horse must have travelled on the way to the stable at Mapleton.
3. **Investigation**: he carries out the test by examining some soft ground over which, if his hypothesis is correct, Silver Blaze must have travelled.

MARSHALLING INFORMATION TO FACILITATE INVESTIGATION

[4.60] Abductive reasoning is creative and involves the use of our imagination; but our imagination can not operate in a vacuum. It has to be based on the evidence available to us, and we can facilitate our reasoning processes by organising or marshalling the information in ways that tend to highlight connections between different pieces of information. In "A Theory of Preliminary Fact Investigation", Tillers and Schum identify a number of different ways in which items of evidence can be organised or marshalled in order to bring to light connections between them. The methods that follow do not correspond exactly with those identified by Tillers and Schum, but they do draw very heavily on their work. The methods described in this chapter involve marshalling according to *sources* of information, according to *scenarios*, *narratives* and *"clues"*, and according to *legal rules* and *factual issues*.

Marshalling according to sources

[4.70] As Chapter 7 explains, the sources of information in litigation fall into three main classes – namely testimony, real evidence and documents. Separate marshalling systems will usually be required for each of these classes. Marshalling according to the source of information is actually a very common method of marshalling for lawyers, although this typically will just take the form of a series of witness statements or an exhibit list. The information to be obtained *from* a source is, however, only one side of the information we can usefully marshal; the other side is information *about* that source, such as information about the credibility of a witness, or the authenticity of an item of real evidence.

Witnesses and other "actors"

[4.80] As already noted, a witness statement is one method of recording the information to be obtained from that witness. Statements can be prolix, however, and it is sometimes useful to record, in summary form, the various facts about which a particular witness might be able to give evidence. In addition, when the information-gathering phase is still in progress, we can for each witness or possible witness, record the additional areas about which we would like to interview them.

Equally helpful is to create what might be called a "who's who" or "cast list" of the witnesses and other "actors" in the case. "Actor" is here being used to encompass not only persons who are able to give evidence about the events that are the subject of the litigation, but all of the actors in that drama, including those who can not testify because they are incompetent, deceased, unavailable or because they are not human (for example, legal persons such as corporations, or animals). A "who's who" is often a useful adjunct to a chronology, particularly in cases where there are such a large number of witnesses or actors that it is difficult to keep track of them all.

At its bare minimum the "who's who" would record the actor's name, contact details, any abbreviations that are used to designate them in the chronology, and a brief description of their role in the drama. Other details that may be useful to marshal include the actor's employment, relationship to the parties and/or to other witnesses, dates on which they have made statements, detailed cross-references to any such statements or other documents or exhibits that they might be able to produce, and so on.

These details help to keep track of who a particular actor is, and to keep on top of the paperwork and exhibits. However, we may want to know even more than this about each actor. For every witness, or potential witness, or indeed for any person whose behaviour, or whose reasons for behaviour, might be relevant in the litigation (such as the deceased in a murder case), the "who's who" can be used to record a whole host of information that is relevant to their credibility – such as prior criminal history, reasons to lie, and so on – or that sheds light on whether they are likely to have behaved in the manner alleged or claimed. The gathering of this kind of information fleshes out the actors in the drama, and may therefore lead to a richer and more plausible case theory.

Real and documentary evidence

[4.90] It is always useful to keep track of those documents or objects that may be entered into evidence as exhibits. At the very least, such an exhibit list should record the identity of the witness who will be used as a vehicle for getting the exhibit into evidence. However, there are a number of other details that it is also useful to record. These include the substance or significance of a document or object: what will it prove?

Just as it is useful to record credibility-related information about witnesses, so it is useful to record information relevant to the authenticity of a document or object. There are very often conditions that have to be satisfied before a document or object can be tendered in evidence; for example, evidence may have to be led in relation to the signing or witnessing of a document. It is important to identify what these conditions are – they are determined by the law of evidence – and to record in our real evidence log details of how we intend to go about proving that those conditions are satisfied.

Marshalling according to scenarios and narratives

[4.100] A chronology is probably the single most important method of marshalling information. If we only have time do one of the things suggested in this and the previous chapter, it should be a chronology. A chronology is not the only method of organising information according to time of occurrence, however. Scenario marshalling can also be classified as a method of marshalling according to time, since scenarios are narratives with a beginning, middle and end – in other words, because they unfold over time.

Sometimes the very comprehensiveness of a chronology can be an obstacle to its usefulness: the sheer number of items of information recorded in the chronology may conceal rather than reveal connections between the items of information. We may want to strip down the chronology to reveal the skeleton of a story contained in it, and thus marshal the information according to a scenario.

As we examine the information, possible scenarios that explain that information may come to mind. These scenarios will be a mixture of events or facts for which we have evidence, and events or "facts" which we have conjectured. The facts for which we have evidence will have been selected from the chronology on the basis that they seem to belong to the same scenario or story. But the scenario is more than just the sequence of these facts: in a scenario, facts are causally related.

Moreover, it is unlikely that our chronology will contain evidence of all of the elements of the scenario we have imagined. The additional "facts" suggested by the scenario for which we presently have no evidence are called "gap-fillers" by Tillers and Schum. We may now construct a pared-down chronology for our scenario, incorporating both the facts pruned and selected from our main chronology and the "gap-fillers"; or we may just write down a version of the scenario in narrative form.

In any case, with the "gap-fillers" identified, we can now look for evidence to support those facts. If the evidence is found, then this tends to confirm the scenario. If no evidence to support the "gap-fillers" can be found, then we may discard the scenario in favour of others that have stronger evidential support.

As the information is added to the scenario it may slowly develop into a more complete narrative. A narrative like this can easily be incorporated into an Advice on Evidence. The development of such a narrative will simultaneously enable us to marshall all of the relevant evidence, explain what the case is about to our instructor or client, and highlight the strengths and weaknesses of the case. It will also provide a starting point for the writing of other documents such as a statement of material facts or an opening address.

Marshalling for "clues"

[4.110] Typically, the issues to be determined in litigation revolve around the occurrence or nature of a past event. Binder and Bergman (p 368) call such events the "moment (or moments) of substantive importance". Marshalling for "clues" rests on the idea that no event, or moment, occurs in isolation. There is a build-up to the event, other things happen at the same time as the event, and the event continues to have effects into the future, like the ripples on a pond after a stone has been thrown in.

If we have an idea of the event in question (a working theory of the case, or scenario), we can look for the items of evidence that we imagine would precede, accompany or follow such an event. To the extent that we find those items of evidence, this supports the theory or scenario we are investigating. There may even be some items of evidence the existence of which seems necessary to our theory – that is, if these items of evidence do not exist, then our theory must be wrong. In a criminal proceeding, for example, opportunity is such a detail: if it can be proved that the accused did not have the opportunity to commit the crime, then the accused must be innocent, no matter how much other evidence there is suggesting that the accused is guilty.

We can, then, divide the surrounding circumstances into three main timeframes, in terms of their relation to the event or events in question:

- Circumstances that precede the event in question and that seem to point forward in time to it having occurred or having occurred in a particular way. This might be because events like the event in question are usually preceded by such items of evidence, or because such items of evidence are usually followed by an event such as the event in question.
- Circumstances that occur or exist at the same time as the event in question, the relevance of which stems from the fact that they are the kinds of items of evidence that typically accompany events such as the event in question; or are the kinds of items of evidence without which the event in question could not have occurred; or are the kinds of items of evidence that would not normally exist or occur if an event like the event in question had not also occurred.
- Circumstances that follow the event in question and that seem to point back in time to the event in question. This might be because events like the event in question are usually followed by such items of evidence; or because items of evidence such as these do not normally occur or exist if an event like the event in question had not also occurred.

With typical disdain for plain English, Wigmore called these three types of evidence *prospectant* (forward looking) evidence, *concomitant* (accompanying) evidence and *retrospectant* (backward looking) evidence. In the *Science of Judicial Proof*, Wigmore identified four common classes of "probanda" (his word for the objects of proof in a trial: that is, the things that we are trying to prove in order to succeed); one of these was the "doing of a human act". Wigmore then identified a number of different kinds of circumstantial evidence that could be used to prove each of the classes of probanda. His classification scheme for the doing of a human act was roughly as follows:

- **Prospectant evidence**
  - Character or disposition
  - Motive or emotion
  - Intention, design or plan
  - Habit or custom
- **Concomitant evidence**
  - Time and place: opportunity
  - Personality, tools, clothing, surroundings etc

- **Retrospectant evidence**
  - Mechanical and physical traces
  - Mental traces

We can think of each of these types of evidence as a kind of "clue". This idea of clues can then be used in two ways. First, we can use it to select from our main chronology those items of evidence that seem to support (or to eliminate) the theory of the case or scenario we have in mind. Second, with an idea of the kinds of items of evidence we would expect to precede, accompany or follow an event like the event in question, we can look for evidence to show that those items of evidence did or did not exist. The heads of evidence Wigmore included in each of the categories provide both useful mental prompts – what to look for – and headings under which evidence can be organised. For example, all evidence suggesting motive can be grouped together under that heading, rather than in strict chronological order. This way of grouping evidence is a precursor to the identification of the "main arguments" that we will use to prove our case: see Chapter 6.

Marshalling according to legal rules

[4.120] Marshalling according to legal rules has an obvious and intuitive appeal to lawyers. It involves identifying all of the possible causes of action, criminal offences, or defences that might arise on the information available to us. The next step is to identify all of the elements of each of these causes of action, offences or defences. The information is then grouped under these elements. In case theory terms, this is a method of marshalling according to the legal case, where scenario marshalling is a method of marshalling according to the factual theory. There are numerous advantages to this method of marshalling information according to legal rules:

- The stories clients and witnesses tell do not always fit neatly with the "stories" recognised by the law as constituting a cause of action or offence. Keeping in our mind the elements of the actions or offences we may ultimately have to prove is a useful means of prompting ourselves to ask the client or witness questions about those elements that may not form a natural part of their story but which are essential to proper proof of their case.
- This method enables us to identify the elements in relation to which there is a paucity of evidence. This may lead us to seek further evidence to support those elements, or ultimately to abandon a particular cause of action or offence that has elements we can not prove in favour of a cause of action or offence the elements of which we can prove.
- Marshalling according to legal rules enables us to identify those elements in relation to which there is a conflict of evidence.

- This method may disclose that we have a number of different ways of proving a particular element: that we have, in effect, more than one possible theory of the case open to us. In relation to the drafting of pleading, this may result in there being a variety of particulars to support one pleaded fact; or it may lead us to plead facts in the alternative.
- This method also enables us to assess whether we are complying with our ethical obligation to only plead facts that are based on our client's instructions or that we reasonably believe to exist.

Sometimes there is some legal uncertainty about one or more of the elements of a cause of action or offence. Perhaps there is a conflict of authority over exactly what must be proved in order to make out the element; or perhaps the most recent appellate pronouncement on the issue lacked clarity. In such cases, it is important to note the uncertainty and see whether, on the evidence available to us, it is likely to matter. If it does matter, then we may need to take some further steps, such as:

- develop a legal argument to support the version of the legal rule that is best for our case; and
- have a fallback position to deal with the possibility that our legal argument will be rejected by the court.

Marshalling according to factual issues

[4.130] Sometimes time is short and the issues obvious. This may be because the evidence to prove certain elements of the action or offence is so obviously incontrovertible that we can assume that no attempt will be made by our opponent to controvert it. Alternatively, the pleadings and other interlocutory procedures, such as notices to admit, may have narrowed the issues to just one or two. In such cases we may choose to focus our efforts on the issues that are likely to be the subject of dispute at the trial, and give more cursory attention to the remaining issues or elements of the cause of action or offence.

In order to marshal according to factual issues, we must first select the issues of importance. Sometimes these issues may closely correlate to a legal element of an action or offence. For example, did the plaintiff have a pre-existing injury? Did the defendant's negligence cause the plaintiff's injury? What was the accused's intention in doing the act he or she undoubtedly did? Where a crime has undoubtedly been committed by someone, was it the accused who committed it? In other cases, the issues may be more removed from the legal elements. For example, did the accused own the knife used in the attack? Did a meeting between the plaintiff and the defendant take place on a particular date?

The danger in marshalling according to factual issues rather than legal rules, however, is the obvious one: somehow overlooking the fact that there is no evidence to prove an element of the cause of action or offence. Marshalling according to factual issues can, however, be combined with marshalling according to legal rules by identifying the factual issues that arise in respect of each of the legal elements: the factual issues thus become subheadings of the legal elements.

Summary

[4.140] This chapter identified three steps that are involved in investigation:

1. **Abduction**: the imagining of a hypothesis or working theory of the case that provides an explanation of the evidence currently available to us;
2. **Retroduction**: the identification of "tests" that might confirm or disprove the hypothesis;
3. **Investigation**: the carrying out of the above "tests" through the application of appropriate investigative techniques.

The chapter then identified several different ways of marshalling information in order to facilitate investigative thinking (these were in addition to the creation of a chronology, the subject of the previous chapter):

- marshalling according to **sources** of evidence, including marshalling according to witnesses and other actors (the "who's who"), and marshalling according to real and documentary evidence;
- marshalling according to **scenarios** and **narratives**;
- marshalling for "**clues**";
- marshalling according to **legal rules**; and
- marshalling according to **factual issues**.

Theory and Proof

Developing a case theory 5

Introduction

[5.10] A theory of the case, or case theory, provides the blueprint for the conduct of the proceedings. While advocacy texts are in universal agreement that we need a case theory in order to run a trial, they do not always explain how to go about getting one. That is the subject of this chapter. The next two chapters explain how to go about proving the case theory. The three chapters should be read in conjunction. This chapter is divided into two main parts. The first contains a general discussion of case theory, distinguishing between two aspects of the case theory – the legal case, and the factual theory – and describing the ideal attributes of both. The second part describes a method for matching the legal case to the factual theory, thereby ensuring that we clearly identify what it is that we have to prove in order to succeed.

Although this "theory and proof" part of the book comes after the chapters on chronologies and investigation, in many cases the process of identifying a theory of the case and the means of proving it are likely to happen concurrently with investigative steps such as the interviewing of witnesses. When we commence our "theory and proof" analysis, for example, we may be working from a series of witness statements. At the same time that we are carrying out our "theory and proof" analysis we may also be interviewing those witnesses in order to clarify their statements, obtain further information from them, or just prepare them for the process of giving evidence at trial.

What this means is that the evidence we are analysing is seldom fixed or final; nor is it likely to be complete. This is because, apart from the committal in criminal proceedings, and in contrast to the United States system of taking depositions, Australian trial procedure provides no opportunity for a party to question its opponent's witnesses prior to the trial. As a consequence, it will not be until the close of the evidence at the trial itself that we will know what the evidence in the case actually is. This does not make the theory and proof analysis any less important; but we should be careful to remember that all we can do, prior to the trial, is analyse the evidence that we believe is likely to be adduced at the trial.

For similar reasons, this chapter and those following generally refer to "facts in issue" and "factual propositions" rather than "facts" as a reminder that at the outset of a trial the only "facts" are the things that the parties agree or admit to be facts; everything else is just an allegation – that is, a factual proposition that must be proved. Not until judgment is handed down are the "facts" known. Although this chapter and the next use a variety of terminology to describe propositions at different levels of our analysis – including legal case, factual theory, facts in issue, material facts, main arguments and items of evidence – it is important to remember that all these different kinds of propositions are factual propositions that must be proved.

CHOOSING A THEORY OF THE CASE

What is a case theory?

[5.20] Most trials are disputes about facts – that is, the parties disagree about what happened. Because the events to which the disagreements relate are (generally) in the past, the court can not perceive those events for itself and can never truly "know" what happened. Even when the events happen to have been recorded (for example, the video footage of Rodney King being beaten by Los Angeles Police, or security camera footage of an armed robbery), there can still be uncertainty about the nature of the event or the identity of the participants. Thus, factual uncertainty is a condition of litigation.

Compared to factual uncertainty, uncertainty about the law is usually relatively minor. That is, while the occurrence or nature of the events in question might be uncertain, the legal consequences of the event having occurred (or not) in a particular way are usually reasonably clear. If the accused did act in the way alleged by the prosecution, then he will be guilty of crime X; but did he do so? Of course, there are cases where the parties agree about what happened, but disagree about the legal consequences of what happened; but this kind of dispute raises different kinds of issues and requires different kinds of methods from those that are covered in this text.

Typically, then, a common law trial is an adversarial contest between two or more parties each of which is attempting to persuade the court to accept its version of events or (particularly in the case of the defence in criminal proceedings) to *not* accept the version of events put forward its opponent. This highlights the difference between a party who carries the burden of proof in a trial and a party who is free of that burden. The party with the onus of proof has to put forward a positive version of events. The party without the onus of proof may choose to put forward a version of events, but will frequently (and particularly in the case of the defence in criminal proceedings) instead attempt to raise doubt about its opponent's version of events without putting forward a positive alternative.

A positive case theory, then, is a version of events put forward by a party; it is a "theory" about what happened. It is a story, but it is a legally significant story – that is, it is a story that, if accepted, has legal consequences. In criminal proceedings, if the prosecution's story is true, then the accused is guilty of the offence charged; if the defence's story is true, then the accused is innocent, or guilty of a lesser offence. In the conditions of uncertainty that prevail in common law trials, however, the truth can never truly be known. It is therefore more accurate to say that if the prosecution's case theory is accepted, then the accused will be convicted; whereas if the defence's case theory is accepted then the accused will be acquitted. Even if the defence chooses not to put forward a positive version of events, however, it will still need a theory of the case: but the theory of the case might instead focus on identifying the elements of the opponent's case theory that will be targeted for doubt.

In terms of its role as a blueprint for the conduct of the trial, the case theory provides the answer to the first of the two key questions that must be addressed before trial (the answer to the second question is the subject of the next two chapters):

1. What do we have to prove in order to succeed?
2. How are we going to prove that?

It is the case theory that we are setting out to prove, and knowing what we are trying to prove from the outset of the trial enables us to know what evidence we need to adduce from each of our witnesses, to know whether we need to cross-examine our opponent's witnesses and, if so, to know what it is that we need to cross-examine them about. In the theory of the case is purely defensive these key questions might instead be formulated as:

- What are the facts about which we must raise doubt in order to succeed?
- How are we going to raise doubt about those facts?

If we do not know what our theory of the case is when, for example, we stand up to cross-examine our opponent's witness, then we will not know whether we agree with some or all of the things that they have said; accordingly, we will not know whether we need to damage their credibility in general, or on particular points, or indeed whether we need to cross-examine them at all. In these circumstances, our conduct of the trial is likely to be inconsistent, incoherent and unpersuasive. In short, if we do not know what we are trying to prove, we are unlikely to prove it!

The two aspects of case theory: case and theory

[5.30] In discussing the theory of the case, it is useful to distinguish between two different aspects. We will call these two aspects the "legal case" or "case", and the "factual theory" or "theory". There is nothing preordained about these terms; Anderson, Schum and Twining, for example, use the terms "theory" and "story" instead of "case" and "theory"; and Berger et al, talk about the "legal theory" and the "factual theory". I am using "case" and "theory" in a way that I hope corresponds to the manner in which a lawyer would ordinarily respond to the questions from the bench – that is, along the lines of "What is your case?" and "What is your theory?"

The "case" (or "legal case"), then, is an encapsulation of the theory of the case in a single factual proposition, the case in its essence, a proposition to the effect that an event with legal consequences has occurred. It is a succinct statement of the theory of the case in language that corresponds to the substantive law: an action for breach of contract, a case of murder, a defence of contributory negligence. For example, in a homicide trial the prosecution's case might be that "the accused murdered the deceased". In a contract case, the plaintiff's case might be that "the defendant breached its contract with the plaintiff, and thereby caused the plaintiff to suffer loss".

The legal case can be broken down into the elements laid down by the substantive law: the elements of a cause of action, the elements of a criminal offence, and the elements of a defence. These elements of the case constitute the "facts in issue" in the trial. Legal cases can thus be said to be based on "templates" established by the substantive law which set out the features that a narrative or factual theory must have in order to be recognised as being of legal consequence, in the sense that a narrative with these elements is actionable, or constitutes a crime, or provides a defence to a cause of action or criminal prosecution.

The "theory" (or "factual theory"), on the other hand, is a narrative or story that is capable of filling all the holes in the template, and thus ensuring that all of the elements of the legal case are present. It is a "theory" in the sense that it is a theory about what happened, an explanation for all of the evidence. We can distinguish between two types of factual theory – the purely descriptive and the explanatory: see Binder and Bergman (1984, p 177). A descriptive theory is simply a story about *what* happened. An explanatory theory also attempts to explain *why* this happened. As discussed below, a factual theory with both descriptive and explanatory elements is more complete, and therefore more plausible, than a purely descriptive theory.

The theory of the case is the combination of these two aspects, the case and the theory. In order to succeed at trial, it is the case that we must make out, the case that we must prove. The theory, however, provides the means of proving the case. In other words, if we can persuade the court to accept our theory about what happened – that is, our narrative – then (assuming we have done our work correctly) our case will also be established. To put it another way, the theory is the answer to the question "what do you say happened?"; and the case enables us to answer the question "what is the legal significance of that?"

Defence theories of the case

[5.40] There are a number of ways in which defendants, civil or criminal, can respond to a positive theory of the case put forward by the party with the onus of proof, namely the plaintiff or prosecution. For instance, defendants may:

- deny that the plaintiff's/prosecution's legal case has a proper foundation in law – that is, they may argue that even if the facts were as alleged, they would still not constitute a cause of action or offence;
- put forward a legal case of their own in the form of a legally-recognised defence to the legal case of the plaintiff/prosecution. Such a case effectively "trumps" the legal case of the plaintiff/prosecution. Examples of such defences are contributory negligence, voluntary assumption of risk, and self-defence. These defences are their own independent legal cases, with elements that must be satisfied by a factual theory, just like the legal case of the plaintiff/prosecution (although the burden of proof in criminal proceedings may mean that once the defence is properly open on the evidence, the onus is on the prosecution to disprove it);

- attack the plaintiff's/prosecution's factual theory by arguing that the evidence adduced does not address one or more of the elements of the legal case – in other words, argue that there is no case to answer;
- attack the persuasiveness of the factual theory. This may involve putting forward a factual theory to compete with that put forward by the plaintiff/prosecution, or it may simply involve reliance on an argument that the plaintiff/prosecution has not satisfied its burden of proof.

If we are acting for the defence, then in order to take either of the last two options above, we will have to carry out the same analysis of the plaintiff's/prosecution's legal case and factual theory as the plaintiff or prosecutor would have had to do. One major difference between the roles, though, is that the plaintiff/prosecution will only succeed if every element of the legal case is satisfied; the defence can succeed by defeating any one of those elements. It may be a legitimate time-saving choice, then, to focus our analysis and efforts on that element of the plaintiff's/ prosecution's legal case we regard as weakest, and to effectively concede the other elements.

Anticipating the opponent's theory of the case

[5.50] We should always attempt to anticipate our opponent's case theory, both in legal and factual terms. In a civil proceeding, the pleadings should give us some idea of our opponent's case theory; in criminal proceedings, the prosecution might get some idea of the likely defence case theory from the accused's record of interview or, in jurisdictions that provide for these procedures, from the defence response to a prosecution case statement. At other times, it may be necessary for us to use our imagination and ask ourselves the question: "If I were my opponent, how would I run their case?"

If our opponent's case theory is simply a contradiction of our own factual theory, then we may be able simply to note the areas of contradiction when mapping our own case, rather than creating an independent map of our opponent's case. Where our opponent is advancing his or her own legal case, however, or where their factual theory is more than just a contradiction of ours, then separate mapping may be necessary. Methods of mapping case theories are discussed in the next chapter.

Researching and selecting the legal case

[5.60] A legal case is not simply plucked from thin air: it is suggested by the stories told by the client and/or witnesses, and the factual theory that we build from that material. We may also believe that there are a number of possible legal cases open to us. With some idea of the legal case in mind, there are several steps we now need to take:

- Ensure that our case has a solid **foundation in law** – that is, that it corresponds to a legally recognised cause of action, criminal offence, or defence.
- Identify, and set out, all of the **elements** of the legal case. Where there is more than one legal case, the elements of each should be set out separately. By doing this, we are providing ourselves with the answer to the question: "What do we have to prove in order to succeed?" Methods for setting out the case are discussed in the next chapter.
- Carry out any **legal research** into areas of uncertainty associated with the legal case or cases. The legal research required here is in terms of the substantive law, rather than the law of evidence. It may be that there is uncertainty about exactly what must be proved in order to satisfy one or more of the elements of a legal case: this uncertainty should be noted, and we might choose to set out the competing versions of the element in question.
- Check that the legal case, if successful, will provide the client with the **remedy** they are seeking. If we are acting for a plaintiff in potential civil proceedings, it is also important, as a matter of practical reality, that we select as a defendant a person who will be capable of satisfying a judgment against them.
- Match the factual theory to the legal case. This means ensuring that the factual theory, or story, we will present to the court is capable of satisfying all the elements of the legal case. This is discussed in the second part of this chapter.
- Analyse the evidence from the point of view of proving the case: this is the subject of the next chapter.

Choosing the factual theory

[5.70] Before discussing how we should go about proving our case theory, it is worth describing the criteria by which a factual theory, or story, will be judged – that is, what makes a factual theory a good factual theory? This is particularly important where we are faced with a choice of possible theories.

Consistency with instructions

[5.80] Our factual theory must be consistent with our instructions from our client: there is no point in developing a theory of self-defence when our client is adamant that he or she was not the person involved.

Legal significance

[5.90] Human experience is infinite in its variety; in terms of legal significance, however, only certain kinds of "stories" count. The stories that count are those that can be fitted into the framework or pattern of one of the templates recognised by the law as constituting a cause of action, criminal offence, or defence. These standard templates have certain elements, and their acceptance by the court entails certain results or remedies.

In order for a factual theory of the case to be legally significant, it must be made to fit into one of these standard templates, and it must be capable of satisfying all the necessary elements of that template. A story involving a complaint about an invasion of the client's privacy is not legally significant if the law provides no remedy for a breach of privacy. Similarly, a story about a breach of contract is not legally significant unless it contains all the elements necessary to make out a breach of contract claim: offer and acceptance, consideration, loss and so on.

Comprehensiveness

[5.100] A factual theory must be capable of accounting for all of the evidence in the case. Evidence that is inconsistent with the factual theory can not simply be ignored in the hope that it will go away: it will not! This does not mean that the factual theory has to be consistent with all of the evidence: that will usually be impossible. It does mean, however, that the factual theory must be comprehensive in the sense that it is able to account for all of the evidence, to provide an explanation for everything.

Thus, the factual theory will dictate our "attitude" to all of the evidence in the case. The evidence is either consistent with our theory (and therefore to be accepted) or inconsistent with our theory (and therefore to be rejected). If it is to be rejected, our theory should tell us why: is the witness mistaken or lying? Is the document a forgery or did our client sign it without understanding what it was?

Evidential support

[5.110] Comprehensiveness is not enough, however. For example, a factual theory that posits that the witnesses are all lying, the documents are all forged, and the real evidence was all planted or manufactured by the police is comprehensive in the sense described above, but it is also likely to be lacking in evidential support. A good factual theory is not only able to account for all the evidence, it is also supported by that evidence. The more evidence we have to explain away, the weaker the factual theory will be. Ideally, our factual theory will require us to explain away the smallest amount of evidence consistent with victory.

It is also important that our theory stays "close" to the evidence, in the sense that we avoid over-elaborating, or setting out to prove something that is in truth a matter of speculation or conjecture rather than inference, particularly where that something is unnecessary to our case. If we have no basis for attributing motive, for example, then it is counter-productive to do so.

Plausibility

[5.120] The stronger the evidential support for a theory, the more plausible the court will find it. Independently of the degree of evidential support, however, some stories are inherently more plausible than others. Plausible stories conform to commonly held views about the ways in which human beings behave, or how the world operates; implausible stories are at odds with those views.

Research by psychologists suggests that juries make sense of evidence presented at trial by imposing a narrative on it. This narrative will be constructed out of a combination of the trial evidence, the jury's collective knowledge about similar events, and the jury's generic expectations about what makes a complete story: see Pennington and Hastie (1991). The more a party's case theory conforms to the jury's knowledge about similar events, and their expectations about what makes a complete story, the more likely it is to be accepted. There is no reason to believe that judges or magistrates are any different from juries in this regard.

Plausible stories are thus "complete" stories; they explain, for example, *why* people acted as they did. It is for this reason, rather than because it is an element of any offence, that evidence of motive is so important in the construction of a plausible case theory. Similarly, it is for this reason that when a case theory involves a person acting in a way that seems to be out of character, either their "true" character should be revealed, or the circumstances should be shown to have been exceptional.

A story is complete when it provides answers to questions such as "Why would that person have done this?" If the story is incomplete, this may have to be acknowledged in the opening or closing addresses – for example, "we cannot know why this person acted as they did, but the evidence clearly shows that they did". This is because – as was discussed above at [5.110] in relation to the need for evidential support – it is important not to promise to prove more than we can prove; so if we are unable to say exactly how, or when, or why, a particular event occurred, then we should not do so.

In *Weissensteiner v The Queen* (1993) 178 CLR 217, for example, the accused was charged with the murder of a couple with whom he had gone on a yachting trip. The three had sailed off together; the accused returned alone. The couple's bodies were never found. If the accused had murdered the couple, then there was no evidence to say exactly when, or how, he had done this. The story presented by the prosecution was therefore unavoidably incomplete, but the accused was convicted nevertheless.

Plausible stories also conform to the jury's beliefs about similar events. Sometimes those beliefs may be stereotyped, ignorant or prejudiced. This presents a great challenge that there is no simple way of addressing. If our client's instructions are that "a dingo took my baby", then we have little choice but to attempt to persuade the jury that, notwithstanding their beliefs that dingoes do not do things like that, this is precisely what happened.

Sometimes the reasons for the apparent implausibility may have to be addressed head-on. Battered woman syndrome evidence, for example, is essentially used to overcome stereotyped views about how people who are subjected to violence are likely to behave – namely by removing themselves from the situation in which the violence is occurring. The use of battered woman syndrome evidence is an attempt to change the tribunal's views on this point, and so open the door to the acceptance of a story that might otherwise seem implausible.

Minimalism

[5.130] As already discussed, we should generally avoid setting out to prove any fact that we do not have to prove in order to succeed. For example, in *Weissensteiner v The Queen* (1993) 178 CLR 54 if the prosecution had put forward a positive factual theory about the time, location or cause of death of the two people who had disappeared, they would have created an easy target for the defence. And if the defence had been able to cast doubt on the prosecution's theory on these details (as they inevitably would have), this would have affected the credibility of its entire case. Given that the criminal law did not require the prosecution to prove these facts, it would have breached the principle of minimalism to set out to prove them.

Of course, it is sometimes helpful to include in our theory of the case a fact that, strictly speaking, is unnecessary. Motive, as already discussed, is a common example of this. Motive is not an element of any criminal offence; but if the prosecution can prove that there was a motive this will answer one of the questions that a jury will almost inevitably ask itself: why would the accused have done that? However, as soon as we assert a motive as a fact, we have effectively included it in our theory of the case and taken on the onus of proving it. If our opponent is able to cast doubt on the motive, then this will cast doubt on our entire factual theory, even though motive is not an element of the legal case.

It is possible, however, to incorporate unnecessary (but helpful) facts such as motive into our factual theory without taking on the onus of proving them. We can do this by being careful when we address the tribunal of fact to avoid asserting that the particular fact is true, but instead offering it to the tribunal as a possible explanation. For example, rather than saying "the accused did this because ...", we might instead say something along the lines of "you might wonder whether the reason the accused did this could be because ...", or "you might think ...". By using words such as this we can offer the explanation without damaging our case if we fail to positively prove it. Similarly in *Weissensteiner* it was possible for the prosecution to point out that the accused had the means to kill his companions (there was a rifle on board, for example), without positively asserting that this was how he had done it.

The principle of minimalism is particularly important to the party that does not have the onus of proof, namely the defence. If the defence puts forward a positive factual theory in the eyes of the tribunal of fact it takes on the onus of proving that theory. This is so even though as a matter of law, the onus of proof will remain on the prosecution. This is because the tribunal of fact is likely to evaluate the prosecution and defence theories of the case as if they were equal competitors, choosing the theory that they consider to be more probable. The accused may thus be convicted because the defence theory was less probable than the prosecution theory, rather than because the tribunal was satisfied that the prosecution had proved its theory beyond reasonable doubt. There is therefore a risk for the defence in offering an alternative version of events – such as that someone else was the real perpetrator, that the accused was framed, or that the accused was elsewhere at the time (alibi) – rather than simply seeking to raise doubt about the prosecution case.

For the same reason, the prosecution and defence will often attempt to characterise the issues in the trial in fundamentally different ways. The prosecution will usually want to characterise the issues as being about what really happened, the truth; the defence, on the other hand, will usually want to characterise the issues as being about whether or not the prosecution can prove their case beyond reasonable doubt. This difference is likely to flow through into the way in which each party addresses the tribunal of fact: the prosecution will usually want to talk about what really happened (while acknowledging its duty to prove its case beyond reasonable doubt); the defence, on the other hand, will usually want to talk about whether the facts in issue have been proved beyond reasonable doubt.

Simplicity

[5.140] The principle of "Ockham's Razor" is that the simpler an explanation is, the more likely it is to be true. For example, where something has gone wrong, it is more likely to have been due to a stuff-up than to a conspiracy. Complexities should only be introduced if the simpler theory fails to provide an adequate explanation for all of the evidence: in other words, complexities should only be introduced to the extent that they are necessary.

The same is true of a theory that requires the tribunal of fact to make a distasteful finding of fact. If we can succeed without alleging fraud, for example, then in general fraud should not be alleged; if we can show that a witness might have been mistaken, it is unnecessary to try and persuade the tribunal of fact that he or she is lying. This is reflected in the oft-quoted dictum of the High Court of Australia in *Briginshaw v Briginshaw* (1938) 60 CLR 336 to the effect that particular care and caution are required before the tribunal of fact should find that a serious allegation, such as fraud or adultery, has been made out.

Consistency

[5.150] It is sometimes tempting to want to run a number of alternative theories: my client was not there; and if he was, then he did not do it; and if he did, then he was acting in self-defence. On their own, each of these factual theories might be plausible; failure to choose one of them, however, is likely to mean that none is accepted. This is because they can not all be true: the three theories are mutually inconsistent.

In determining whether reliance on alternative theories will contravene the requirement of consistency, the test is really this: is the very fact of a party offering alternatives likely to make the tribunal of fact suspect that the party does not really know what happened, or that the party has no interest in the truth? In applying this test, it is necessary to distinguish between the legal case and the factual theory. The example in the paragraph above is one involving inconsistent factual theories.

The problem of inconsistency is likely to arise where alternative legal cases are based on alternative factual theories. Frequently, however, one factual theory can give rise to a number of alternative legal cases – in the form of different causes of action or offences, such as actions for breach of contract, for misleading and deceptive conduct under the *Competition and Consumer Act 2010* (Cth), or for deceit. Alternative legal cases are frequently put forward in pleadings, or relied on by police when charging a number of offences for the same conduct. If there is a problem in reliance on alternative legal cases, it is not a problem of inconsistency, but of lack of clarity.

There are also occasions when it is possible to rely on alternative factual theories without contravening the requirement of consistency. There may be a number of different ways in which a particular aspect of the legal case can be proven: for example, statements of claim in negligence actions frequently plead numerous particulars of the allegation of breach of duty, any one of which would be capable of satisfying this aspect of the cause of action. In effect, the pleadings allege that there were numerous breaches of duty.

Similarly, in criminal proceedings, it may be quite reasonable for the prosecution to assert that the accused intended to kill the deceased; but that if the jury is not completely satisfied on this point, then they should at least be persuaded that the accused was reckless in regard to the possibility of death. The two mental states, while distinct, lie on the same continuum. The alternative theory can be offered to the jury without undermining the primary theory.

Clarity

[5.160] It should be possible to state our factual theory succinctly – that is, to encapsulate it in a few pithy sentences, no matter how complex the issues in the trial or voluminous the evidence. It is perfectly legitimate in an adversarial system of justice to leave out detail that is unnecessary to our factual theory in order to present a story that is clearer and more easily understood: in any trial there is an almost infinite amount of information and detail that could be presented, and failure to leave out some of that material may create the risk that our factual theory will be lost in the clutter of detail. There is only a danger in doing this if the details we have left out are likely to jump up and bite us when raised, for example, in cross-examination.

Clarity may also require the abandonment of some of the alternative legal cases, particularly where the tribunal of fact is a jury. It may simply confuse a jury to be presented with a whole range of possible causes of action or offences constituted by the alleged conduct. Unless there is a very good reason to advance alternative theories – such as the desirability of certain remedies only available on certain causes of action – then it may be wise to choose the strongest legal case and drop the others.

Flexibility

[5.170] The best laid plans can go awry. Witnesses fail to turn up, fail to testify in accordance with their earlier statements, fail to be as credible as we had hoped they would, or give evidence that we did not anticipate them giving. Evidence we had hoped to rely on may be ruled inadmissible; or evidence of our opponent that we had hoped to be able to exclude may be admitted. Our factual theory must be sufficiently flexible to enable us to adapt to these circumstances. For example, if certain aspects of our factual theory are rejected, can we construct an alternative case based on our opponent's factual theory? The need for flexibility should particularly be borne in mind when drafting our opening address: it is damaging to promise to prove something and then be unable to prove it.

MATCHING FACTUAL THEORY TO LEGAL CASE

[5.180] With both a legal case and factual theory in mind, it is now possible to carry out a detailed analysis in which the elements of the factual theory are matched to the elements of the legal case. The purpose of carrying out such an analysis is to enable us to:

- be confident that proof of our factual theory will satisfy the elements of our legal case; and
- identify the elements of our factual theory that are crucial to the proof of our legal case.

The analysis is divided into three main steps:

1. stating the legal case;
2. breaking the legal case into its elements (the "facts in issue"); and
3. identifying the elements of the factual theory that will be used to prove each of the facts in issue.

State the legal case

[5.190] The "case" or "legal case" is the ultimate factual proposition that we must prove in order to succeed. This factual proposition corresponds to the substantive law, and might – in, for example, a homicide trial – be a proposition such as that "the accused intentionally killed the deceased". In cases where there is more than one legal case – for example, if the plaintiff is relying on theories of breach of contract, fraudulent misrepresentation and misleading and deceptive conduct – then each case will require its own analysis. The legal case provides the touchstone for relevance and should be drafted carefully. It is also important to check that the legal case has sound foundations in the substantive law: this was discussed earlier in this chapter.

Identify the facts in issue

[5.200] It is well known that proof of a cause of action or offence requires proof of several distinct elements. In order to ensure that we clearly identify all the different factual propositions that we must prove in order to succeed, the legal case should be broken down into these elements. The **elements of the case** are laid down by the substantive law: the elements of the cause of action, criminal offence or defence. These elements of the case are often called the "**facts in issue**"; they are "in issue" in the sense that they provide the focus of the dispute between the parties, and are crucial to the outcome of the litigation. This is because proof of all of the facts in issue should necessarily entail proof of the legal case (if this is not the case, then there is something wrong with our analysis). As McHugh J said in *Goldsmith v Sandilands* (2001) 190 ALR 370; [2002] HCA 31 at [31]:

> The facts in issue reflect the material facts that constitute the claimant's cause of action – which may be defined as the set of facts to which the law attaches the legal consequences that the claimant asserts. The facts in issue also include those material facts that provide any justification or excuse for, or a defence to, the cause of action.

Similarly, in the criminal context, Gleeson CJ, Gaudron, Gummow and Hayne JJ said in *Smith v The Queen* (2001) 206 CLR 650; [2001] HCA 50 at [7], that:

> [o]n a criminal trial the ultimate issues will be expressed in terms of the elements of the offence with which the accused stands charged. They will, therefore, be issues about the facts which constitute those elements.

The facts in issue, or elements of the case, are thus case-specific factual propositions couched in legally significant language: for example, in a homicide trial, among the facts in issue might be propositions to the effect that "the accused caused the death of the deceased"; in a rape trial, propositions to the effect that "the accused sexually penetrated the complainant" and "the complainant did not consent to this"; in a breach of contract case, propositions to the effect that "the parties had entered into a legally binding agreement" (which would itself require proof of several subsidiary facts in issue relating to offer and acceptance, consideration and so on) and "the defendant breached this contract"; and in a negligence action, propositions to the effect that "the defendant owed the plaintiff a duty of care", "the defendant breached the duty of care" and the "defendant's breach of duty caused the plaintiff to suffer loss and damage".

It is the facts in issue that form the basis of the **pleadings** in a civil case, and of the **presentment** or **indictment** in a criminal case. However, although the facts in issue are "factual" propositions, they are not so much elements of a narrative as they are assertions that an element of a legally recognised criminal offence or cause of action is present. For example, assertions to the effect that "the accused caused the death of the deceased, and did so intending to kill the deceased", or that "the defendant breached its contract with the plaintiff thereby causing the plaintiff to suffer loss and damage" tell us virtually nothing about the narratives that will be used to substantiate these assertions. This is because the facts in issue are the elements of the legal case, not the factual theory.

Indeed, the facts in issue will be essentially the same for every homicide, and for every breach of contract case, and for this reason we often just use shorthand to designate the facts in issue. In a negligence case, for example, we may use labels like "duty of care", "breach of duty", "causation" and "damage" as shorthand for the propositions set out in full above. This is fine, provided we remember that the labels are only shorthand for facts that must be proved.

Although the facts in issue are essentially the same for all actions or prosecutions of a particular type, it is often useful to identify the facts in issue in order to ensure that we have the means of proving them. Few things are more embarrassing than being no-cased by an opponent because of a failure to lead evidence to prove one of the elements of the legal case, particularly if the means were available to do so.

[5.210] Where a **defence** is being raised, there are additional facts in issue. For example, a prosecution theory of the case in which the defence is self-defence, should also have as a fact in issue the proposition that "the accused was not acting in self-defence". This is because if self-defence is open on the evidence, the onus of disproving it rests on the prosecution. In civil proceedings, by contrast, the onus of proving a defence rests on the defence, so disproof of the defence is not a necessary element of the plaintiff's case; but it may still be convenient to include it in our own analysis.

There are sometimes also some **technical matters** that must be proved (or admitted); for example, if one of the parties is not a human being, it may be necessary to prove that the party in question is a "legal person" capable of suing or being sued. Whether or not such matters are included as facts in issue is not important, provided that they are not overlooked.

In some cases there may be a number of **alternatives** available in respect of a particular element of the cause of action or offence. In a homicide trial in Victoria, for example, the mens rea for murder can be described as "intent or recklessness as to death or grievous bodily harm". It can immediately be seen that mens rea can be satisfied in a number of alternative ways: by showing that the accused intended to kill the deceased; intended to cause grievous bodily harm to the deceased; or performed the actus reus knowing that it was probable that death or grievous bodily harm would result from it. If the prosecution is uncertain that it will be able to show that the accused intended to kill the deceased, then it might rely on recklessness or intention to cause grievous bodily harm as an alternative. Although the same evidence might be used to prove each of these alternative facts in issue, it is useful to identify them separately. Of course, if the prosecution case is that the accused did in fact intend to kill the deceased, then there might be no need to consider the alternatives.

With the legal case now broken into its elements, attention turns to the factual theory. The factual theory, too, must be broken into its elements.

Identify the key elements of the factual theory

[5.220] We will assume that we have already selected a factual theory that has as many as possible of the attributes described earlier in this chapter. This factual theory is a story or narrative, a version of events advanced by us. It is by proving the factual theory that we satisfy the elements of the legal case. We must therefore check that the proof of the factual theory will indeed satisfy the elements of the legal case. The process involves looking at each of the facts in issue in turn, and identifying the element or elements of the factual theory that satisfy each of those facts in issue.

Any element of the factual theory that is essential to the proof of one or more of the facts in issue is crucial to our case: if we fail to prove that element of the factual theory, we will fail to prove one or more of the facts in issue, and our case will fail. We can call the elements of the factual theory that are crucial to our success in this way the "**material facts**". The material facts are the parts of the factual theory that we must prove if we are to succeed. In a civil case, the material facts have a loose correspondence with the **pleadings** and the **particulars** of the pleadings.

The material facts differ from the facts in issue in that they are elements of an actual narrative being presented to the court. For example, where one of the facts in issue in a homicide case might be a proposition to the effect that "the accused caused the death of the deceased", the equivalent material fact might be a proposition to the effect that "the accused stabbed the deceased fifteen times in the chest". In the latter proposition we have moved away from the language of the law into the language of a narrative.

What the "facts in issue" and "material facts" have in common, however, is that they are both likely to be "in issue" – that is, the subject of dispute – between the parties. For this reason, courts and the parties to litigation frequently use the phrase "facts in issue" to refer to the contested elements of both the legal case and the factual theory. As McHugh J indicated in the passage from *Goldsmith v Sandilands* quoted above, the facts in issue in a trial effectively "include" the material facts because it is the material facts that must be proved in order to make out the elements of the cause of action, offence or defence in question. So, while this text does draw a distinction between the facts in issue and the material facts, the distinction need not be strictly adhered to, and the phrase "facts in issue" can safely be used to encompass both the elements of the legal case and the elements of the factual theory that are necessary to the proof of that case.

In any event, it is in connecting the material facts to the facts in issue that we construct the relationship between the legal case and the factual theory. What is required of us is to identify precisely which elements of the factual theory are relevant to prove precisely which elements of the legal case. For example, in a case where the defence was one of self-defence, the fact that "the accused attacked the deceased first" might be relevant to prove the fact in issue that "the accused was not acting in self-defence".

Sometimes there may be more than one element of the factual theory that is capable of satisfying a particular fact in issue; in such cases, we are blessed with **alternatives**. In a negligence action, for example, numerous particulars of breach of duty are often pleaded: proof of any one of these material facts will satisfy this element of the legal case. Similarly, in a prosecution for assault, there may be several acts that are capable of constituting the assault. Sometimes, we also need to identify **fall-back** positions: if we are unable to prove our primary factual proposition, is there a fall-back proposition that may also satisfy the particular fact in issue? Having fall-back positions is consistent with the need for flexibility in our factual theory.

Reflect on the objects of proof

[5.230] Through our analysis we have now identified those things we must prove in order to succeed. These "objects of proof" fall into two categories:

1. the elements of the legal case or facts in issue; and
2. the elements of the factual theory or material facts.

We prove the material facts by means of evidence, and thus satisfy the elements of the legal case. Chapter 6 describes a generalised method for analysing evidence in order to prove our material facts. Before delving into the nitty-gritty of the evidence, however, it is often useful to take the time to think a little more reflectively about the objects of proof we have identified, asking ourselves a question such as "What kind of evidence would we need to prove such a fact?"

For example, among the elements of the case may be a requirement of causation, or the possession of a particular mental state; no doubt our factual theory will also contain factual propositions that satisfy these elements (if not, then our factual theory is defective). But how do we go about proving that one event caused another? Or that a person had a particular mental state at the time of doing an act? Of course, the objects of proof that can arise in litigation are infinite in their variety. They vary according to the particular area of practice, influenced or determined by the content of specific rules of substantive law, and by the custom or habit of those who practise within a particular field. Indeed, often the easiest way to find out how to go about proving the objects of proof that arise in a particular area of practice is to ask a practitioner with experience in that area.

Some objects of proof do, nevertheless, arise in numerous different areas of practice. These include:

- that an event occurred, or occurred in a particular way;
- that a person did an act, or did an act in a particular way;
- that one event caused another event to occur;
- that a person had a particular state of mind at a time of interest to us;
- that an object or course of conduct conformed, or did not conform, to a particular standard; and
- the identity of persons or things.

In Chapter 4, under the heading "Marshalling for 'clues'" (at [4.110]), we discussed the circumstantial evidence that Wigmore argued was relevant to prove the doing of a human act. This included such things as motive, intention, opportunity and so on. Wigmore, in fact, attempted to classify the objects of proof that arise in litigation into a series of categories and subcategories which, between them, "covered the field"; and he also attempted to identify systematically the kind of evidence that could be used to prove each of these categories and subcategories. This aspect of his work makes interesting reading. It is often helpful to take a similar approach to the propositions we are required to prove in the litigation in which we are involved. The essence of the approach is to ask ourselves, for instance, "How would I know whether one event caused another?" or, "How would I know what a person's state of mind was at a particular point in time?"

[5.240] Taking state of mind first, the well-known dictum of Megarry J in *Re Flynn (deceased); Flynn v Flynn* [1968] 1 WLR 103 at 107 that the "state of a man's mind is as much a fact as the state of his digestion" does not take us very far because it begs the question of how we are to prove that fact. Although different states of mind must be proved in different ways, common to all of them is the fact that the only person who can give direct evidence about a person's state of mind is that particular person (the phrase "direct evidence" is defined at [6.40]). This evidence may take the form of contemporaneous statements, or it might be given in the witness box. Apart from this common element, different states of mind require different kinds of evidence.

If, for example, one of our objects of proof is the proposition that a person knew of a particular fact (for example, that a machine was unsafe, or that the person was insolvent), we might be able to prove this by leading evidence to show that the person must have actually perceived the fact in question, or by leading evidence to show that someone had told them about the fact. Alternatively, we might be able to prove the fact of their knowledge by relying on their conduct on the basis that they had behaved in a manner that suggested that they knew of the fact in question.

If, on the other hand, we are required to prove intent, then the best means of proving this might again be to rely on the evidence of the person's conduct, but this time on the basis that what a person says or does is evidence of what they intended to do. To take an obvious example, if the person in question has shot another in the head at point blank range, this usually provides a strong foundation for an inference that they intended to kill that person. This inference obviously rests in part on the fact that it is a matter of common knowledge that shooting someone in the head is likely to kill them. Of course, as Megarry J pointed out, in "one sense there is no end to the evidence that may be adduced; for the whole of a man's life and all that he has said and done, however trivial, may be prayed in aid in determining what his intention was at any given moment in time"; realistically, however, "[a]ll that the courts can do is to draw inferences from what has been said and done; and in doing this, too much detail may stultify".

Turning to the causation example, the aetiology of many events is well known and understood: for example, a court will have no difficulty in seeing that a spill of cooking oil on a supermarket floor might cause someone to slip and fall when they would not otherwise have done so. Often, however, we may conclude that expert evidence is necessary to establish a causal link between one event and another; for example, medical evidence to establish that the accused's stabbing of the deceased was the cause of the deceased's death. Sometimes even the experts might be uncertain about the aetiology of certain events, such as cancers and other illnesses. The most they may be able to point to is a statistical correlation between exposure to a particular risk and the occurrence of the illness, and correlation is not the same as causation. If we do not have any evidence to the effect that a particular event definitely did cause the event in question, then we may have to focus our attention on the other possible causes: if we can eliminate all of the other possible causes, then the event we have identified as the cause must have been the cause (the elimination of alternatives is discussed further at [7.160]-[7.210] under the heading "Arguments about inferences").

Summary

[5.250] A number of terms and concepts have been introduced in this chapter. These include:

- the **theory of the case**, or case theory: the combination of the legal case and the factual theory;
- the **legal case**: the statement of the case in its essence, a proposition to the effect that an event recognised by the law as being of consequence has occurred;
- the **facts in issue**: the **elements of the legal case**, derived from the substantive law;
- the **factual theory**: the "theory" of what happened, a party's version of events, a narrative or story capable of satisfying the elements of the legal case;
- the **material facts**: the elements of the factual theory that are essential to the proof of one or more of the facts in issue (the material facts are also sometimes referred to as the "facts in issue"); and
- the **objects of proof**: the facts in issue and material facts.

The method described in this chapter can be summarised as follows:

1. state the legal case;
2. identify the elements of the legal case (the facts in issue);
3. identify the key elements of the factual theory (the material facts); and
4. reflect on the means of proving the objects of proof.

Finally, the chapter argued that the prospects of a factual theory being accepted by a court were likely to be determined by the degree to which the theory possessed the following attributes:

- consistency with instructions;
- legal significance;
- comprehensiveness;
- evidential support;
- plausibility;
- minimalism;
- simplicity;
- consistency;
- clarity; and
- flexibility.

Proving the theory   6

Introduction

[6.10]   Chapter 5 explained how to go about choosing a case theory, and attempted to describe what it is that distinguishes a good case theory from a bad one. It also drew a distinction between two aspects of the case theory: the legal case and the factual theory, explaining how the factual theory is our means of proving the legal case. With the case theory now selected, this chapter explains how to go about proving it. Like the methods described in Chapters 3 and 4, the methods expounded in this chapter are a form of evidence marshalling – that is, the evidence is marshalled according to the case theory. Marshalling the evidence in this way forces us to think about how we are going to prove our theory of the case, and thereby provides us with the answer to the second of the two key questions that must be addressed before trial. Those questions are, it will be recalled:

1. What do we have to prove in order to succeed?
2. How are we going to prove that?

If our theory of the case is purely defensive these questions might instead be formulated as:

1. What are the facts about which we must raise doubt in order to succeed?
2. How are we going to raise doubt about those facts?

What we are really doing at this stage, however, is identifying the arguments on which we hope to be able to rely in our closing address to the court. Thinking ahead to the arguments we want to make in the closing address forces us to identify the evidence we will need to adduce during the course of the trial in order to be able to make those arguments. This is very important because our arguments about what happened must be based on evidence: if we neglect to lead the evidence, then we will be unable to make the argument.

The first part of the chapter describes, in general terms, how to go about marshalling evidence according to the factual theory. The second part of the chapter describes three different methods for "outputting" the fruits of this analysis:

1. the prose method;
2. the chart method; and
3. the outline method.

Each of these methods can be used to produce a "map" of our arguments in the case, which can then be used both to structure and record our analysis, and to communicate that analysis to others.

The analytical methods described in this chapter are concerned with the "big picture" of the case as a whole – thus, they are a form of macro-analysis. Sometimes, however, it is helpful to descend into the details, to micro-analyse individual items, or particular combinations, of evidence. The micro-analysis of evidence is the subject of Chapter 7. The two chapters are complementary, and the preparation of a complete case map usually requires both macro- and micro-analyses.

MATCHING EVIDENCE TO FACTUAL THEORY

[6.20] Following Chapter 5, we should have already selected a legal case and factual theory. We will also have identified the key elements of the factual theory (the material facts) – that is, the elements of the factual theory that satisfy the elements of the legal case (the facts in issue), and on which proof of the legal case therefore depends. So how will we prove the material facts? The answer is obvious: by means of evidence.

The aim of the analysis described in this part of the chapter, then, is to develop the evidence-based arguments that we will use to persuade the court to accept our factual theory. These are the arguments that we want to be able to make in our closing address to the court. We can develop these arguments by analysing the relationship between the factual theory and the evidence (just as in the second part of Chapter 5 we analysed the relationship between the factual theory and the legal case).

Focus on the real issues

[6.30] In some cases, we can immediately identify the fact that some of the "facts in issue" are not really in "issue" at all. In civil proceedings, in particular, the pleadings will generally narrow the issues, and render some of the facts in issue uncontentious. The pleadings should therefore be carefully scrutinised in order to identify the propositions that our opponent denies, admits, or does not admit. Similarly, the parties may have made formal admissions, or made agreements about the existence of certain facts that constitute key elements of our factual theory. It is often helpful to construct a table that summarises the effect of each of the main pleadings in the statement of claim (and any defence or counterclaim), together with the various parties' responses to those pleadings.

Our previous analysis of the evidence may also suggest that the evidence in relation to some of our material facts is so overwhelming that they can not be seriously contested. In a criminal proceeding, for example, the fact that the crime was committed may effectively be beyond dispute; the real issue may simply be whether it was the accused who committed the crime. If the nature of the actus reus, or the circumstances in which it was committed, are themselves evidence of the mens rea, then proof of identity may provide sufficient proof of all the necessary facts in issue. Conversely, the evidence that the accused committed the actus reus may be overwhelming (including reliable admissions by the accused), and the issue may be one of mens rea, or of the availability of an affirmative defence.

As long as our analysis is sound, and we still remember at trial to lead all the evidence that proves the "uncontentious" facts in issue, then we can focus on the material facts that are likely to be the real subject of dispute in the trial.

Proving the material facts with evidence

[6.40] Our factual theory is the answer to the question "What happened?" But we must now answer the next question: "How do we know that this is what happened?" Or, to put it another way, "What reasons can we give the court to believe or accept that this is what happened?" In order to answer these questions, and thereby persuade the court to accept our factual theory, we must develop arguments based on the evidence. We should already have carried out some sort of analysis in which we have identified all the items of evidence available to us. This "inventory" of evidence might take the form of a chronology, or it might take the form of one of the other marshalling methods described in Chapter 4. We will use the label "item of evidence" to describe any factual proposition for which we have a direct source – for example a witness who can testify to that effect.

In broad terms, the items of evidence available to us will fall into two main categories:

1. **Direct evidence:** this form of evidence is presented by witnesses who claim to have actually witnessed the events in question. If they are believed by the court, then their testimony may conclusively establish the truth of one or more of the material facts. Testimonial evidence – that is, the evidence of a witness – is "direct" when the witness narrates his or her actual observation of a material fact – that is, a factual proposition that satisfies one or more of the elements of the case.

2. **Circumstantial evidence:** this is evidence that supports our factual theory as a matter of inference – that is, from the evidence that one fact exists or one event occurred, we may ask the court to infer that one or more of the material facts also occurred. Facts or events from which such inferences can be drawn are often referred to by courts as "facts relevant to facts in issue".

These two types of evidence provide different kinds of arguments that we can use to persuade the court to accept our factual theory. With direct evidence, we are effectively saying to the court: "you should accept that this event happened because this witness, who is a credible witness, says that they saw it happen". With circumstantial evidence, on the other hand, we are effectively saying to the court: "you should accept that this event happened because the circumstances suggest that it must have happened".

Keeping this difference in mind, what we are aiming to do is to identify the arguments we can advance that will persuade the court to accept our factual theory (and, in particular, its key elements, the material facts) in preference to that of our opponent. In cases where there is a conflict of testimony between witnesses who both claim to have witnessed the events in question and very little circumstantial evidence (many sexual offence trials are like this), then our arguments are likely to revolve around the credibility of our main witnesses and the plausibility and consistency of their testimony. Moreover, the testimony of the witnesses may effectively cover all of the material facts. In addition to the direct evidence, however, we may also have a certain amount of circumstantial evidence that supports or undermines the direct evidence of the witnesses in relation to one or more of the material facts.

In other cases, however, there is either no direct evidence at all, or the direct evidence only deals with some of the material facts. In such cases, a much more important role is played by the circumstantial evidence. In some cases – such as a homicide – there may be literally hundreds of items of evidence that are in some way relevant to the proof or disproof of the various material facts. The unstructured enumeration of such items of evidence as reasons for the court to accept our factual theory is more likely to leave the court dazed and confused, than it is to persuade.

In such cases we may have to structure our argument more carefully than in a case based on direct evidence. We may want to group the items of evidence under headings that reflect the main arguments we are likely to make. For example, rather than listing all the items of evidence that go to prove motive, means, opportunity and so on, we may choose to summarise this evidence with broader factual propositions, such as "the accused had a motive to kill the deceased", "the accused had the opportunity to kill the deceased", "the accused had the means to kill the deceased", "the accused exhibited a consciousness of guilt", "traces of the deceased's blood were found on the accused's clothing", or "the accused confessed to the crime".

We will call such factual propositions "**main arguments**" in order to emphasise the fact that the "main arguments" are the pillars of the argument that we will ultimately use to try to persuade the court to accept our case – that is, the reasons why the court should find our factual theory proven. We should draft our main arguments with this in mind and, given that they are arguments, we should ensure that they are phrased as persuasively as the evidence will allow, and in a form that corresponds to the way in which we are likely to want to use them. For example, if the evidence allows it, the proposition that "the accused, and the accused alone, had the opportunity to commit this crime" is a much stronger reason for the court to find the accused guilty than the bare proposition that the accused had opportunity.

Because of their role as arguments, it is also important when drafting the main arguments to bear in mind an important principle about organising information – that is, human beings struggle to grasp more than seven ideas, categories or concepts at one time: see Minto (1991). This means that for each material fact or fact in issue we should try to avoid having more than seven arguments or reasons. This may require us to choose main arguments that are capable of summarising the effect of a large body of diverse evidence. For example, in a case where there is a significant amount of forensic evidence, a proposition like the one above that "traces of the deceased's blood were found on the accused's clothing" might need to be subsumed under a more general proposition, such as that "there is a body of forensic evidence linking the accused to the crime".

Filling in the gaps

[6.50] By definition, a material fact is crucial to the satisfaction of one or more of the elements of the legal case. Failure to prove one of our material facts may therefore result in failure to prove our case as a whole. So what do we do if we find that we appear to have no means of proving one or more of our material facts? The first step may be to look for further evidence: the methods we can use in order to find additional evidence were discussed in Chapter 4. But we may not find anything further of use.

The next step is to look again at the evidence we already have. Is there any way in which this evidence can be used to provide the foundation for an inference in relation to the material fact for which there is a paucity of evidence? For example, in a criminal proceeding we may appear to have no evidence to prove mens rea. In such a situation we should consider whether the very nature of the actus reus, or the circumstances in which it was committed, provide the foundation for an inference that the accused also possessed the necessary mens rea. If so, then we do have a means of proving the mens rea. Proof of mens rea would depend on the persuasiveness of some generalisation to the effect that a person performing such an act would usually have such a state of mind. The construction of inferences is discussed in more detail in Chapter 7.

If we are still at a loss as to how to prove a particular material fact – and it really is a *material fact*, crucial to the success of our case – then we are in trouble. We may try to look for an alternative legal case, one for which we do have the necessary evidence; but if this is not possible, then it may be time to settle!

Leftover evidence

[6.60] At the end of our analysis we may find that there are some items of evidence that we have not used and which do not appear to be relevant to prove any of our material facts. It is possible, of course, that the evidence simply is irrelevant; but there are two other possibilities we should always consider. The first is that the evidence *is* relevant, albeit in some way we have not yet identified, either to support or to undermine our case. If it can be used to support our case, then we should consider using it: the stronger our case is, the better. If, on the other hand, it could be used to undermine our case, then our opponent is likely to use it for that purpose. The other possibility is that the leftover evidence could be used to support a different legal case characterised by different elements. For example, the leftover evidence might be capable of proving the additional element that is required to transform an assault into a *serious* assault.

Defence theories

[6.70] So far the discussion has assumed that we are attempting to prove all the material facts necessary to establish the elements of a legal case. This is always true of the plaintiff or prosecution; but it is not always true of the defence in either civil or criminal proceedings. The various types of defence theories were discussed in Chapter 5. One type of defence theory involves advancing a competing factual theory that may have its own material facts. The method of proving such a theory is the same as that described above.

Another type of defence involves arguing that the evidence adduced by the plaintiff/prosecution does not address one or more of the elements of the legal case, so that there is no case to answer. Such a defence involves careful analysis of the elements of the plaintiff's/prosecution's legal case, and the evidence adduced to prove it. It can either be argued that the factual theory simply does not satisfy all of the facts in issue – that is, that the factual theory does not contain any material facts that address one or more of the facts in issue. Or it can be argued that there is no evidence to support a material fact crucial to the plaintiff's/prosecution's case.

If such a submission is not open, or if it fails, then it is still possible to attack the persuasiveness of the plaintiff's/prosecution's factual theory by arguing that the court should not be satisfied as to one or more of the material facts relied on by the plaintiff/prosecution to satisfy the elements of its legal case. In any case, reliance on such a defence requires a very close analysis of the prosecution's case in order to find its weak points – that is, the element or elements in relation to which there is a paucity of evidence. Once the weak points are found, we can focus all of our efforts on them.

Negating an opponent's factual theory

[6.80] It is not only the defence that is required to contest its opponent's factual theory. Given that a common law trial is an adversarial contest between parties who (typically) present competing factual theories, one of the best and most effective ways of persuading the court to accept our factual theory is to provide it with reasons for not accepting our opponent's factual theory. Remember that our factual theory is our answer to the question: "What happened?" If we can eliminate all the other possible answers, then the answer we are putting forward must be correct. As Sherlock Holmes remarked to Dr Watson in *The Adventure of the Beryl Coronet* "It is an old maxim of mine that when you have excluded the impossible, whatever remains, however improbable, must be the truth."

One of the best ways of persuading the court to accept our factual theory, then, is to lead evidence to show that the alternative possibility or possibilities did *not* happen. The ways of identifying evidence that can be used to eliminate a possibility were discussed in Chapter 4 and there is some further discussion in Chapter 7 in relation to the elimination of alternative explanations.

At this point it is enough to remember that we may want to include, among our main arguments, the negation of our opponent's factual theory. For example, if we are acting for the prosecution in a murder trial where the defence is one of accidental shooting, we may want to include as one of our main arguments a proposition that "the shooting was not accidental". By including the negative of our opponent's factual theory among the main arguments for accepting our factual theory, we can treat our opponent's factual theory as a target on which we can focus our ammunition.

Sourcing items of evidence

[6.90]   In the terminology we are using, an item of evidence is a factual proposition for which we have a direct source, as opposed to one that has to be inferred from another factual proposition. In relating the evidence to the material facts, we should therefore make sure that we identify the source or justification for each item of evidence, just as we did when preparing a chronology. In general, an item of evidence must be proved or justified by:

- the testimony of a witness;
- a document (that will usually have to be tendered through a witness);
- an item of real evidence (that will also usually have to be tendered through a witness);
- formal admissions made by the opposing party, or by agreements between the parties as to the facts;
- the court taking judicial notice of the fact; and
- the operation of a presumption of law following proof of a fact that triggers the presumption.

Different sources raise different kinds of issues – for example, credibility of witnesses, authenticity of documents and real evidence, and so on. These are discussed in more detail at [7.20]-[7.90] under the heading "Arguments about witnesses and other sources of evidence".

The impact of the law of evidence

[6.100]   As we identify the evidence we want to use, we are always likely to have in the back of our minds the possibility that certain uses of certain types of evidence may be prohibited by the law of evidence. The application of the law of evidence is discussed in some detail in Chapter 8; but it often also operates at the subliminal or intuitive level. We may instinctively sense that a particular use of a particular item of evidence is likely to infringe the hearsay rule, or the rule against non-expert opinion evidence. We should never be content, however, to jettison such evidence without some further analysis or thought.

This is because evidence is often relevant in more than one way. If there is an item of evidence that would be helpful to our case, and it appears to fall foul of an exclusionary rule, we should therefore ask ourselves whether there is any other way in which the evidence could be used. As long as we can identify a use of the evidence that does not contravene an exclusionary rule, then the evidence is likely to be admissible even if there are other (perhaps more obvious) uses that would contravene an exclusionary rule.

Another way in which the law of evidence is likely to impact on our analysis at this early stage is in relation to the use of documentary and real evidence. As is discussed in Chapter 7, real evidence and documents must usually be tendered through a witness who lays a foundation for their admission into evidence. When we find a document or item of real evidence on which we wish to rely, therefore, we should identify the witness through whom we will seek to tender it.

Summary

[6.110] The aim of the analysis we have been describing, then, is to create arguments based on the evidence available to us, which we can use to persuade the court to accept our factual theory. We do this by relating each of our items of evidence to one or more of the material facts, or to the factual theory as a whole. The precise nature of that relationship will vary according to the following questions:

- Is the evidence **directly** relevant to one or more of the material facts or to the factual theory as a whole – that is, does the witness claim to have actually perceived the events in question?
- Alternatively, is the item of evidence only **circumstantially** relevant to one or more of the material facts – that is, must we draw an inference or inferences from the item of evidence in order to connect it to the material fact or elements?
- Are there so many items of evidence that we need to group them into **main arguments** that summarise their effect?

Through this process of relating the evidence to the material facts, we construct the arguments we will use to try and persuade the court to accept our factual theory. Every case is different – both in terms of the material facts we are trying to prove and the items of evidence we have available to prove them – so it is not possible to lay down a standard template for such arguments. There are, however, some techniques we can apply to create a "map" of this argument and the basic methods of doing so are discussed in the next part of this chapter. Refinements will be added in Chapter 7.

MAPPING THE ARGUMENTS

[6.120] There are several methods for recording our analysis and thereby creating a "map" of the arguments we intend to use in our closing address. The creation of a case map will enable us to:

- identify the evidence we will have to lead in order to ensure that we prove each and every one of our material facts;
- identify the material facts in relation to which there is a paucity of evidence;
- identify the material facts in relation to which there is a conflict of evidence;

- identify the material facts in relation to which there is a preponderance of consistent evidence; and
- communicate the results of our analysis to others, such as clients, instructing solicitors or counsel.

Each of the methods set out in this chapter has its own advantages, and it is ultimately a matter of personal preference as to which method you choose to use. The prose method is essentially an extended argument in prose form that can be rendered with as much or as little rigour as you choose. The chart method is diagrammatic, and is best for those who most easily digest information in visual form; it also facilitates more rigorous analysis. The outline method is more akin to point form, and is probably the easiest to do quickly, but the hardest to do well. Remember, however, that the most important thing you are doing in creating a case map is helping yourself to structure an argument based on evidence. In light of this, what follows should not be treated as an inflexible prescription of technique. Do whatever works for you!

The prose method

[6.130] In essence, the prose method requires us to draft our closing address to the court. Many lawyers are more comfortable analysing evidence in prose, rather than in the form of a chart or outline, and there is no inherent reason for a case map in prose not to be as rigorous as a case map in either of the other two forms. Indeed, in prose the precise nature of the connections between factual propositions may have to be properly argued and explained; whereas in an outline, in particular, subtleties can sometimes be glossed over or ignored.

If we are carrying out our analysis as part of an advice on evidence in which we have been asked to consider the merits of the competing cases, then our approach is likely to be a little more judicial in approach – that is, assessing the merits of both cases, rather than seeking to advance the arguments in favour of one. However, if we are preparing for trial, then we are truly constructing an argument. Nevertheless, we should also remember that an argument that fails to account for all of the evidence, including the unfavourable evidence, is not truly persuasive. If we are drafting our closing argument, then our case map is likely to do the following:

- explain the relationship between the legal case and the factual theory – that is, explain how the factual theory satisfies the elements of the legal case;
- provide reasons based on the evidence for the court to find each of the material facts proven;
- explain, if appropriate, how we will go about disproving our opponent's factual theory;
- where witnesses have given **contradictory** testimony, explain why one witness or set of witnesses ought to be preferred over another, for reasons based on:

- the relative **credibility** of the witnesses;
- the **inherent plausibility** of their testimony; and
- the absence or presence of **corroboration**;
• in a case involving **circumstantial** evidence, explain why one inference or conclusion ought to be favoured over another, for reasons based on:
  - the **inferential force** of particular items of evidence;
  - the fact that there are numerous separate and independent strands of evidence, all pointing towards the same conclusion;
  - the accumulated weight of a **body of convergent evidence**;
  - the absence or presence of **conflicting** evidence; and
  - the degree to which any **alternative explanations** for the accumulated circumstances can be said to have been eliminated.

The conceptual bases for all these arguments are either discussed below, in relation to the chart method, or in Chapter 7.

The chart method

[6.140] Many people find it easiest to absorb information when it is presented in a visual form. This means that the chart method – which involves the translation of the analysis described earlier in this chapter into a visual diagram or series of diagrams – is particularly useful when we intend to use our case map as a basis for communicating our analysis to others. The diagrams may be "vertical", in which case we work down from material facts to main arguments, to items of evidence, to sources of evidence. Alternatively, they may be "horizontal", in which case we work across from material facts to main arguments, to items of evidence, to sources of evidence. The basic component of both kinds of chart, however, is the relationship between two or more factual propositions.

Different shaped nodes can be used to distinguish, for example, between material facts, main arguments, items of evidence, and sources of evidence. This is not essential – but it can be an aid to understanding (to do this, you would need to develop your own "palette" of differentiated nodes: this chapter does not prescribe one). What is essential, though, is to understand the nature of **the relationships between nodes at different levels** of the chart. In vertical charts, the usual relationship between two nodes connected by a vertical line is as follows: if the factual proposition at the bottom of the connecting line is true then this makes it more likely than it would otherwise have been that the proposition at the top of the connecting line is true. In other words, the proposition at the bottom is probative of the proposition at the top – the arrowhead on the connecting line serves to highlight the nature of this relationship. If the opposite is true – that is, if the proposition below makes it *less* likely that the proposition above is true – then this can be indicated by the use of a negative sign, or by the use of a different shaped or coloured node. Horizontal charts are the same, except that proof flows from right to left, rather than from bottom to top. The charts in this text are a mixture of horizontal and vertical.

[6.150]   In this chapter and in Chapters 7 and 8, the charts are generally fragments of more complex arguments; a more complete set of charts for a sample case can be found in the Appendix, and even more complete case maps can be accessed by clicking the "sample analyses" link at www.evidence.com.au. All the charts in this text were prepared using argument mapping software called **bCisive** (there are links to bCisive and other argument mapping software such as **Rationale** at www.evidence.com.au). bCisive uses colour (which has been converted to greyscale in this text), labels and icons to distinguish between different kinds of factual propositions, including:

- **contention**: the proposition the arguments for which are being mapped in the particular chart; depending on the chart, this might be the legal case, the factual theory, a fact in issue, a material fact, a main argument, or some other fact relevant to a fact in issue (in other words, it need not be the case itself);
- **reason**: a factual proposition that makes the proposition above it *more* likely;
- **objection**: a factual proposition that make the proposition above it *less* likely (so there could be an objection to an objection);
- **rebuttal**: a factual proposition used to rebut a reason or, more commonly, an objection;
- **compound** reasons and objections: a reason or objection made up of two or more "conjunctive" or "linked" co-premises (the meaning of these terms is discussed at [6.220]);
- **co-premises**: indicated by the use of an ampersand, "&"; and
- **evidence**: the actual evidence for the reason, objection or rebuttal and, in particular, the **source** of the evidence (bCisive also includes specific icons for some common sources of information such as experts or publications).

In the charts in this text, the source of an item of evidence is usually only described in the most general terms. In some cases, however, it can be useful to describe the source of the evidence in the same sort of detail that we used in preparing the chronology: see Chapter 3, "Cross-reference the source material" at [3.60]. Where the source is a document or item of real evidence, we might also want to include the name of the witness who will authenticate the evidence.

[6.160]   We will begin with a very simple chart of the evidence used to prove one of our material facts. In this example, the means of proving one of our material facts is the testimony of a single witness who claims to have actually perceived the occurrence of that event. This is an example of direct evidence: with direct evidence, the "item of evidence" being given by the witness is actually the truth of the "material fact" itself. To put it another way, the witness is narrating an event (a material fact) that satisfies one of the elements of the legal case (the facts in issue). For instance, in an assault prosecution, the main witness might be the victim of the alleged assault, giving direct evidence of the fact that the accused hit him or her. The means of charting this is shown in Figure 6.1.

Contention
The accused hit the victim

Evidence
Testimony of victim

Figure 6.1: Direct evidence in an assault case

In the example shown in Figure 6.1, the only issue for the court is to decide whether or not to believe the witness. If the court believes the witness, then it will find the material fact proven, and this will in turn satisfy whichever facts in issue the material fact is being used to prove. The assessment of **credibility** is not always as straightforward as it sounds, however, and a number of its subtleties are explored in Chapter 7.

[6.170] If we have no witness claiming to have perceived the particular event, however, then we will have to rely on **circumstantial** evidence to prove the material fact. In the simple example shown in Figure 6.2 we are attempting to prove a material fact by means of a single item of circumstantial evidence. In this example – which we can assume is part of a homicide trial – the material fact is that the accused shot the deceased. The prosecution is leading an item of evidence from "Witness A" to the effect that the accused owned a gun of the type used in the shooting. Obviously, this evidence would be insufficient on its own to justify a conviction. Moreover, treating it as a single item of evidence is slightly misleading. In fact, we are likely to require at least two items of evidence: first, evidence to establish what kind of weapon was used; and second, evidence to establish that the accused owned such a weapon. Nevertheless, treating it for the moment as a single item of evidence, Figure 6.2 illustrates a method of charting it.

In Figure 6.2, there is an extra step. This is because the witness is unable to testify that the material fact occurred: all they can do is testify as to the existence of a circumstance from which the occurrence of the material fact can be inferred.

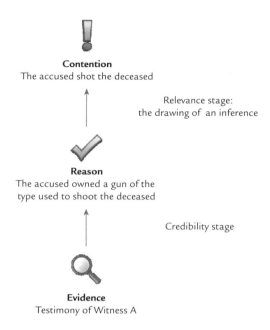

Figure 6.2: Circumstantial evidence in a homicide trial

Not only must the court decide whether the witness is credible (if it does, it will find that the accused did own such a gun), it must also decide what this circumstance means: does it indeed provide a basis for inferring that the accused shot the deceased? In Chapter 7 these two decisions will be referred to as the "credibility stage" and the "relevance stage".

A number of subtleties and complications arise in relation to circumstantial evidence. These are considered in detail in Chapter 7 and include the following:

- The relevance of circumstantial evidence is not always self-evident and may have to be justified or explained: see "Arguments about relevance" at [7.100]-[7.150]. For example, Figure 6.2 does not explain the connection between the factual proposition that the accused owned a gun of the type used to shoot the deceased, and the factual proposition that the accused shot the deceased.
- Sometimes the reasoning required to connect an item of evidence with a material fact takes more than one step: indeed, a whole chain of inferences may have to be drawn before we can be satisfied that we have demonstrated that an item of evidence does actually render more probable the existence of a material fact. These are also discussed in "Arguments about relevance" at [7.100]-[7.150].
- Unlike direct evidence, circumstantial evidence is always inconclusive: the inference for which we are contending is never the only possible explanation for an item of evidence. In order to persuade the court to draw the inference for which we

are contending, we may have to "eliminate" these alternative explanations. This is discussed in "Arguments about inferences" at [7.160]-[7.210].

[6.180] In some cases, we may have a combination of both direct and circumstantial evidence to prove a particular material fact. The direct and the circumstantial evidence provide independent reasons for the court to accept the material fact. Such a combination might be charted according to Figure 6.3. As far as the direct evidence is concerned, we can again proceed by a single step from the evidence to the material fact; whereas the circumstantial evidence requires (at least) two steps.

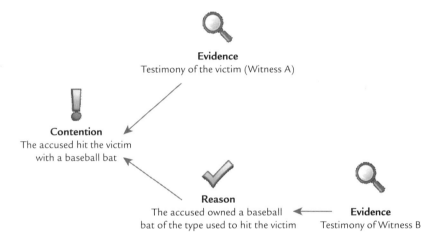

Figure 6.3: Direct and circumstantial evidence

There are other kinds of **combinations** of evidence that are worth mentioning. To use the language adopted by Schum (1994), the relationship between items of evidence and their sources can be either "harmonious" or "dissonant"; harmonious evidence can be either "corroborative" or "convergent"; and dissonant evidence can be either "contradictory" or "conflicting".

[6.190] **Corroboration** occurs when we have more than one witness testifying to the same item of evidence. Corroboration is about the relationship between **sources of evidence**: two sources who testify to the same item of evidence are said to corroborate each other (in the law of evidence the word "corroboration" is used rather more loosely, as we shall see in Chapter 8). For example, two witnesses who both report that they saw the accused enter the deceased's home in Melbourne at 5 pm on the day of a murder with which the accused is charged are corroborating each other. They are testifying to the same event. Note that in this case the item of evidence is not itself a material fact: rather, it is an item of circumstantial evidence which, together with other items of circumstantial evidence, will be used as the basis from which the material fact (presumably, that it was the accused who did the act that caused the death of the deceased) can be inferred. Figure 6.4 shows how this might be charted. Separate nodes have been used for each witness to indicate that the witnesses are independent, the testimony of each providing an independent reason for finding the proposition proved. By contrast, the two factual propositions are "conjunctive" or "linked", the relevance of each depending on the other, so that between them they provide a "compound" reason for finding the inference of opportunity: this is discussed further at [6.220].

[6.200] Another common combination of evidence occurs when two or more witnesses give **contradictory** evidence. There is contradiction between two sources when the items of evidence they report cannot both be true. In other words, corroboration and contradiction exist when witnesses or other sources of evidence are, respectively, in agreement or in disagreement with each other. There

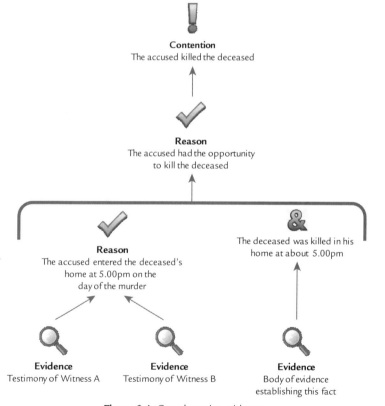

Figure 6.4: Corroborative evidence

are two types of contradiction: first, flat contradiction of the "yes, he did; no, he did not" variety. Figure 6.5 is an example of flat contradiction in a rape trial where the issue is one of consent.

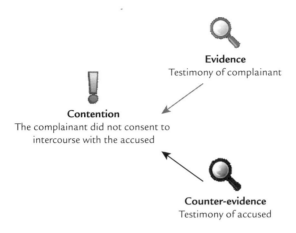

Evidence
Testimony of complainant

Contention
The complainant did not consent to
intercourse with the accused

Counter-evidence
Testimony of accused

Figure 6.5: Contradictory evidence

The second type of contradictory evidence is when two sources report items of evidence that are logically incompatible in the sense that they cannot both be true: for example, witness A says that he or she saw the accused enter the deceased's home at 5 pm, and witness B says that he or she saw the accused in Sydney at that time. At least one of the witnesses must be either mistaken or lying (I say *at least* one, because there is of course the possibility that they are both wrong). Figure 6.6 is an example of witnesses contradicting each other by giving logically incompatible evidence.

[6.210] Another common relationship between items of circumstantial evidence, in particular, is that of **convergence**. Evidence is convergent when it points in the same direction – that is, when it favours the same conclusion or when the same inference can be drawn from it. In Figure 6.7, two separate items of circumstantial evidence are being used to support two separate chains of reasoning – one of opportunity, one of motive – which both, independently of each other, support the existence of a material fact.

Evidence can be convergent at different "levels" of the case. For example, "main arguments", such as "the accused had a motive to kill the deceased", "the accused had the opportunity to kill the deceased" and "the accused had the means to kill the deceased" are convergent in that they all favour the same conclusion: that the accused killed the deceased. Items of evidence can also be convergent. For example, lower level factual propositions such as "the accused entered the deceased's home at 5 pm" (as testified by witness A) and "the accused left the deceased's home

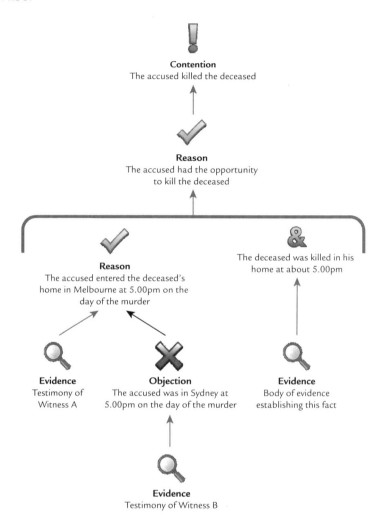

Figure 6.6: Logically incompatible evidence

at 5.30 pm" (as testified by witness B) together provide a basis for inferring that "the accused was inside the deceased's home from 5.00–5.30 pm". This factual proposition in turn combines with a proposition such as "death occurred sometime between 3 pm and 7 pm" (as testified by the forensic pathologist) to provide a basis for inferring that "the accused had the opportunity to kill the deceased".

If further evidence is available to show that no-one else entered the house during that timeframe, then this provides a basis for the even stronger main argument that "the accused, and the accused alone, had the opportunity to kill the deceased". If suicide and accidental or natural death can be eliminated as possibilities, then all this evidence converges very strongly on the material fact: that it was the accused who killed the deceased.

With convergent evidence, the various items of evidence provide the foundation for independent, or separate, arguments. Of course, the effect of all these independent arguments is cumulative, but they nevertheless act like separate strands of a rope or cable, each independently adding its weight to the case as a whole. For example, evidence of opportunity may be probative, even if the evidence of motive is rejected. This means that the court may find a fact proven even if it rejects some of the items of evidence being offered in support of that case. Evidence that operates independently in this way is often said to have a **cable** structure (the significance of this for the standard of proof is discussed in Chapter 7).

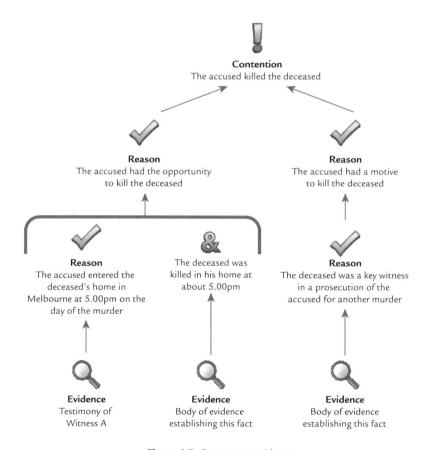

Figure 6.7: Convergent evidence

[6.220] Sometimes, however, evidence is only probative when combined with other evidence. Instead of providing independent or separate reasons, two or more items of evidence may be said to provide a "conjoint" reason. This is sometimes called a relationship of "**conjunction**": such a relationship exists if a court must find all the propositions on one level proven before it is entitled to find the proposition above proven (see Anderson, Schum and Twining (2005), pp 103-104). For example, a court can only find the legal case proven if it finds that all the elements of that case have been established: the relationship between the facts in issue is therefore one of conjunction. Walton (1996a, pp 85-86) instead uses the word "**linked**" to describe such a relationship: in a linked argument "each premise supports the conclusion through the mediation of the other premise. Both are needed, and neither supports the conclusion independently – the two premises work 'co-operatively rather than 'independently'." In bCisive two or more factual propositions that have such a relationship together form a "**compound** reason" (or objection). Whichever terminology we use, however, the basic idea is the same.

At the evidence level, the relationship between the various items of evidence used to found a tendency or coincidence argument is often one of conjunction or linkage. In *Sutton v The Queen* (1984) 152 CLR 528, for example, the prosecution combined the proposition that one person must have committed a series of three rapes (based on the similarities between them), with a proposition that the accused had committed two of the rapes (based on identity evidence from the complainants), in order to establish his identity as the perpetrator of the third rape. If either of these propositions failed – that is, if the court was not satisfied both that there was only one rapist, and that the accused had committed two of the rapes – then the argument would collapse. Accordingly, the relationship between the two propositions was not one of convergence, but one of conjunction or linkage. In the charts shown in Figures 6.4, 6.6 and 6.7, the fact that two items of evidence provide conjoint or linked, rather than independent, reasons is indicated by the fact that they are bound together into a single compound reason.

[6.230] **Conflicting** evidence is really the opposite of convergent evidence – that is, two items of evidence are conflicting when they point in different directions, favour different conclusions, or provide the foundation for different inferences. As with convergent evidence, a conflict between evidence can occur at any level of the case. For example, the main arguments that "the accused had the opportunity to kill the deceased" and "the accused had the means to kill the deceased" might conflict with a main argument established by the defence, or revealed by the evidence, such as "the accused had no motive to kill the deceased", or "the accused and the deceased were in a loving relationship". These latter two propositions do not support the conclusion that "the accused killed the deceased", but instead favour the conclusion that "the accused did not kill the deceased".

Conflicting evidence differs from contradictory evidence because it is possible for two items of conflicting evidence to both be true. For example, while it is not possible for the accused to be in both Melbourne and Sydney at the same time, it is possible for the accused to have had the opportunity to kill the deceased, and for the accused and the deceased to have been in a loving relationship; indeed it is possible for the accused to have been in a loving relationship with the deceased, and to have killed him or her.

Bearing in mind that a good case theory is comprehensive, in the sense of being capable of accounting for all the evidence in the case, our map of the case should not be limited to the evidence that favours our case, but should also include unfavourable evidence. In Figure 6.8, the conflict occurs at the level of the main arguments – that is, between the opportunity and means arguments on the one hand and the loving relationship argument on the other. Note that as far as the opportunity argument is concerned, there are two independent convergent reasons for accepting this argument; but that each of these reasons is itself a compound reason.

[6.240] So far we have only been drawing charts of a single material fact. If we want to create a chart of the **case as a whole**, then we have to subsume all the material facts and the means of proving them under a single, larger proposition, such as the legal case or the factual theory. Such a chart might look like Figure 6.9 – because the facts in issue are the elements of the case, they are conjointly required. That is, we have to prove all of them in order to prove our case. However, it is seldom practical to map our entire case in a single chart because the chart becomes unworkably large and complex, and impossible to read when printed. It is therefore better to break our case map into several separate charts, each mapping a different aspect of the case. For this reason, the chart in Figure 6.9 really just provides an overview of, or key to, the case map. Sometimes we will not even be able to fit all of the evidence used to prove a particular material fact on a page, and we may need separate charts for each of the main arguments, and even for different aspects of those arguments. For example, the "Chart 3" referred to in Figure 6.9 might in turn refer to Charts 3A, 3B and 3C, or 3.1, 3.2, 3.3, and so on. Provided that our reader can understand how all the charts fit together, this is not a problem.

This discussion has been intended to provide an introduction to the creation of evidence charts: further complexities and refinements to the chart are discussed in Chapter 7, and the Appendix contains a more complete example of a case map. It also identifies and explains how to avoid some of the **mistakes** most commonly made in the preparation of charts.

The outline method

[6.250] We do not always have the time to fully articulate, either in prose or by creating a chart, the arguments on which we will rely. In such cases we may choose to simply set out in point form the evidence we will use to prove each of the material facts, without worrying too much about the subtleties of the relationships between the various factual propositions. If we take this approach,

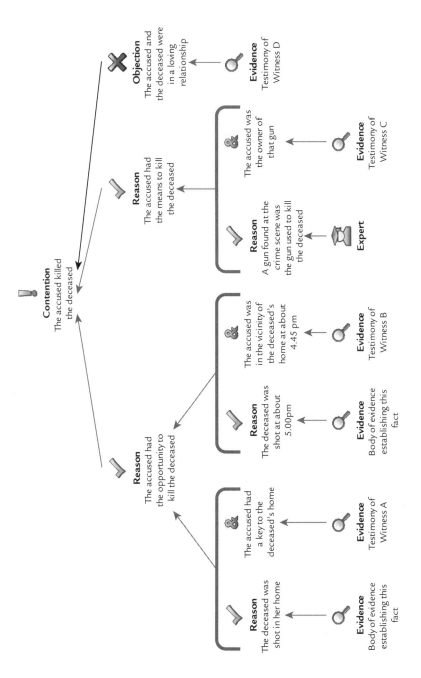

Figure 6.8: Conflicting evidence

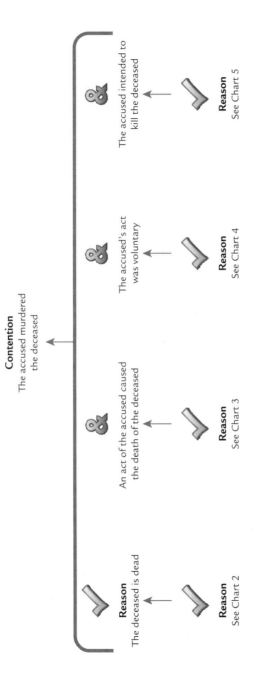

Figure 6.9: Mapping the entire case

then an outline can be a very effective method for carrying out a quick analysis for our own benefit.

Of course it is possible to construct an outline that uses numbered headings, different fonts or point sizes, indentations and so on to distinguish between the different levels of the analysis, to capture relationships such as convergence, conjunction and conflict, and to distinguish between the different types of sources: see "Sourcing items of evidence" at [6.90]. We might do this, for example, by using a code, such as the following:

- FT – for factual testimony;
- OE – for opinion evidence;
- RE – for real evidence;
- DE – for documentary evidence;
- JN – for a factual proposition of which judicial notice can be taken;
- FA – for a factual proposition in respect of which a formal admission has been made;
- AF – for a factual proposition that has been agreed between the parties;
- PL – for a factual proposition proved by the operation of a presumption of law; and
- G – for a generalisation (the role of generalisations is discussed at [7.110]).

However, constructing an outline with this degree of rigour is not easy; nor will it usually provide an effective and easy-to-understand means for communicating the results of our analysis to others.

Checking the case map

[6.260] There is never one right way to put together a chart, outline or case map in prose. That said, it is possible to distinguish between a good (or effective) and a bad (or ineffective) map of the case. Remember that the whole purpose of the analysis is to map arguments that can be used to persuade the court to accept our factual theory. Thus, the real tests are whether the case map accounts for all of the evidence, and whether the relationships between the material facts, the main arguments and the items of evidence are natural, logical and persuasive.

Is there a simple objection to our case map, along the lines of "you have not accounted for item of evidence X"? And would another person reviewing the case map be able to understand, as a matter of logic, why we say that the main arguments are reasons for finding the facts in issue proven? Further, are they likely, on the basis of those propositions, to agree that the facts in issue are proven?

If the material facts do not flow naturally, logically and persuasively from the evidence, then either the case is hopeless and should be settled, or the case map needs more work. In particular, it may require the application of some of the methods for the micro-analysis of evidence discussed in the next chapter.

Summary

[6.270] A number of concepts and ideas have been introduced in this chapter. These include:

- An **item of evidence**: a factual proposition for which we have a direct **source**, such as a witness who can testify to that effect. (We also saw that there are a variety of sources for evidence, including real and documentary evidence.)
- **Direct** evidence: a witness provides direct evidence when their testimony narrates their actual observation of a material fact – that is, a factual proposition that satisfies one or more elements of the legal case. (Real evidence can also be direct: real evidence is discussed in Chapter 7.)
- **Circumstantial** evidence: evidence that supports or undermines the existence of one or more of the facts in issue by a process of inference.
- **Main arguments**: arguments used to summarise the effect of a body of (usually convergent) evidence.

We have also examined a variety of **arguments** we can use to support our case:

- Arguments based on **direct** evidence ask the court to accept that an event happened because a witness says he or she saw it happen.
- Arguments based on **circumstantial** evidence ask the court to accept that an event happened because the circumstances suggest that it must have happened.
- An important way of persuading the court to accept our factual theory is to **negate** or disprove our opponent's theory.
- Our case will usually depend on a combination of these different kinds of arguments.

We also examined three different ways of creating a **map of the arguments** we would like to be able to use in our closing address in order to persuade the court to accept our theory:

1. The **prose** method effectively requires us to draft our closing address.
2. The **chart** method requires us to create a visual diagram of our arguments.
3. The **outline** method uses point form.

Finally, we saw that evidence can **combine** in a number of different ways:

- Evidence is **corroborative** when two or more sources report the same event or item of evidence.
- Evidence is **contradictory** when the items of evidence reported by two or more sources cannot both be true.

- Two or more items of evidence (or other factual propositions) are **convergent** when they independently favour the same conclusion.
- There is a relationship of **conjunction** or **linkage** between two or more items of evidence (or other factual propositions) when proof of the proposition on the level above them requires proof of them all.
- Two or more items of evidence (or other factual propositions) are **conflicting** when they favour different conclusions.

Arguing from and about evidence

7

Introduction

[7.10] This part of the book is concerned with the process of identifying and constructing the arguments we want to be able to make in our closing address. The focus of the previous chapter was on the big picture, the macro-analysis of the structure of our case as a whole. The focus of this chapter, on the other hand, is on the minutiae, the details, on the micro-analysis of individual items, or combinations, of evidence. In particular, we will examine the following types of arguments we may want to be able to make from and about the evidence:

- arguments about the **credibility** of witnesses and other sources of evidence;
- arguments about the **relevance** of evidence;
- arguments about whether or not particular **inferences** should be drawn;
- arguments about **missing** and **negative** evidence; and
- arguments about the **probative value** of evidence and the application of the **standard of proof** to a case.

By identifying these arguments in advance we provide ourselves with a blueprint for the conduct of the trial. In particular, this will enable us to identify the evidence we need to adduce from each witness, identify our aims for the cross-examination of our opponent's witnesses, and so on. Although the focus of this chapter is on the construction of arguments from and about evidence, knowing how arguments about evidence are constructed is also helpful when we come to apply the law of evidence, particularly when an item of evidence is, or may be, subject to the application of a rule of evidence that turns on the use that is made of the particular piece of evidence. If we are unable to make arguments about how evidence is being used, then we will be unable to make arguments about the application of such rules.

Many of the concepts discussed in this chapter are explained through the use of diagrams: this has not been done because the chapter is intended to constitute an extended lesson in evidence charting (although it can serve that purpose), but in the belief that the various concepts dealt with can be explained more clearly through a combination of words and diagrams, rather than through words alone.

ARGUMENTS ABOUT WITNESSES AND OTHER SOURCES OF EVIDENCE

[7.20] Because evidence must always have a source – for example, a witness – one of the most important and common kinds of argument we can make about evidence is an argument about the credibility of its sources. Indeed, it could be argued that the first question a court must ask itself in relation to each item of evidence adduced is "How credible is the source?" If the source of an item of evidence is not credible, then the item of evidence can not safely be relied on. Source credibility is one of the two main attributes that determine the probative value of an item of evidence (the other is its degree of relevance, or "inferential force": see the discussion of probative value at the end of the chapter). Thus, credibility questions can arise in relation to any item of evidence, whether we characterise it as direct or circumstantial.

In a common law trial, credibility is generally treated as a matter of weight for the tribunal of fact to assess, rather than a matter of admissibility for the tribunal of law to determine (two apparent exceptions to this – the rule against opinion evidence, and the tendency and coincidence rules – are discussed in Chapter 8). This means that the court does not take source credibility into account in deciding whether or not an item of evidence is relevant for the purposes of determining its admissibility. Instead, the approach taken by a court can be characterised as follows: "Assuming that the source is credible and that the item of evidence is therefore true, would the item of evidence affect our assessment of the probabilities of the existence of the facts in issue?"

Typically, then, arguments about source credibility are used as part of the process of persuading the court to accept or reject a factual theory, rather than as part of the process of determining the admissibility of evidence. This part of the chapter examines the different kinds of arguments about credibility that can be made in relation to the different kinds of sources of evidence; it begins by identifying what those sources are. Remember, however, that one of the main purposes of thinking ahead to the arguments we may want to make in our closing address is to ensure that we identify the evidence we will need to adduce in order to be able to make those arguments. If we want to be able to argue, for example, that a particular witness was lying or mistaken, then some foundation for that argument will have to be laid during the course of the trial.

The three main sources of evidence

[7.30] In a common law trial, there are three main sources of evidence:

1. **Testimonial** evidence: that is, evidence given by witnesses reporting their perceptions (or opinions) to the court.
2. **Real** or tangible evidence: that is, evidence that the court perceives with its own senses. All exhibits in a trial are real evidence.
3. **Documentary** evidence: of course, documents are always in some sense a form of "real evidence" in that the court is able to examine a document for itself; and the contents of a document are often used in the same way as witness testimony (for example, expert reports or admissible documentary hearsay). Nevertheless, documents do raise distinct issues, and it is convenient to recognise them as a separate category of evidence.

Of these three classes of evidence, the oral testimony of witnesses is, in a common law trial at any rate, regarded as the "primary" source. This is not to say that a court will always give more weight to the testimony of a witness than to either real or documentary evidence; indeed, contemporaneous documentary evidence is often regarded as more reliable. But witnesses are the primary source in the sense that both the other forms of evidence must usually be tendered through a witness who "authenticates" the item of real evidence or the document. We will now examine the kinds of arguments that can be made about each of these kinds of sources.

Arguments about witness credibility

[7.40] In determining the credibility of a witness, there are three main questions the court might ask itself:

1. How **honest** is the witness?
2. How **accurate** was the witness's original **observation** of the event in question?
3. How **reliable** is the witness's **memory** of that observation?

The first question concerns whether the witness is, or might be, lying; the second and third concern the possibility that the witness is mistaken. Mistake may arise either from weaknesses in the original perception of the fact about which the witness is giving evidence, or from a faulty recollection of that perception. In order to persuade the court to accept the testimony of a witness, we may need to satisfy it in relation to each of these issues; on the other hand, in order to persuade the court to reject the testimony of the witness, we may only need to raise doubt in relation to one of them.

In terms of the witness's **honesty**, depending on the rules of evidence applying in our jurisdiction, we may be able to make arguments based on:

*   the witness's record of **honest or dishonest behaviour**, including, most obviously, any **convictions** for dishonesty-related offences;
*   the witness's **reputation** for honesty or dishonesty;
*   any **motive** the witness may have for being untruthful in the particular proceeding, or in the absence of any such motive – that is, **bias** or the absence of bias; and
*   any **consistency or inconsistency** on the part of the witness in the description of the event in question.

In terms of the accuracy of the witness's original **observation**, we may be able to make arguments based on:

*   the witness's **capacity** for accurate observation, based on the quality of their senses (good or poor eyesight, for example);
*   the witness's **opportunity** for observation (how long did they have, for example, or were they even there);

- the **conditions** in which the observation occurred, which may be characterised as having been either favourable or unfavourable for accurate observation;
- any **expertise** on the part of the witness in making such observations;
- any **expectations** the witness may have had about what they were going to observe (based, for example, on what they had been told by others, or on their own prejudices and biases); or
- any **interest** the witness may have had in a particular perception (for example, an expert witness instructed by a party, who might have an interest in perceiving a test result that favours that party).

In arguing that a party expected to see a particular event, or had an interest in perceiving it, we need not argue that they are necessarily being dishonest; instead, we can argue that their mind was not a "blank slate", that their expectations or interests coloured their perceptions and rendered them unreliable.

In terms of the reliability of the witness's **memory**, we may be able to make arguments based on:

- the witness's **capacity** for accurate recollection;
- the degree to which the witness's recollection of the event in question may have been **affected or influenced** by subsequent events, including discussions with investigators or other witnesses, or media reporting of the events in question; or
- any **consistency or inconsistency** on the part of the witness in the description of the event in question.

More generally – in the sense that they may be relevant to honesty, accuracy or reliability – credibility-related arguments may be based on any of the following:

- The **inherent plausibility** of the events to which the witness is testifying. In general, if a witness is testifying to an event that is inherently unlikely, then we will look for strong indicias of credibility before accepting his or her testimony. This is related to the point made in Chapter 5 – that it is more difficult to persuade a court to accept a case theory that requires it to make a distasteful finding of fact, such as fraud. This is partly because fraud is seen as an uncommon, and therefore unlikely, event.
- The ability of the witness to place the event of interest within a context of plausible **collateral detail** – that is, of detail that is incidental to the event of interest. A witness who can not provide such collateral details is likely to be suspected by the tribunal of fact of either having made up their testimony, of having made a poor initial observation of the events in question, or of having an unreliable memory of those events.
- The degree to which such collateral details are shown to be true or false. If the collateral details can be shown to be false, then this will cast doubt on the witness's entire testimony.

- The witness's **demeanour** in the witness box.
- The degree to which the witness's testimony is **corroborated** or **contradicted** by the testimony of other witnesses: is there an "odd man out"?
- The degree to which the witness's testimony is **consistent with the other evidence** in the case.
- Where the witness is one of the actors in the event in question – such as the victim of an alleged assault – the degree to which the witness's testimony is consistent with his or her **conduct** before, during or after the event in question.

Of course, there has to be a **foundation in evidence** for all of these arguments. In order to be able to make such arguments during our closing address, we must, therefore, ensure that we have obtained the necessary evidential ingredients during the examination and cross-examination of the various witnesses. If, for example, we want to be able to argue that the conditions for observation were good so that an observation is likely to have been accurate, then we need to ensure that we have established the foundations for such an argument when we examined the various witnesses concerned. Similarly, if we wish to be able to argue in closing that a witness had no motive to lie, then the absence of that motive is a fact that we must establish during our examination of that witness.

Arguments about real evidence

[7.50] The issues associated with real evidence are similar, but not identical, to the issues that arise in relation to human sources. Whereas the components of witness credibility can be described as honesty, observational accuracy and reliability of memory, any assessment of the credibility of real evidence gives rise to the following questions:

- How **authentic** is the item of evidence – in particular, is it what it purports to be?
- Where the evidence was produced as a result of some sort of process, how **accurate** is the item of evidence?

In terms of authenticity, we may be able to make arguments based on the integrity of the chain of custody of an exhibit or sample, including the possibility that an item of evidence has been planted, fabricated, substituted or tampered with. Any break in the chain of custody of an item of evidence can completely destroy its probative value. If it is our item of real evidence, we therefore need to diligently ensure that there are no such breaks, and that every individual through whose hands an item of real evidence passed is available to give evidence about what they did with the item.

In terms of accuracy, we may be able to make arguments based on the reliability of a mechanical device or measuring instrument used to produce or analyse the item of real evidence. Where real evidence is produced through some mechanical or electronic process we may be able to characterise it as having an "objectivity" lacking in the evidence derived from human sources.

Structurally, evidence relating to the authenticity and accuracy of real evidence performs the same function as evidence relating to the credibility of a witness. The main point of distinction to note is that whereas the law of evidence generally limits the admissibility of evidence relating to the credibility of a witness, it often requires the leading of evidence relating to the authenticity and accuracy of real evidence: see the discussion of admissibility at [7.70].

Arguments about documentary evidence

[7.60] Documentary evidence raises issues similar to both testimonial and real evidence. Like real evidence, documentary evidence gives rise to issues of authenticity. However, because the content of documents is often used in a way that is equivalent to the way in which the testimony of witnesses is used, it often makes as much sense to talk about the "credibility" of documents (and their human creators) as it does to talk about their "accuracy".

Documentary evidence is usually used to supplement, support or rebut the oral testimony of witnesses. Where our documentary evidence is consistent with the oral testimony of the witnesses, our argument is straightforward. More complex arguments must be developed when the documentary evidence and the testimony are at odds with each other. All of these arguments are likely to be subject, of course, to the hearsay rule, which may prevent us from relying on the contents of a document as evidence of its truth (rather than as evidence relevant to the credibility of a witness). The hearsay rule is discussed in Chapter 8.

Sometimes we may want to argue that the court should prefer the documentary evidence to the oral testimony of the witnesses. In making such arguments we are likely to rely on some combination of the following factors (as always, some evidential foundation must have been laid during the examination of the witnesses):

- the **contemporaneity** of the documents with the events they describe – so that the documents can be said to have been made while the events were still fresh in the memory of their creator;
- the fact that they were **created before litigation was contemplated** – so that they are less likely to be self-serving than the oral testimony;
- the degree to which the documents were to be **relied on** by their creator or someone else, and the consequent **need for them to be accurate**; and
- the **steps taken to ensure the accuracy** of the documents, either in relation to a specific document, or in relation to the class of documents to which the document belongs.

On other occasions we may have to argue that the oral testimony should be preferred to the documentary evidence. In making such arguments we are likely to rely on some combination of the following factors:

- the fact that the oral testimony was given on **oath** in the presence of the tribunal of fact, allowing the court to assess the witnesses' **demeanour**, and exposing the witnesses to prosecution for perjury if they did not tell the truth;
- the fact that the oral testimony was tested by **cross-examination**; and
- the possibility that the creator of the documents **may not have realised the importance** of their contents at the time they were created, and may not therefore have been scrupulous about accuracy.

Admissibility requirements for sources

[7.70] Each class of source has its own admissibility requirements. We are here discussing the rules that apply to the source, rather than to the content of the evidence they provide. Rules relating to the substance of the evidence that the source will provide – such as the hearsay rule – are discussed in Chapter 8 (the rules that regulate the admission of evidence relevant only to the credibility of a witness are discussed later in this chapter). If we intend to adduce an item of evidence, we should always check the admissibility requirements that apply to evidence of that type; and we should identify the means we will use to satisfy those requirements. To do this, we will need to consult the evidence texts or statute relevant to the jurisdiction in which we are litigating. What follows is a very general discussion that is in no way intended as a substitute for such texts.

The rules that apply to **witnesses** are the most straightforward. In general, a witness will be competent to give evidence if they understand that in doing so they are under an obligation to tell the truth. Competence issues only really arise in relation to children and intellectually disabled witnesses. Generally, a competent witness can be compelled to give evidence: the only real exceptions to this rule concern the accused (and sometimes members of the accused's family) in criminal proceedings. A different form of "competence" issue arises in relation to the testimony of experts, who must be "qualified" to give expert testimony: this generally requires us to lead evidence (usually from the particular expert) to show that the witness has some relevant expertise.

Real and **documentary** evidence do not just walk themselves into evidence, and they can not simply be tendered from the Bar table. First, some foundation for their admission into evidence must usually be laid, and that foundation is usually laid through the testimony of witnesses. This means that before we can rely on any document or item of real evidence, we must usually identify the witness through whom we will tender that evidence. Usually the foundation required by the law of evidence relates to the authenticity and accuracy of the real or documentary evidence. For example, before photographs of a crime scene can be tendered, evidence will usually have to be adduced from the photographer to establish what it is that the photographs are photographs of, and that they accurately record the state of the scene at the time at which they were taken. Similarly, if the relevance of a document depends on it having been properly executed or attested – for example, a will or a contract – then this will have to be established. If we only have secondary evidence of a document – for example, a copy – there may be additional requirements.

The effect of admissibility requirements like these is to require us to prove certain facts before an item can be received in evidence. In Chapter 8, facts that must be proved before an item can be received in evidence are called "**foundational facts**". It is an important part of our preparation for trial to identify all the foundational facts that must be proved before an item of evidence on which we wish to rely can be admitted; and to identify the means we will use to prove those facts. Often it is simply a matter of asking a series of questions of the witness through whom the evidence is being adduced. A general approach to the proof of foundational facts is discussed in Chapter 8.

Charting credibility evidence

[7.80] A case map should always include both favourable and unfavourable credibility-related evidence, as this evidence is often crucial to the outcome of the case. In terms of its logical classification, credibility-related evidence is a form of **ancillary** evidence (see Schum, 1994). Ancillary evidence is evidence that has no direct bearing on the facts in issue, but can be used to determine the credibility or inferential force of evidence that does have such a bearing. It is **collateral** to the main issues. Where the evidence relates to the credibility of a particular witness, for example, the relevance of that evidence to the proceedings depends on the fact that that witness happens to be testifying in the proceedings. If the witness was not testifying, then information about his or her credibility would be irrelevant. Thus, ancillary evidence has no "inherent" relevance; rather its relevance is "derived" from its relationship to other evidence that is inherently relevant. All of this is equally true of evidence relevant to the "credibility" of real and documentary evidence. However, for convenience, we will focus our attention on examples involving evidence relevant to the credibility of witnesses.

If we want to incorporate credibility-related evidence in a chart, we must recognise that there is a difference between a witness testifying to a factual proposition and that factual proposition being true. The very first step in any chain of reasoning from the testimony of a witness is therefore the step that goes from a witness testifying to a factual proposition, to that proposition being true. Whether or not a court will choose to take that step will depend on its assessment of the credibility of the witness; for this reason, we will call this first step the "credibility stage". This step is common to all evidence, whether it is characterised as direct or circumstantial.

Credibility evidence, then, is evidence that has a bearing on whether the court should take the credibility step – that is, the court has to decide, on the basis that a witness says that fact X occurred, that fact X did indeed occur. For example, with an eyewitness in an armed robbery case:

- the witness's opportunity for observation may only have been brief;
- there may have been an object obscuring the witness's view of the perpetrator; and
- the witness may have been expecting to see the accused (perhaps the witness is a police officer who had had the accused under surveillance).

There are several different ways in which such credibility evidence could be charted, but the simplest, and least confusing, way is probably to show them as objections to the testimony of the witness. Figure 7.1 shows how this might be done (I have not bothered to include sources for the various items of ancillary evidence, but some of it we will no doubt elicit from the witness in cross-examination).

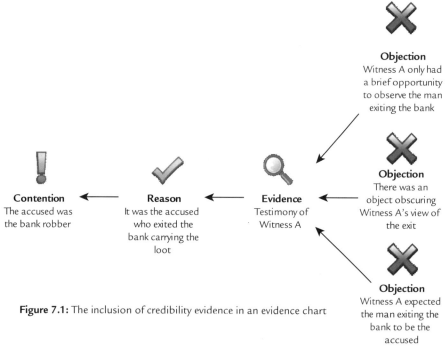

Figure 7.1: The inclusion of credibility evidence in an evidence chart

Figure 7.2 shows an alternative, but slightly clunkier, way of charting the same credibility evidence. As both charts show, however, each of the items of credibility evidence in this example provides a separate and independent reason for rejecting the witness's credibility, rather than one conjoint or linked reason (the difference between convergent and conjunctive evidence was discussed in the previous chapter).

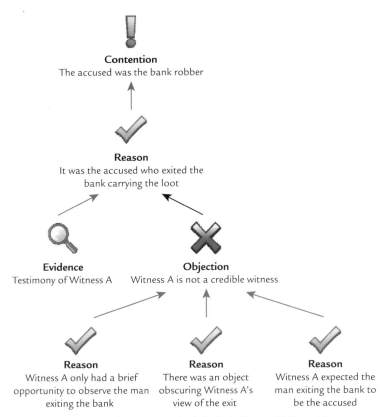

Figure 7.2: An alternative method for including credibility evidence

Favourable credibility evidence can also be included in our case map, as in Figure 7.3. In this chart, the favourable evidence has been included as a co-premise of the testimony, although it could equally well have been included as a reason relating to the testimony of the witness, as in Figure 7.4. As long as we remember that credibility evidence is evidence that has a bearing on whether or not the court should make a finding of fact based on the testimony of a witness, then the particular conventions we adopt to map credibility evidence are not important.

Incidentally, it is important not to be blind to the weaknesses of our own witnesses. If the credibility of one of our witnesses is likely to be attacked by our opponent during cross-examination, we may prefer to draw the sting of that attack by having our witness disclose during examination-in-chief any negative credibility evidence. If, for example, our witness has a previous conviction for perjury, and our opponent knows this, then we should probably not leave that conviction as a grenade for our opponent to lob at the witness. Instead, we should try and limit the damage by defusing the grenade, or at least conducting a controlled explosion, during our own examination of the witness.

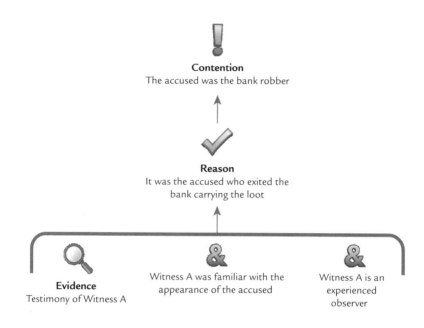

Figure 7.3: Favourable credibility evidence

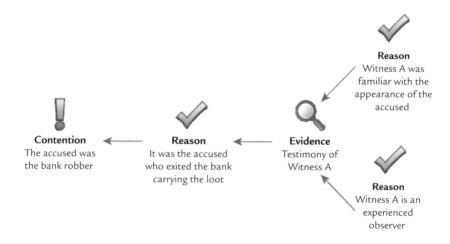

Figure 7.4: An alternative method for including favourable credibility evidence

Admissibility of credibility evidence

[7.90] Much of the foundation for any arguments we may wish to make about the credibility of a witness can be laid during the examination or cross-examination of that witness. Sometimes, however, we may wish to lead additional evidence relevant to the credibility of a witness. At this point we will need to consider the law of evidence, which limits our freedom to lead evidence that is relevant only to the credibility of a witness. For example, it is generally not permitted to lead evidence of prior consistent statements made by the witness in order to persuade the court that the witness is credible. Similarly, if a witness has made a statement about a collateral detail that we can prove to be false, we may be prevented by the "collateral issues" or "finality" rule from doing so: this is because a lie about such a detail is only relevant to the credibility of the witness.

Because of the restrictions imposed by the law of evidence on credibility evidence, it is important to be able to determine whether evidence is relevant only to the credibility of a witness, or whether it has some other relevance to the facts in issue. One way of testing whether evidence is only relevant to the credibility of a witness is to conduct the following thought experiment: imagine that this witness was not testifying. Would the evidence still be relevant to the facts in issue? For example, evidence to show that an eyewitness has poor eyesight clearly has no connection to the facts in issue if that witness is not testifying. Its relevance is only "derived", rather than "inherent". If an item of evidence is relevant only to show that our own witness is credible, then we will generally not be allowed to adduce that item of evidence (of course, we may be able to surreptitiously elicit credibility-enhancing details from our witness during the course of their examination-in-chief).

The primary method sanctioned by the law for impeaching the credibility of our opponent's witness is to put allegations to them in cross-examination. Subject to any overriding statutory limitations (such as rape-shield laws), questions on matters relevant only to credit are usually proper if they are indeed relevant to credit – that is, if they would tend to weaken confidence in the witness's testimony, as a matter of logic and rationality, rather than prejudice and emotion. If the witness denies the allegation, however, then we will only be able to lead evidence to prove the truth of the allegation if it falls within the limited class of exceptions to the "collateral issues" or "finality" rule (the uniform evidence legislation's version of this rule and its exceptions are found in ss 102 and 106). These exceptions include such matters as bias, prior convictions and prior inconsistent statements; but do not include matters such as proving that the witness has lied or is mistaken about a collateral detail of his or her testimony.

ARGUMENTS ABOUT RELEVANCE

Using circumstantial evidence

[7.100] An item of evidence is relevant if it rationally affects the assessment of the probability of the existence of one or more of the facts in issue – that is, if it makes more or less likely the existence of one of the facts in issue. Relevance is, in fact, a prerequisite to the admissibility of evidence, so arguments about relevance are not arguments we are likely to make during our closing address, but during the course of the trial itself. Therefore, there is a case for leaving our discussion of relevance to the next chapter, which deals with arguments about admissibility. However, the discussion of relevance also provides a foundation for the discussion of arguments about inferences, one of the main subjects of this chapter. For that reason, we will deal with relevance now.

Chapter 6 drew a distinction between direct and circumstantial evidence. Direct evidence was defined as testimony in which a witness narrates his or her actual observation of a material fact. Real evidence can also be direct – for example, security camera footage that records the commission of a crime. Questions of relevance do not arise in relation to direct evidence: if a witness claims to have perceived the very events that are the subject of the proceedings, then clearly his or her evidence is relevant. The issue for the court is one of credibility rather than relevance.

However, questions of relevance do arise in relation to circumstantial evidence. The process of using circumstantial evidence is actually a very familiar one that we rely on every day in our ordinary lives. For example, if we wake up in the morning to find that the ground outside is wet, we will probably infer that it must have rained during the night, even if we did not see or hear it raining. Whenever we form a belief that an event occurred, and we do so not on a basis of our own or someone else's perception of the event, but on the basis of "clues" or "signs" that suggest the event must have occurred, we are relying on circumstantial evidence.

The Duke of Wellington once said: "All the business of war, and indeed all the business of life, is to endeavour to find out what you don't know by what you do." His words are equally apt to describe the process of using circumstantial evidence, which also involves using traces, clues or signs – the things we do know – to reconstruct an event that we did not actually witness. Questions of relevance arise in relation to circumstantial evidence because people do not always agree about the meaning of these clues or signs – that is, they do not always agree about whether or not one event provides a basis for inferring that another event has occurred. As Sherlock Holmes told Dr Watson in *The Boscombe Valley Mystery*:

> Circumstantial evidence is a very tricky thing. It can seem to point very straight to one thing, but if you shift your own point of view a little, you may find it pointing in an equally uncompromising manner to something entirely different.

This means that as well as challenging the credibility of the source of an item of circumstantial evidence, a party may also argue about the inferences that should be drawn from that item of evidence. Indeed, they may argue that no inference can be drawn from the item of evidence at all, that it is simply irrelevant. Thus, we must always be prepared to defend the relevance of an item of circumstantial evidence.

The role of generalisations

[7.110] If our opponent does challenge the relevance of an item of circumstantial evidence we wish to lead, how can we demonstrate that it is indeed relevant? If, for example, one of our main arguments is that "the accused had a motive to kill the deceased", and our opponent or the court replies "so what?", how do we defend the relevance of this evidence? (Of course, we are unlikely to be called on to justify the relevance of motive evidence, but the process of justification is the same for all kinds of circumstantial evidence.)

We first need to be able to identify the factual proposition that we say should be inferred from the evidence – that is, what is the item of evidence being used to prove? Second, we need to be able to identify a **generalisation** that shows how the item of evidence is relevant to prove that factual proposition – in other words, that explains the connection between the item of evidence and the factual proposition inferred from it.

For example, if asked to justify the relevance of motive, we might reply that "motive is relevant because a person with a motive to kill someone is more likely to do so than a person without such a motive". When combined with such a generalisation, our evidence of motive places the accused in a restricted class of people ("people with a motive") who are more likely to have murdered the deceased than people who are not in that class. It can therefore be said to have increased the probability of the accused's guilt; and the smaller the class is, the more it will have done so.

As Schum (1994, p 83) notes, generalisations like this are the "glue" that connects items of circumstantial evidence with the factual propositions inferred from them. In some disciplines, a generalisation like this is called the "warrant" for the drawing of the inference, or the "relevancy authorisation". Generalisations or warrants usually include a "hedge" or "qualifier", such as "sometimes", "usually", or "often". For example, our generalisation about motive might be restated as "people with a motive to kill other persons *sometimes* do so". The relevance of all circumstantial evidence depends on generalisations or warrants; it is just that these are usually left unstated. When asked to defend the relevance of an item of circumstantial evidence, however, the generalisation or warrant may be forced out into the open.

Including generalisations in a chart

[7.120] There are many ways of illustrating in a chart generalisations of the evidence; in bCisive, however, the easiest way is to include the generalisation as a co-premise or assumption. This is because the relationship between an item of evidence and the generalisation that justifies the drawing of an inference from that item of evidence is always one of conjunction: they are two parts of a single compound reason, and if we do not accept the generalisation, then we should not draw the inference. Using this method, our earlier example of the inference that it had rained during the night might be charted as follows:

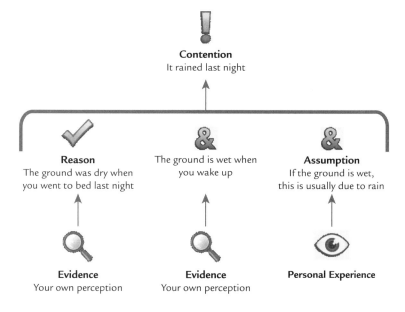

Figure 7.5: Generalisations as co-premises

In this example, the single compound reason is made up of two factual propositions based on the evidence of your own eyes together with a generalisation that is unsupported by any specific evidence, but which is based on your personal experience as a human being: it could also have been shown as a "common belief", as in Figure 7.7.

Where do generalisations come from?

[7.130] Most of the unstated generalisations that provide the justification for the drawing of inferences are indeed based on our common sense and experience of life. That is why there is often disagreement about generalisations once they are forced out into the open: "common sense" is not always "common", and different people have different experiences of life. Sometimes the disagreement is about the choice of hedge or qualifier; sometimes it is about whether a generalisation of that type is ever true. Such a disagreement can, for example, be seen in views about sexual history evidence in rape trials – some assert that sexual history evidence is relevant, others deny it. This is because they disagree about the acceptability of any generalisation that appears to connect the sexual history of the complainant in a sexual offence trial with the facts in issue in such a trial.

Nevertheless, our system of proof assumes that judges and jurors come to court with a ready stock of such generalisations they can draw on to make sense of the evidence presented to them. Although it might be possible to produce evidence to "back-up" these generalisations, it is in fact very unusual for a party to produce "backing" evidence for a generalisation; indeed, it is unlikely that the court would allow backing evidence to be adduced.

It is different where expert opinion evidence is concerned. The inferences drawn by experts will also depend on generalisations – for example, the identification of the accused from a fingerprint depends on the generalisation that "no two people have the same fingerprints". To take another example, an expert might, on the basis that a sample taken from the accused's hand had tested positive for lead, barium and antimony, be prepared to express the opinion that the accused had discharged a firearm no more than three hours prior to the sample being taken. This inference depends on a generalisation to the effect that when a sample tests positive for those substances, it indicates that the person has discharged a firearm within a particular timeframe. Generalisations of this kind are usually proved by the evidence of the expert concerned – that is, the expert will provide the "backing" evidence for the generalisation. In the language of the law of evidence, the general information relied on by the expert forms part of the "basis" of his or her opinion. Figure 7.6 shows how the firearms discharge residue example might be charted. Note that because this generalisation is supported by evidence, it has not been shown as an "assumption".

Backing evidence is also sometimes adduced in cases where the prosecution seeks to rely on tendency or coincidence evidence on the basis that a particular modus operandi for a crime is an unusual or rare one. In such cases, police officers or other appropriate witnesses may be permitted to testify about the relative rarity of the commission of crimes using such a modus operandi.

Chains of inferences

[7.140] So far we have been looking at single inferences, but with most items of circumstantial evidence several reasoning steps are actually necessary to connect the item of evidence with one of the material facts and, through that, to one of the facts in issue. In the firearms residue example in Figure 7.6, for example, the diagram

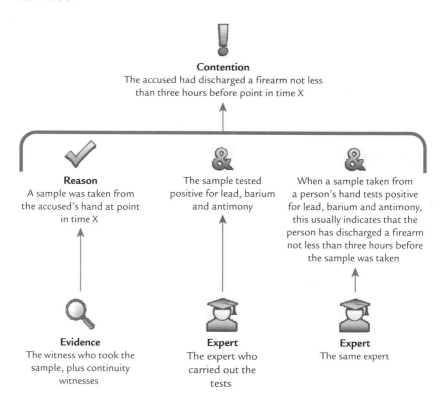

Figure 7.6: Backing for a generalisation relied on by an expert

only takes us to the stage where we have established that the accused probably discharged a firearm within a three-hour period prior to the taking of the sample. But this inferred factual proposition must still be connected to the facts in issue. On the assumption that the evidence is being adduced in a murder trial, the fact that the accused discharged a firearm is neither a fact in issue, nor a material fact: it is only a fact relevant to a fact in issue, circumstantial evidence from which a material fact – such as that it was the accused who shot the deceased – can be inferred.

Because several steps are usually required to connect an item of circumstantial evidence to a material fact, we may be forced, when defending the relevance of an item of circumstantial evidence, to spell out all of these steps. There is another benefit to doing this: it enables us to identify the points at which our opponent may attempt to break the chain of inferences by offering alternative explanations for an inference. Once we have identified these possible "escape routes" we can look around for further evidence to try and block them off. This is discussed in the next part of this chapter, which deals with arguments about inferences.

For the moment, however, our focus is on relevance. Where several steps are required to connect an item of evidence to a material fact, each of the steps will involve the drawing of an inference, first from the item of evidence itself, and then from a factual proposition that has previously been inferred. The relevance of the item of evidence depends on the acceptability of the chain of inferences as a whole. Wigmore called such chains of inferences "catenate", or chain-like, which seems apt to describe a process of working up step by step, link by link, from an item of evidence to the facts in issue. Walton (1996a, p 89), on the other hand, uses the phrase "serial argument" to describe an argument that "is composed of two or more stages (subarguments [or inferences]) where the conclusion of the first argument also functions as a premise to the second argument".

Sometimes the series or chain of inferences can be quite long: imagine, for example, the chain of reasoning required to connect an item of evidence, such as OJ Simpson's televised freeway drive, to the proposition that he murdered his wife. Presumably the argument would be along the lines that Simpson's behaviour demonstrated a consciousness of guilt, but at every step along the way there may be an alternative explanation: indeed, we may end up concluding that it is unsafe to draw any inferences from the conduct at all.

[7.150] To appreciate just how tenuous serial arguments can be, we can look at an item of evidence relied on by the prosecution in a case that is perhaps the most notorious miscarriage of justice in the history of the United States: the Sacco and Vanzetti trial. In this trial, Sacco and Vanzetti, two Italian migrant anarchists, were charged in relation to an armed robbery and murder that occurred in South Braintree, Massachusetts in 1920. The two were convicted, sentenced to death, and ultimately executed. The item of evidence in question was provided by Officer Connolly, one of the officers who arrested Sacco. Officer Connolly testified that Sacco attempted on several occasions to put his hand under his overcoat in spite of being warned not to do so. As it happened, there was a revolver concealed under Sacco's overcoat. As an exercise in defending the relevance of this item of evidence, Schum (1994, p 88) suggests that eight steps would be required to connect it to the only real fact in issue in the trial, that of identity. Schum's best attempt to defend the relevance of the item of evidence, including the generalisations relied on, is shown in Figure 7.7.

The first step, the credibility stage, is concerned with the credibility of Officer Connolly. The remaining seven steps constitute the relevance stage: the stage in which we attempt to justify or explain the relevance of the item of evidence to the facts in issue. Each of the steps is "justified" by a generalisation, which is shown as a "common belief". As Schum notes, we are likely to disagree about the acceptability of the generalisations he uses to justify the drawing of the various inferences; at the very least we are likely to disagree about his choice of hedges or qualifiers. Alternatively, we may concede the truth of a generalisation but deny

Continued on next page

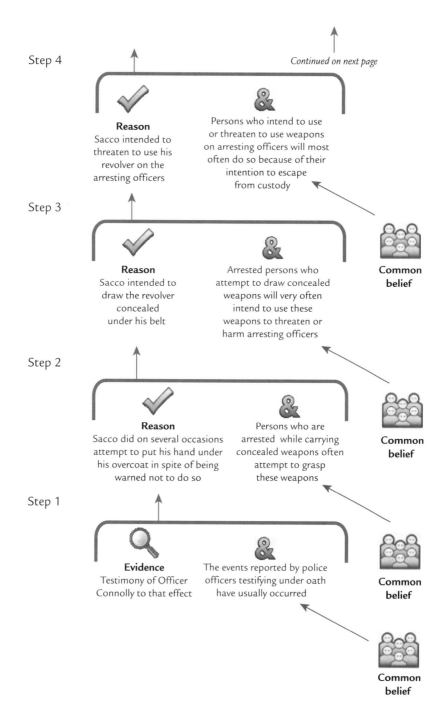

Step 4

Reason
Sacco intended to threaten to use his revolver on the arresting officers

&

Persons who intend to use or threaten to use weapons on arresting officers will most often do so because of their intention to escape from custody

Step 3

Reason
Sacco intended to draw the revolver concealed under his belt

&

Arrested persons who attempt to draw concealed weapons will very often intend to use these weapons to threaten or harm arresting officers

Common belief

Step 2

Reason
Sacco did on several occasions attempt to put his hand under his overcoat in spite of being warned not to do so

&

Persons who are arrested while carrying concealed weapons often attempt to grasp these weapons

Common belief

Step 1

Evidence
Testimony of Officer Connolly to that effect

&

The events reported by police officers testifying under oath have usually occurred

Common belief

Common belief

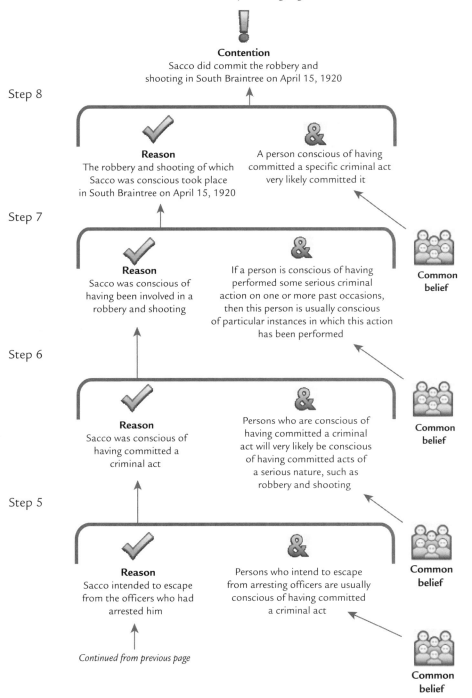

Step 8

Step 7

Step 6

Step 5

Figure 7.7: Schum's analysis of Sacco's hand movements

that it provides a justification for the inference sought. It is difficult to see, for example, how the generalisations relied on by Schum to justify Steps 6 and 7 can in fact justify the inferences drawn. This is no criticism of Schum: indeed, it is reasonable to assume that part of Schum's purpose in "defending" the relevance of the item of evidence was to demonstrate that no defence is possible. In other words, the example is partly intended to demonstrate to the reader that, properly analysed, the fact of Sacco attempting to put his hand under his overcoat had no rational bearing on the issues to be determined by the court and should not have been admitted into evidence.

Instead of objecting to a generalisation, however, we may concede it as a general truth, but deny its application in the present case. Sacco, for example, claimed that the first questions he and Vanzetti were asked by the arresting officers concerned their political beliefs. It will be remembered that the two were committed anarchists at a time of significant social and labour unrest. We can also imagine that the Massachusetts constabulary may have had a reputation for violence or maltreatment among migrant anarchist workers, and that Sacco was aware of this reputation. On the basis of Sacco's evidence we can therefore identify an alternative explanation for the inferred factual proposition that Sacco was attempting to draw his revolver in order to escape from custody – that is, he was doing so not because of a consciousness of guilt, but from a fear of maltreatment. In other words, even if we concede the truth of the generalisation used to justify Step 5, that "persons who intend to escape from arresting officers are usually conscious of having committed a criminal act", there is a basis for arguing that the generalisation did not apply to Sacco. This does not necessarily mean that the evidence is irrelevant, but it does suggest that there may be an alternative explanation for it. The significance of alternative explanations for an item of evidence in the overall proof of a case is our next topic.

In terms of relevance, however, we can observe that Sacco's testimony about the questions he was asked, and evidence about the reputation of the Massachusetts police for violence, are relevant even though they do not provide a foundation for an inference that a material fact exists. Rather, they are relevant because they provide the basis for an alternative explanation for such an inference. Evidence would also be relevant if it could be used to eliminate an alternative explanation and thereby support the drawing of the inference.

In classificatory terms, evidence that supports or eliminates the existence of an alternative explanation for an inference is "**ancillary**" evidence (Schum, 1994, pp 109-114). This classification is not especially important for lawyers, however, because the law of evidence does not draw any distinction between circumstantial evidence and this kind of ancillary evidence (as opposed to credibility-related ancillary evidence, to which special rules do apply). The most important thing, then, is that we are able to articulate how an item of evidence is relevant to support or eliminate an alternative explanation, rather than necessarily being able to correctly classify it as ancillary evidence.

ARGUMENTS ABOUT INFERENCES

Two kinds of arguments about inferences

[7.160] The fact that an item of evidence has been admitted on the basis that it provides the foundation for a relevant inference does not necessarily mean that the court will draw that inference. The previous part of this chapter explained that sometimes the chain of inferences required to connect an item of evidence to the facts in issue can involve several steps. It further explained that, because circumstantial evidence is never conclusive, there is always the possibility of there being an alternative explanation for the evidence (alternative, that is, to the explanation we are advancing). Given all this, how can we persuade a court to draw the inference for which we are contending; and how can we persuade the court not to draw an inference for which our opponent is contending?

To put it another way, how do we go about defending and strengthening or, alternatively, attacking and weakening, a chain of inferences? The first and most obvious form of defence is to use several independent but convergent chains of inferences (motive, means, opportunity and so on) to prove each of our material facts. By this means, no single chain has to bear the entire weight of the case – the separate chains instead become like the strands in a cable of proof, each contributing their strength to the strength of the case as a whole. Equally, an obvious form of attack is to offer a rival body of evidence – such as evidence of an alibi – that is inconsistent with our opponent's case.

But there are also methods we can use to strengthen or weaken a single chain of inferences. The key to these methods is to be found in a feature of circumstantial evidence we have already noted: the fact that at every step in a chain of inferences there is the possibility of an alternative explanation for the evidence.

To use a metaphor, we can think of a chain of inferences as a path down which we are trying to lead the court, a "path" that "ends" in a finding that a material fact exists. For every step we are asking the court to take, there is an alternative, an "escape route" into which our opponent may try to lure the court. If the court takes any of these alternative paths it will fail to arrive at the destination to which we are leading it. If, however, we are able to block off all of these alternative paths, all of these escape routes, then the court will have no choice but to follow us. Of course, the roles may be reversed, and it may be we who are trying to find an escape route from a chain of inferences on which our opponent is attempting to rely.

There are, then, two possible kinds of arguments about inferences:

1. An argument that the court should not draw an inference. In order to make such an argument we can identify a possible alternative explanation for the inference (this may be provided by our client's instructions), and then lead evidence to support it.

2. An argument that a court should draw an inference. In order to make that kind of argument we must lead evidence to eliminate any of the alternative explanations on which our opponent is, or might be, relying.

In either case, we must begin by identifying what those possible explanations are. It is important to note at the outset, however, that there is a fundamental difference between the position of the party seeking to defend a chain of inferences, and the position of the party seeking to attack it. The defending party – that is, the party seeking to persuade the court to draw the chain of inferences that connects the item of evidence to the facts in issue – must be ready to defend every single link in the chain, every single inference in the series of inferences. The attacking party, on the other hand – that is, the party seeking to persuade the court to accept an alternative explanation for the evidence – need only attack one link in the chain. From the point of view of the attacking party, therefore, only one escape route needs to be found. From the point of view of the defending party, on the other hand, every possible escape route must be identified and, where possible, blocked off.

Identifying alternative explanations

[7.170] The most straightforward way of identifying alternative explanations is simply to ask ourselves, our client, or an appropriate expert, the following question: "What other explanations might there be for this item of evidence?" Indeed, we may well be restricted in the explanations we can advance by our client's instructions, or by the statements that our client has already made to others (such as the police). Assuming that we are not so limited, however, we can be a little more creative, in a systematic way. In particular, if we have gone to the trouble of identifying all the steps in the chain of inferences needed to connect an item of evidence to the facts in issue, then we can look for alternative explanations at every single step of the chain.

Examining each of the steps closely, we may conclude that some steps are so strong that no alternative explanation is likely to be credible, but that others are vulnerable to attack. For example, there is unlikely to be a plausible alternative to Step 4 in the chain of inferences Schum used to defend the relevance of Officer Connolly's testimony about Sacco's hand movements. If the court is prepared to find that Sacco intended to draw and use his concealed revolver, then it is also likely to find that he would have done so for the purposes of escape. Step 4 is not a weak point. But there are obvious weaknesses with each of Steps 5, 6 and 7. Indeed, it was as an alternative explanation for Step 5 that the relevance of Sacco's testimony about the questions asked by Officer Connolly could be defended. And if the court rejected that explanation, and found that Sacco's conduct was demonstrative of a consciousness of guilt, then an obvious alternative explanation for each of Steps 6 and 7 is the possibility that he was conscious of having committed some other criminal act.

We can apply a similar analysis to any chain of inferences. For example, in the firearms discharge example at Figure 7.6, the drawing of the inference that the accused had discharged a firearm within a period of three hours prior to the taking of the sample rested on a generalisation to the effect that "when a sample taken from a person's hand tests positive for lead, barium and antimony, that usually indicates that the person has discharged a firearm not less than three hours before the sample was taken". The generalisation is not absolute, being qualified by the word "usually". Indeed, one of the ways of thinking about alternative explanations is to think of them as exceptions to the generalisation that justifies the drawing of an inference, or as evidence that shows that the generalisation does not apply in the particular instance.

For example, the inclusion of the qualifier "usually" within the generalisation above immediately alerts us to the possibility that there must be other possible explanations for the positive result than that the accused had discharged a firearm. The "Birmingham Six", for example, first became serious suspects in the 1974 IRA bombings in Birmingham because the hands of two of them tested "positive" for nitro-glycerine; one possible explanation for this fact was that the test also reacted positively to a substance coating a pack of cards with which they had been playing. Similarly, the Royal Commission into Lindy Chamberlain's conviction for the murder of her daughter, Azaria, ultimately found that the substance in the car that had tested "positive" for foetal haemoglobin was actually a sound deadener.

Moreover, the inference in our example that the accused had discharged a firearm was only one step in a chain of inferences needed to connect the positive result to a material fact, such as that it was the accused who had shot the deceased. Even if the accused did discharge a firearm, there are still alternative explanations for this fact: perhaps he or she discharged a firearm for some other reason within the relevant time period.

Substantiating alternative explanations

[7.180] If we are merely identifying alternative explanations for the purpose of eliminating them, then we can go on to the next topic below. But if we are intending to rely on an alternative explanation as a means of persuading a court not to draw an inference for which our opponent is contending, then it is not enough to simply identify possible alternative explanations. The mere enumeration of a list of possible explanations, unsupported by any evidence, is unlikely to deflect the court from the path of drawing the inference in question. We need to choose a point of attack, and we need to lead evidence to give substance to the attack. We need to entice the court down the alternative path, and arguments that are not substantiated by evidence are unlikely to be enticing.

If, for instance, we were acting for the defence in the firearms discharge residue example, and we wanted to avoid the inference that the accused had discharged a firearm, we would need to lead evidence, either from our own expert or from the prosecution's expert during cross-examination, to the effect that there are other substances that may also test positive. We would also need to lead evidence to show how the accused might have had such a substance on his or her hands at the time the sample was taken. If we are unable to lead credible evidence on both of these points, then the court is likely to draw the inference that the accused had indeed discharged a firearm. If, on the other hand, we are conceding that the accused had discharged a firearm, but are attempting to avoid the inference that the accused shot the deceased, we will need to lead credible evidence to show that the accused had discharged a firearm for some other purpose during the relevant timeframe. Without such evidence, we are relying on a mere theoretical possibility, and a mere theoretical possibility is always likely to be defeated by a possibility backed up by evidence.

Eliminating alternative explanations

[7.190]   The approach is different when we are trying to persuade the court to draw the inference. Rather than identifying and substantiating one or more alternative explanations, we must identify and eliminate all alternative explanations. If some of the possible alternative explanations have not been eliminated, then the tribunal of fact is likely to be left in a state of doubt about our case. By eliminating the alternatives, we leave the tribunal of fact with no choice but to draw the inferences for which we contend. The process is, thus, analogous to "closing the gates" in cross-examination and thereby forcing a witness down a particular path.

This process of elimination is required from the highest level of the case, in relation to alternative explanations for the body of evidence as a whole, to the lowest, in relation to alternative explanations for specific inferences. We will begin with the elimination of alternative explanations for the case as a whole. In a case involving a death by shooting, for example, in order to persuade the court to find that the deceased had been murdered by the accused, we might have to eliminate possibilities such as suicide, accident, or murder by a third party (such explanations are examples of defences that involve putting forward a factual theory to compete with that of the prosecution). Similarly, in *Weissensteiner v The Queen* (1993) 178 CLR 217, the accused was charged with the murder of a couple with whom he had gone on a yachting trip. The three had sailed off together; the accused returned alone. The couple's bodies were never found. Clearly, in such a case a major part of the prosecution task was to eliminate any explanation for the couple's disappearance other than that they were murdered by the accused.

Usually, however, we do not have to eliminate the entire universe of conceivable explanations. The circumstances may be such as to reduce some explanations to no more than mere theoretical possibilities: if the person was shot in the back of the head with a long-barrelled firearm, then suicide is unlikely (although it might be just as well to have this confirmed in passing by an appropriate expert witness). Other explanations are inherently implausible: the prosecution in *Weissensteiner* did not, for example, bother to eliminate the possibility of alien abduction. The universe of possible explanations that we must confront is also reduced by the conduct of our opponent. It is an unusual case in which the pleadings, records of interview or other evidence do not provide us with an indication of the explanation on which our opponent is likely to rely.

As a matter of practical advocacy, past reliance by our opponent on one explanation will make it difficult for him or her to rely at trial on a different explanation. If, for example, the story originally told by the accused was one of accidental shooting, then it will be very difficult for him or her to switch to a story of murder by a third party, or suicide. At the very least, any such switch will come at considerable cost to his or her credibility. Of course it is always prudent to consider the possibility that some such switch might be attempted, and to make contingency plans accordingly. If, in the circumstances, however, it seems reasonable for us to assume that "if this explanation was true then our opponent would already have relied on it", then our opponent's failure to rely on it can be treated as evidence of its untruth, and we can instead focus our efforts of elimination on the explanation or explanations on which our opponent has relied, or is likely to rely.

It is sometimes helpful to cast an alternative explanation we are seeking to eliminate in the negative, and to include it as part of our own case. So, for example, if the defence is likely to be one of accidental shooting, it may be helpful to incorporate into our case a main argument, such as "the shooting was *not* accidental". We can then marshal evidence according to this proposition. Thinking of the explanation in this way will often correspond to the way in which we argue the case in our closing address. This was discussed at [6.80] under the heading "Negating our opponent's factual theory".

[7.200] So far we have been considering the elimination of alternative explanations for the case as a whole. The process can also be required at the lower levels of a case in relation to specific inferences. As we know, circumstantial evidence is always inconclusive – for every inference, there is an alternative. We also know that as the proponent of a chain of inferences, our opponent need only break one link in that chain in order to destroy the value of the evidence, whereas we must be ready to defend every single link. We should therefore be prepared to analyse every step of a chain of inferences in order to identify the possible means by which our opponent will seek to "escape" from the path down which we are attempting to lead the court.

Assuming we have already examined the case for weak points – places where our opponent may seek to derail a chain of inferences by offering an alternative explanation – we can now go on to consider how we will eliminate these alternative explanations. Each possible alternative explanation is a potential escape route, and we must block them all. Blocking off these escape routes is essentially the same process, in miniature, as that required to eliminate explanations for the case as a whole. We can again include the negative of the explanation as something that we lead evidence to prove. For example, if we are prosecuting in the firearms discharge residue example and are able to prove that the accused did discharge a firearm, and that the only time he or she could have done so was in shooting the deceased, then the accused must have shot the deceased. We may therefore include among the propositions we are trying to prove the proposition that the accused did *not* discharge a firearm for some other purpose during the relevant timeframe.

Similarly, we can imagine a case where it is important to establish that the accused was inside particular premises at a particular time. We have a witness who testifies that she saw the accused entering the premises half an hour before the time of importance to us. This provides the basis for an inference that the accused may still have been inside the premises half an hour later. But there are other explanations, in particular the possibility that the accused left the premises during that time. Perhaps our witness was observing the door through which the accused entered the premises for that entire half hour and is able to testify not only that she saw the accused enter the premises, but also that she did not see the accused leave the premises. But this still leaves open the possibility that the accused may have exited through some other door. To eliminate the possibility that the accused left the premises, we would therefore also need evidence from someone who was watching those other exits, or who had examined the premises and can testify that there are no other exits. If we can prove all these propositions, then the conclusion is inescapable: the accused was in the premises at the time of importance. The evidence in this example is charted in Figure 7.11.

Of course, we have to accept the reality that we will not always have available to us the evidence to eliminate all the possible alternative explanations for each of the inferences we are asking the court to draw. We can console ourselves with the thought that there is a difference between our opponent offering an alternative explanation and the court accepting that explanation: some explanations are simply implausible. Moreover, the gradual accumulation of circumstances will itself go some way towards reducing the plausibility of any innocent explanation for them. That said, if we have the means to eliminate an alternative explanation, we should use it.

Charting alternative explanations

[7.210] Structurally, an alternative explanation is an "exception" to a generalisation that justifies the drawing of an inference – that is, it is a reason why the generalisation does not apply in the particular case. In terms of logical classification, the evidence used to substantiate or eliminate alternative explanations is ancillary evidence; again, however, nothing turns on this classification. All of this is, however, useful to remember if we want to include an alternative explanation, and the evidence used to support or eliminate it, in an evidence chart. For example, the alternative explanation for Sacco's conduct could be charted as shown in Figure 7.8 (like all the charts that follow, this is obviously only a fragment of the complete chart; and none of them include the "source" for the generalisation which, as Figure 7.7 showed, would usually be a "common belief").

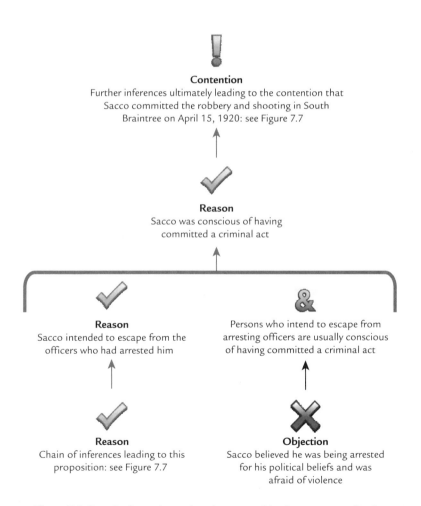

Figure 7.8: Sacco's alternative explanation as an objection to a generalisation

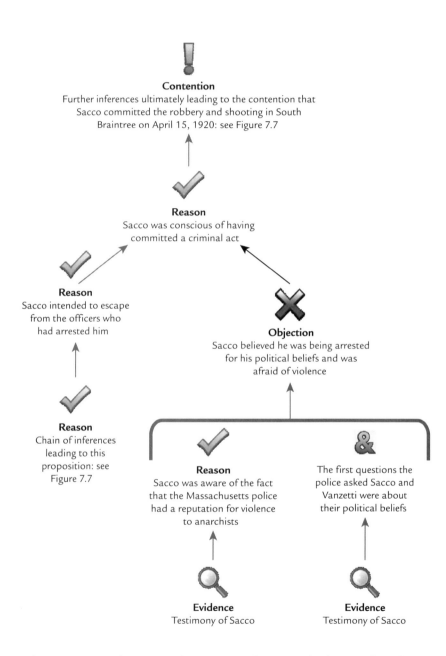

Figure 7.9: Sacco's alternative explanation as an objection to the drawing of an inference

Thus, the alternative explanation is shown as an objection to the application of the generalisation to Sacco (the "objection" is effectively shorthand for the phrase "this generalisation does not apply in the present case because ...").

If the generalisation was not included in the chart, then the alternative explanation may instead be shown simply as an objection to the inference drawn from the factual proposition, as in Figure 7.9, which also includes the items of evidence on which the objection is based. This alerts us to the need to find a method of proving the factual proposition that Sacco was afraid of police violence (this could just be Sacco himself, but we might also want to find other sources of evidence to corroborate Sacco).

If we are eliminating the alternative explanation, we can identify the alternative explanation as an objection to the inference, and then show the evidence we are using to eliminate the explanation as rebuttal of (or objection to) the objection, as in Figure 7.10 (which is based on Figure 7.6).

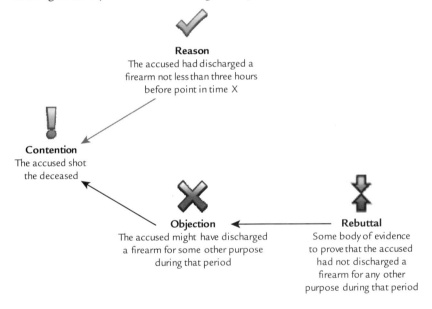

Figure 7.10: Eliminating alternative explanations in the firearms example

Another possibility is to treat the evidence that eliminates the alternative explanations as part of our own case, as in Figure 7.11, which charts the evidence used to eliminate the possibility that the accused had left the premises before the time of importance to us. In this chart the three items of evidence on which we are relying to prove the accused's presence in the premises at the time of importance

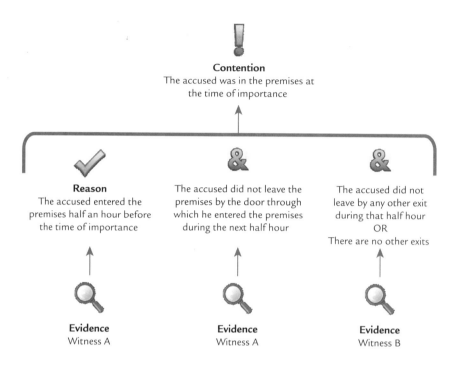

Figure 7.11: Eliminating alternative explanations to prove continued presence in premises

have been shown in a relationship of conjunction, as part of a single compound reason, in order to emphasise the fact that failure to prove any one of them will leave open the alternative explanation that the accused left the premises in the intervening period.

The identification of alternative explanations and the evidence that can be used to support or eliminate them is, then, the key to arguments about inferences.

ARGUMENTS ABOUT NEGATIVE AND MISSING EVIDENCE

[7.220] There are two types of circumstantial evidence that often cause a degree of confusion: negative evidence and missing evidence. Negative evidence is evidence that something did not happen – that is, it is evidence of the non-occurrence of an event. Missing evidence, on the other hand, is the absence of evidence that we might have expected to have had. Although sometimes similar in appearance, they provide the foundation for very different inferences.

For example, prior to the United States' invasion of Iraq in 2003, when United Nations weapons inspectors failed to find weapons of mass destruction, or evidence of their production, was this negative evidence – that is, evidence that Iraq had no weapons of mass destruction? Or was it missing evidence, suggesting that Iraq had hidden or destroyed the incriminating evidence, was not co-operating with the United Nations? Indeed, was the very absence of incriminating evidence in fact evidence that Iraq *did* have weapons of mass destruction? Following the invasion, the failure to find any weapons of mass destruction, or any real evidence of their existence, strongly suggests that it was negative evidence; and, as we shall see, we can only properly classify an absence of evidence as "missing" evidence when there is a proper foundation for our belief that the evidence must have existed.

Negative evidence

[7.230] In Chapter 4 we discussed the processes of abduction and retroduction. Abduction, as you will recall, is the imaginative process of developing working theories of the case; retroduction is the identification of tests that can be used to confirm or disprove these theories. It was suggested in Chapter 4 that one way of approaching the task of gathering evidence is to ask the following question: "If event X, an event of interest to us, had happened, what else would we also expect to have happened?" We might call these other events "indicator events", in the sense that their occurrence points towards the occurrence of the event of interest. Evidence showing the occurrence of the indicator events would tend to show that the event of interest had also occurred; conversely, evidence that the indicator events had not occurred would tend to show that the event of interest had not occurred.

Negative evidence is, thus, evidence that a particular event did not occur. It operates when the non-occurrence of an indicator event is evidence from which it can be inferred that an event of interest to us did not occur. If our opponent's theory of the case is that the event of interest did occur, then we can attack that theory by leading evidence of the non-occurrence of the indicator events. Negative evidence is also a very common way of eliminating alternative explanations – we eliminate the explanation by leading evidence to show that the things that we would have expected to have happened if the explanation was true did not happen. From this we can invite the court to infer that the explanation is not true.

A good example of negative evidence is found in *Silver Blaze*, the case of the missing racehorse. The (bumbling) Inspector Gregory, who is also on the trail of the horse, asks Sherlock Holmes the following question:

"Is there anything else to which you would wish to draw my attention?"
"To the curious incident of the dog in the night-time."
"The dog did nothing in the night-time."
"That was the curious incident," remarked Sherlock Holmes.

Holmes's theory is that if a stranger had entered the stable and stolen the horse, the dog would have barked; as it did not, then the person who removed the horse from the stable must have been known to the dog. This obviously reduced the field of possible suspects. As Schum (1994, p 363) points out, however, in order for this inference to be safe, Holmes should have done some research about the dog. For instance, if it was a lazy, old or docile dog, then there might be no reason for thinking that it would bark at strangers. It is only if the barking of the dog truly is an indicator event for the entrance into the stable of a stranger that an inference from the non-occurrence of that event is sound. The structure of Holmes's reasoning about the dog that did not bark is represented in Figure 7.12.

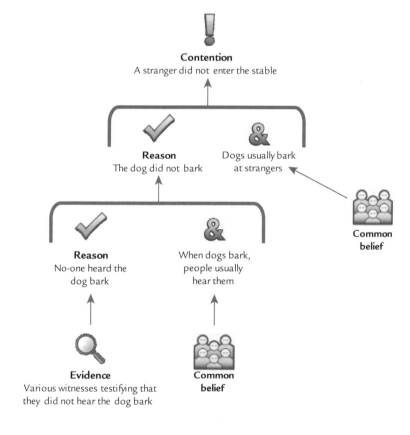

Figure 7.12: Negative evidence: the dog that did not bark

Note that in the example shown in Figure 7.12, we would almost certainly need ancillary evidence to show that the generalisations do apply in the present instance – namely that someone would have heard this dog barking, if it had barked; and that this particular dog would have barked if a stranger had entered the stable.

Missing evidence

[7.240] To say that evidence is "missing" involves two things: first, our failure to find evidence, or our opponent's failure to provide, discover or produce it; and second, a belief that the evidence must exist or have existed. Without the second of these things there is no basis for us to characterise the evidence as "missing" (it may instead be negative evidence). If evidence is properly characterised as missing, however, then this suggests that it has gone missing as a result of some human action, and that the reasons or motives for these actions concern its contents. In other words, it suggests that the reason the evidence is missing is because it was or would have been detrimental to the person who has hidden, destroyed, or failed to produce it. Thus, missing evidence can provide a basis for an inference about the nature of the missing evidence; or about the state of mind of the person responsible for the fact that it is missing.

The fact that the evidence is missing, however, means that we can not know precisely what its content is, was, or would have been. Given this uncertainty, it is often difficult to eliminate alternative explanations for evidence that appears to be missing. Such explanations include the possibility that it never existed, and that there is some other reason for the party's failure to provide, discover or produce it. Even if we feel confident in inferring that the evidence is missing and that the reason for it being missing is that it would have harmed the party who has made it go missing, this will not necessarily entitle us to draw a more specific inference about the contents of the evidence. For example, from the fact that a document is missing we may infer that its contents were damaging; but this will not necessarily enable us to draw an inference as to what the document actually contained.

Similarly, the failure of a party to call as a witness one of its senior employees who was present at a crucial meeting may give rise to the inference shown in Figure 7.13. It is assumed, of course, that it is clear from the evidence that the particular witness would know something about the events in question. If the managing director was not involved in the events that form the subject of the litigation, then there is a perfectly obvious explanation for the defendant's failure to call him or her: he or she has no evidence to contribute. As this suggests, the key to this whole process is the acceptability, and applicability, of the generalisation used to justify the drawing of that inference. The defendant may attempt to advance an alternative explanation for the failure to call that witness. If that alternative explanation is accepted, then the generalisation will not apply and the inference will not be drawn.

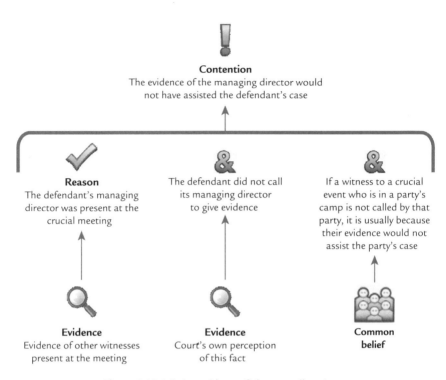

Figure 7.13: Missing evidence: failure to call a witness

It is for these reasons that there are legal rules regulating the drawing of inferences from some of the most common examples of what might be regarded as missing evidence, including the failure of a party to call a particular witness, the accused's failure to testify at trial and the accused's refusal to answer police questions. In Australia, for example, the use of these three types of "missing evidence" is regulated by, respectively:

- the rule in *Jones v Dunkel* (1959) 101 CLR 298 and *Dyers v The Queen* (2002) 210 CLR 285; [2002] HCA 45,
- *Weissensteiner v The Queen* (1993) 178 CLR 217, *RPS v The Queen* (2000) 199 CLR 620; [2000] HCA 3, and *Azzopardi v The Queen; Davis v The Queen* (2001) 205 CLR 50; [2001] HCA 25; and
- the "right to silence", including s 89 of the *Evidence Act 1995* (Cth) and the other "uniform" Evidence Acts. Other examples of missing evidence (although that term is not used) are discussed in the articles by the author (1997a) and by Hamer (2001). Before we can rely on any of these types of missing evidence we must ensure that we have complied with any preconditions imposed by the law of evidence applying in the jurisdiction in which we are litigating.

ARGUMENTS ABOUT PROBATIVE VALUE AND THE STANDARD OF PROOF

[7.250] This final part of the chapter is concerned with arguments about the weight of evidence – that is:

- arguments about the probative value of specific items of evidence; and
- arguments about the standard of proof as it applies to the case as a whole.

Of course, the fundamental purpose of the arguments we make in our closing address is to persuade the court that the standard of proof has (or has not) been met. Nevertheless, there are a few additional points worth observing about the application of the standard of proof to our (or our opponent's) case.

The probative value of specific items of evidence

[7.260] We can define "probative value" as the degree to which an item of evidence affects the probabilities of the existence of the facts in issue – that is, how much does it cause us to revise our previous estimates of those probabilities? To what degree does it persuade us in favour of a theory of the case? Thus, probative value is concerned with the assessment of probabilities. There has been considerable debate over the manner in which probabilities should be assessed and revised in light of evidence. For the reasons set out in the Notes, this text does not attempt to engage with that debate, or even to describe its basic parameters. Nor does it purport to provide any methods for actually calculating probabilities, on the grounds that this is not a task that lawyers preparing for trial are ever required to undertake.

What this text does do is attempt to set out some general considerations that are relevant to the probative value of evidence. These can be used as the basis for arguments about the probative value of specific items of evidence – where, for example, probative value is a criterion of admissibility, as in the tendency and coincidence rules, and the general discretion to exclude evidence on the grounds that it is more prejudicial than probative – or for arguments designed to persuade the tribunal of fact to accept our case or reject that of our opponent. It should come as no surprise that probative value is a function of two attributes: **source credibility** and **inferential force**. These correspond to the credibility and relevance stages of reasoning that we have previously discussed.

Arguments about the credibility of witnesses and other sources were the first topic of this chapter. We will therefore confine our discussion to the second attribute: inferential force. Note that in Australia, where probative value is being assessed by the trial judge for the purposes of determining the *admissibility* of an item of evidence, it is unclear whether or not source credibility can be taken into account (see Gans and Palmer (2014, [16.2.1])).

The inferential force of specific items of evidence

[7.270] Inferential force relates to the relevance stage of reasoning about an item of evidence: assuming the source to be credible, how much does the item of evidence affect the probabilities of the existence of the facts in issue? Evidence is so infinite in its variety that it is really only possible to make some fairly general points:

- A chain of inferences can not be stronger than its weakest link.
- Because every link in a chain of inferences is a source of uncertainty (in the form of alternative explanations), as a general proposition, the longer the chain of inferences required to connect an item of evidence with a fact in issue, the less inferential force that item of evidence has.
- That said, where the links in a chain of inference are supported by "ancillary" evidence, the chain may in fact be quite strong – that is, the item of evidence may have significant inferential force in relation to the facts in issue. The ancillary evidence may take the form of evidence that eliminates alternative explanations, or which shows that the generalisation that justifies the inference does apply in the particular instance. This was discussed in relation to arguments about inferences.
- A chain of inferences that is unsupported by ancillary evidence and rests only on generalisations is unlikely to have very much inferential force. Indeed, unless the chain of inferences is very short, or the generalisations that support the inferences almost universal in their application, such a chain of inferences will border on the speculative.
- Some argue that there is no real difference in overall probative value between a strong argument based on a weak foundation (that is, a source lacking credibility) and a weak argument based on a strong foundation. Others argue that a weak argument based on a strong foundation has more probative value than a strong argument based on a weak foundation: see Schum (1994, pp 301-306).

Standards of proof

[7.280] Depending on who has the burden of proof, there are three main standards of proof that may be applied to our case:

1. proof that there is a case to answer;
2. proof on the balance of probabilities; and
3. proof beyond reasonable doubt.

The first standard may vary according to whether the matter is being tried before a judge and jury, or before a judge alone. If the matter is being tried before a judge and jury, then we can usually satisfy the court that there is a case to answer by showing that there is some evidence capable of proving each of the facts in issue to the required standard. The credibility or inferential force of that evidence is not a question for the judge: provided that there is evidence capable of satisfying all of the elements of the legal case, then the case should be left for the jury. Nor does the judge take into account evidence that undermines the case: thus, the case is assessed at its most favourable.

If the matter is being tried before a judge alone, however, then the question of whether there is a case to answer may require the judge to consider whether he or she is satisfied, on the evidence led by the plaintiff, that all the facts in issue have been proved to the required standard. Such an approach would require the court to assess the credibility and inferential force of the evidence.

The second standard – proof on the balance of probabilities – requires us to prove that it is more likely than not that each of the elements of our case exists. The most interesting issues in relation to the third, criminal, standard – proof beyond reasonable doubt – arise in cases based entirely, or largely, on circumstantial evidence. Proof beyond reasonable doubt in such a case means that there is no reasonable explanation for the evidence that is consistent with the accused's innocence. This obviously means that one of the most important ways of satisfying this standard is by eliminating alternative explanations for the evidence, a process discussed in the section dealing with arguments about inferences at [7.160]–[7.210].

In Australia, at least, questions have arisen as to whether the application of the criminal standard means that all the facts being used to prove guilt must themselves be proved beyond reasonable doubt. The High Court's misleading judgment in *Chamberlain v The Queen (No 2)* (1984) 153 CLR 521 was clarified in the court's later decision in *Shepherd v The Queen* (1990) 170 CLR 573, although some confusion still remains: see Hamer (1997)) and Gans and Palmer (2014, [17.2.1]). What now seems clear is this: the facts in issue must all be proved to the criminal standard. If an "intermediate factual proposition" is **indispensable** to proof of one of the facts in issue, then it, too, must be proved to the criminal standard.

Where there are several independent strands of evidence converging on a fact in issue, then none of them is indispensable to proof of that fact in issue, and none of them needs to be proved to the criminal standard. This is sometimes referred to as a "**cable** of proof". If, on the other hand, proof of one of the facts in issue depends on a single item of evidence or single chain of inferences, then that item of evidence, or every link in that chain of inferences, is indispensable to proof of the fact in issue and must be proved to the criminal standard. The best way to avoid the application of this standard, then, is to persuade the court that there are several independent strands of evidence, all providing a basis for an inference that the fact in issue exists. We should ask ourselves the following question: if we took that item of evidence or chain of inferences away, would we have any other evidence we could use to prove that fact in issue? If not, then the criminal standard applies to that item of evidence or chain of inferences.

Inference vs conjecture

[7.290] In attempting to persuade the court that we have satisfied one of the standards of proof described at [7.280], we may be met with the objection that our case is too speculative. So how do we persuade the court that our case is based on inference, or that our opponent's case is based on speculation and conjecture? In *Holloway v McFeeters* (1956) 94 CLR 470, Dixon CJ attempted to explain the difference. In that case, the plaintiff's husband had been killed by an unidentified vehicle. In order to succeed, the plaintiff had to establish that the driver of the unidentified vehicle had been negligent. The main evidence available to the plaintiff concerned her husband's movements prior to the accident, and some tyre marks on the road. Dixon CJ, albeit in dissent, held (at 475-476) that there was not a proper foundation for the court to infer that the driver had been negligent:

> From the foregoing circumstances certain facts may reasonably be inferred and others perhaps presumed as a matter of probability. It may be inferred that a car proceeding in a westerly direction, a small car, struck the deceased at that part of the road where the dust and debris was found, that the brakes were applied and the car swerved over from the middle of the road to the right-hand side, carrying the deceased for a distance of fourteen yards and that then a wheel or wheels ran over his body. It may be presumed that he was in an upright posture when the car struck him, but on the foregoing assumptions it must be taken that at the moment of impact he was in the middle of the bitumen road. No doubt it might be inferred that the speed of the car at first impact was about thirty miles an hour. Further, the possibility of the accident being caused by some obstruction to vision forming a feature of the locality is excluded. Rain and mist are also excluded.
>
> ... But the real difficulty of the case lies not in finding a foundation for those preliminary inferences, but in the next step. For the state of facts inferred itself leaves room for conflicting conjectures or hypotheses as to the cause of the accident. How came the deceased in the path of the approaching car? Did he move in front of it and into the range of vision suddenly? Was he walking along the middle of the road with his back to it? Did the driver fail to see him until too late by reason of the darkness of his clothes and the upward slope of the road until it levelled out where he was walking? The conjecture that the driver must have been in fault in failing to see him in time to avoid him may be shrewd. But is it more than a conjecture? Before the plaintiff can succeed in such a case as this the circumstances must lead to a satisfactory inference, even though resting on a balance of probabilities, that the accident was caused by some negligence on the part of the driver. In the present case the true cause of the accident is in truth unknown. The state of facts reached by inferences is itself compatible with a number of hypotheses, some of them implying fault on one side, some on the other, some on both sides. Hypotheses of this kind are not inferences. What is required is a basis for some positive inference involving

negligence on the part of the driver as a cause of the deceased's death. The inference may be made only as the most probable deduction from the established facts, but it must at least be a deduction which may reasonably be drawn from them. It need not be an inference as to how precisely the accident occurred, but it must be a reasonable conclusion that the accident in one way or another occurred through the lack of due care on the part of the driver and not otherwise. Reluctant as one is to differ from judges so experienced in such matters [ie the court below], the difficulty seems insuperable of finding a foundation for an inference that the accident was caused in a manner implying negligence in the driver of the unidentified car.

From this passage, several points emerge:

- Inferences have a foundation in evidence; speculation and conjecture run beyond the point where the evidence can take us.
- If we have only established that something *might* have happened, or *might* have happened in a particular way, then we have probably not discharged our burden of proof.
- If there is no reason why the court should prefer one possibility over another – other than that it suits our case better – then we are still in the realm of conjecture.
- If the best that can be said is that a particular inference is "not inconsistent" with the evidence, then the court is unlikely to find that the inference has been proved to the required standard.

It is also worth adding that the "doctrine" of res ipsa loquitur can only be applied – in Australia at any rate – when the "thing" really does "speak for itself", in the sense of providing a solid foundation for an inference that the event was caused by a particular person's negligence: see, for example, *Schellenberg v Tunnel Holdings Pty Ltd* (2000) 200 CLR 121; [2000] HCA 18. As Barwick CJ observed in *Government Insurance Office of NSW v Fredrichberg* (1968) 118 CLR 403 at 413:

> [T]he so-called "doctrine" is no more than a process of logic by which an inference of negligence may be drawn from the circumstance of the occurrence itself where in the ordinary affairs of mankind such an occurrence is not likely to occur without lack of care towards the plaintiff on the part of a person in the position of the defendant.

As this passage makes clear, the inference must always be based on a generalisation similar to the one relied on by the court in *Scott v Londan and St Katherine Docks Co* (1865) 3 H & C 596 at 601; 159 ER 665 at 667: "the accident is such as in the ordinary course of things does not happen if those who have the management use proper care". If such a generalisation is implausible in the circumstances of the case, then it will leave open the possibility that the event might have been caused in some other way, and the onus of proof will not have been discharged.

Summary

[7.300] A number of different types of arguments that can be made from and about evidence have been discussed in this chapter. These arguments were divided into five main categories. A point common to all of these arguments, however, is that a **foundation in evidence** must always be laid for them. The reason our preparation for trial includes the identification of the arguments that we would like to make during our closing address is to enable us to ensure that we lay the necessary foundations for those arguments during the course of the trial.

In terms of arguments about **witnesses and other sources** of evidence, we saw that:

- There are three main sources of evidence in a common law trial: **witnesses, real evidence** and **documents**.
- The **credibility** of a source of evidence is crucial to its probative value.
- There are three main aspects of credibility in relation to **witnesses: honesty, observational accuracy** and **reliability of memory**.
- **Real** evidence gives rise to questions of **authenticity** and **accuracy**.
- **Documentary** evidence also gives rise to questions of **authenticity** and either the **accuracy** of the process that led to their creation, or the **credibility** of their human creators.
- A **foundation** must always be laid through the testimony of a witness before an item of **real** or **documentary** evidence can be tendered.
- It is therefore an important part of our preparation to **identify the witness** through whom we will seek to tender the items of real and documentary evidence on which we wish to rely.

In terms of arguments about **relevance**, we saw that:

- The relevance of **direct** evidence is obvious and need never be defended.
- **Circumstantial** evidence can only be connected to the facts in issue through the drawing of inferences. Because of this, circumstantial evidence is always inconclusive, and its relevance may have to be defended. Sometimes a series or **chain of inferences** is required to connect an item of circumstantial evidence to the facts in issue; in such cases, the entire chain may need to be defended.
- Evidence is also relevant if it can be used to support or eliminate an **alternative explanation** for an item of circumstantial evidence: in classificatory terms, such evidence is ancillary evidence (as is evidence relevant to the credibility of a source).
- All inferences are based on (often unstated) **generalisations**. These generalisations provide the justification or warrant for the drawing of the inference; they are the "glue" that connects an item of evidence or factual proposition to the factual proposition inferred from it.

- In the case of the "generalisations" relied on by **experts** as the basis for their opinions, it is usual for the expert to provide "**backing**" evidence for the generalisation – that is, to give evidence that justifies the generalisation. Backing evidence is not, however, normally led in relation to the (usually unstated) generalisations that underpin the inferences drawn by the tribunal of fact without assistance from an expert.

In terms of arguments about **inferences**, we saw that:

- **circumstantial** evidence is by its nature **inconclusive**, and therefore always susceptible to more than one **explanation**;
- whether we are seeking to defend and strengthen a chain of inferences, or seeking to attack and weaken it, we should attempt to identify all the **alternative explanations** that might be available at every step of the chain;
- one of the best ways of persuading a court not to draw an inference is to lead evidence to **support such an alternative explanation**; and
- one of the best ways of persuading a court to draw a chain of inferences is to lead evidence to **eliminate the possible alternative explanations** that exist at every step of the chain.

We discussed two particular types of circumstantial evidence, namely **negative** and **missing evidence**:

1. **Negative** evidence is evidence of the non-occurrence of an event. If the event is an "indicator event" for an event of interest, then negative evidence can be used to prove that the event of interest did not occur.
2. **Missing** evidence is the absence of evidence that we have reason to believe existed. It is sometimes used as the basis for an inference that the "missing" evidence would have been detrimental to the party who has made it go "missing"; and sometimes as the basis for inferences about the state of mind of the person who made it go "missing".

Special **rules of evidence** often apply to the drawing of inferences from missing evidence, including rules such as the "right to silence".

Finally, the chapter concluded with a discussion of arguments about **probative value** and **the standard of proof**:

- The **probative value** of an item of evidence depends on two attributes: the **credibility of its source**, and its **inferential force** in relation to the facts in issue.
- **Inferential force** depends on a variety of factors, including the degree to which a chain of inferences is supported by ancillary evidence.
- There are a number of different **standards of proof** that the court may apply to a case.

- The application of the criminal standard of **proof beyond reasonable doubt** to a case based largely on **circumstantial** evidence requires the prosecution to exclude as unreasonable any explanations for the evidence that are consistent with innocence.
- Where an item of evidence or chain of inferences is **indispensable** to proof of one or more of the facts in issue, it must be proved to the same standard as applies to that fact in issue.
- A case based on **speculation** or **conjecture**, as opposed to inference, will not satisfy the standard of proof.

Final Preparations

Part
C

Analysing for admissibility [8]

Introduction

[8.10] As a result of the analysis we have carried out in accordance with the preceding chapters, we should by now have identified all the evidence we would like to be able to lead in the trial. This is the evidence that is needed to provide the foundation for the arguments we would ideally make in our closing address. We should also have a good idea of the evidence that our opponent is likely to want to lead in order to prove his or her case. In carrying out this analysis, we have been approaching issues of proof with the law of evidence at the back, rather than at the forefront, of our mind. Now that we have identified all of this evidence, however, it is time to analyse it again in terms of its admissibility. Although admissibility is the focus of this chapter, it is important to state at the outset that this chapter does not purport to be a substitute for a textbook on the law of evidence. Its aims are more limited.

The admissibility of an item of evidence often turns on the question of whether certain "foundational facts" have been established. The first part of the chapter sets out a general method for approaching such questions. Sometimes, however, the admissibility of an item of evidence will instead, or in addition, turn on the issue of how the item of evidence is being used. This is because some of the rules of evidence "prohibit" (prima facie or otherwise) particular uses of evidence. The second part of the chapter contains a brief discussion of some of those rules – specifically, the hearsay rule, the rule against opinion evidence, and the tendency and coincidence rules – attempting, among other things, to describe the structure of the prohibited inferences.

Although the general approach set out in this chapter is applicable in any common law jurisdiction, some of the details of the discussion are specific to the version of the law of evidence that applies in Australia and, in particular, to the version that applies in the "**uniform evidence legislation**" jurisdictions of the Commonwealth, New South Wales, Victoria, Tasmania, Northern Territory, Australian Capital Territory and Norfolk Island, by virtue of the *Evidence Act 1995* (Cth), *Evidence Act 1995* (NSW), *Evidence Act 2008* (Vic), *Evidence Act 2001* (Tas)), *Evidence Act 2011* (ACT), *Evidence (National Uniform Legislation) Act 2011* (NT) and *Evidence Act 2004* (NI) (collectively, the "uniform evidence legislation").

Certain other aspects of the law of evidence were discussed in the previous chapter, including:

- the rules that prescribe the requirements that must be met before evidence from certain sources, in particular real and documentary evidence, can be put into evidence (as was there pointed out, the approach that should be taken to these rules is the approach that is set out in the first part of this chapter);
- the rules that regulate the use of evidence relevant to the credibility of a witness;
- the requirement of relevance, a prerequisite to the admissibility of all evidence;
- the assessment of probative value, which is sometimes taken into account in determining the admissibility of evidence; and
- the application of the standard of proof.

GENERAL APPROACH TO ADMISSIBILITY

[8.20] Textbooks on the law of evidence tend to approach issues of admissibility on the basis that admissibility is a quality that an item of evidence either has, or does not have. Determining admissibility is, thus, a matter of checking off the features of an item of evidence against a list of criteria laid down by the applicable rules of evidence. Sometimes – as, for example, with certain kinds of hearsay – this is easier said than done; but even with difficult-to-apply rules, such as the hearsay rule, admissibility is typically seen as a quality that the evidence either does or does not have.

For a litigator preparing for trial, however, this is not a useful way of thinking about admissibility. This is because the admissibility of an item of evidence is usually determined by the existence of certain foundational facts, facts that must be proved by evidence, and which are often as hotly contested as the other objects of proof in the trial. The labelling of an item of evidence as either admissible or inadmissible should therefore be seen as a statement by the court of a conclusion reached after a process of proof and persuasion by the parties.

In other words, admissibility and inadmissibility are conclusions, not qualities. By proving or disproving the existence of the foundational facts that arise in respect of different kinds of evidence, the parties attempt to persuade the court to reach the conclusion that favours their case. Once this is grasped, it can readily be understood that we can take the same approach to questions of admissibility as we take to any other questions of proof. For this reason, the approach set out at [8.30]-[8.80] is essentially a specific application of the approach set out in Part B of this text.

Identify evidence that may raise questions of admissibility

[8.30] As we analyse the evidence in a case, we should identify two classes of evidence in relation to which we need to carry out some admissibility analysis. The first class comprises the items of evidence that we would like to be able to lead, but which are potentially inadmissible. The second class comprises the items of evidence that our opponent is likely to want to lead, but which we would like to have excluded. Assuming we have a basic degree of familiarity with the law of evidence, this should not be a difficult task. For example, we will automatically know that we will have to give some thought to the admissibility of any document on which we wish to rely; or that any evidence revealing or suggesting other criminal misconduct on the part of the accused will have to be approached with care.

Identify the purpose of the evidence

[8.40] Having identified all the items of evidence in relation to which we are going to carry out some admissibility analysis, the next step is to think clearly about the purpose for which we are adducing each of the items of evidence. What are we using them to prove? If we have analysed our case in accordance with the methods set out in Part B of this book, we should already know this. We need to know the particular purpose of evidence because this is the basis on which admissibility often depends. A document, for example, might be inadmissible hearsay if offered as evidence of its truth; but if we can find another use for the document, then we may be able to have it admitted. This highlights an important truth: never be too quick to give up on an item of evidence that you want to have admitted.

Identify foundational facts relevant to admissibility

[8.50] In general, the rules of evidence are triggered by certain "foundational facts". The word "foundational" is intended to indicate that the proof of these facts is part of the process of laying the foundation for the admission of an item of evidence. We have already seen how a foundation has to be laid for the admission of an item of documentary or real evidence. These are not the only categories in relation to which a foundation has to be laid, however. For example, the exercise of the public policy discretion in relation to illegally or improperly obtained evidence does not need to be exercised by a court unless there is a basis for the court to believe that an item of evidence may have been obtained through an illegality or impropriety. Illegality or impropriety in the obtaining of the evidence is a foundational fact that must be established before the exercise of the public policy discretion arises for consideration. It is not only exclusionary rules and discretions that are triggered by foundational facts; the inclusionary exceptions to those rules also generally require proof of foundational facts. For example, under s 84 of the uniform evidence legislation (which replaces the common law requirement of voluntariness), an admission is not admissible unless the court is satisfied that the admission and the making of the admission were not influenced by violent, oppressive, inhuman or degrading conduct, or a threat of such conduct.

Foundational facts are facts that are relevant to the admissibility of the evidence, rather than to the facts in issue. Although the foundational facts are only relevant to admissibility, however, the evidence used to prove those facts may also be relevant in the trial itself. For example, evidence tending to suggest that an admission was influenced by violent or oppressive conduct, may also be relevant, if the admission is admitted into evidence, to show that the admission is unreliable and should be disregarded. The fact that foundational facts are "only" relevant to admissibility must not, however, be allowed to obscure their importance. Sometimes they can be every bit as significant to the outcome of a trial as any of the other objects of proof. Proof of a foundational fact that leads to the exclusion of a vital piece of evidence may, for example, lead to the collapse of a case (for an example of such a case, see Palmer (1997b)); equally, the admission of a particularly crucial item of evidence may all but guarantee success.

Therefore, foundational facts have to be approached with the same degree of seriousness with which we approach the other objects of proof in the trial. Our method is similar. The first step is always the identification of the foundational facts. If we suspect that an item of evidence falls within the scope of an exclusionary rule, we must identify the facts that trigger the application of that rule. Equally, if we wish to show that an item of evidence that is prima facie inadmissible is actually admissible because of the operation of an inclusionary rule of evidence (that is, an exception to an exclusionary rule), we must identify the foundational facts that trigger the operation of the inclusionary rule. These foundational facts are, in many ways, equivalent to the "elements" of the legal case, except that whereas the elements of the legal case are determined by the substantive law, the foundational facts are usually determined by the law of evidence.

For instance, each of the exceptions to the hearsay rule is triggered by a different set of foundational facts. If we were relying on the common law exception for dying declarations, then one of the foundational facts is that the declarant was under a "settled hopeless expectation of death" at the time of making the declaration. In other words, we would have to establish that a person who is now dead had a particular state of mind at a particular point in time. This is likely to be as difficult to prove as any of the other objects of proof in the trial. If, on the other hand, we are attempting to rely on the exception for contemporaneous representations in s 65(2)(b) of the uniform evidence legislation (the statutory equivalent to the common law res gestae exception), we will have to establish that the representation was made when, or shortly after, the asserted fact occurred, and in circumstances that make it unlikely to have been a fabrication. Similarly, if attempting to have a document admitted under the business records exception, we will have to establish (depending on which jurisdiction we are in) that the document does form part of the records of a business, and that the information it contains was supplied by a person who had personal knowledge of those facts.

Just as legal research is sometimes required in relation to the legal case, so some research into the law of evidence may be required to identify the foundational facts. It is at this point that we will need to consult a text on the law of evidence. Although this chapter does discuss the application of the law of evidence, it only does so in general terms, and makes no attempt to state the law of evidence in a comprehensive or detailed manner. The chapter must, therefore, be used in conjunction with a text on the law of evidence that applies in the jurisdiction in which you are preparing your case. A number of Australian texts are listed in the Notes section at the end of this book; for obvious reasons, the approach taken in this text is most compatible with the approach to the law of evidence taken in Gans and Palmer (2014). Advocacy texts also often detail the facts that must be established before a particular kind of evidence can be adduced or tendered: Mauet and McCrimmon (2011) is particularly helpful in this regard.

Sometimes there may be a degree of uncertainty about what the facts are; again, just as part of our preparation for trial may be the preparation of arguments about the content of the substantive law, part of our preparation for arguments about the admissibility of evidence may be the preparation of arguments about the content or scope of the rules of evidence. Just as we will need to come to court armed with the authorities that support our arguments about the legal case, so we will need to come to court armed with the authorities that support our arguments about the rules of evidence.

Identify the means of proving foundational facts

[8.60] Once we have identified the foundational facts we will have to establish in order to have an item of evidence admitted into evidence, our next focus is on the question of how we will go about proving those foundational facts. In the case of a document or item of real evidence, for example, we must identify the witness through whom we will seek to tender the item of evidence. Will this one witness be able to establish all of the foundational facts, or is more than one witness required? Will we in fact have to call a witness from our opponent's camp in order to establish the foundational facts? What questions must we ask in order to establish the facts? In what order should those questions be asked? Should we apply to the court for a voir dire in order to determine the admissibility of an item or body of evidence? The approach is essentially the same whether we are proving the foundational facts through the examination-in-chief of our own witnesses, or the cross-examination of our opponent's witnesses (as, for example, when we wish to have a prior inconsistent statement of a witness admitted into evidence). Again, Mauet and McCrimmon (2011) is particularly helpful in terms of identifying the precise questions we must ask in order to prove the foundational facts.

At trial: lay the foundation and then adduce the evidence

[8.70] If a voir dire is being held into the admissibility of the evidence, then the evidence can not be adduced until the court's ruling on admissibility has been made. If no voir dire is to be held, however, then the foundation is laid during the ordinary course of the witnesses giving evidence. This is done by asking the witness or witnesses the questions we have identified as being sufficient to lay the foundation for the admission of the item of evidence in question. Once we are satisfied that all the foundational facts have been established, we then go straight on to adduce the evidence. This might involve tendering a document or item of real evidence; or it might, for example, involve asking the witness about the content of a conversation. We do not, however, need to stop and seek the court's or our opponent's permission to adduce the evidence. The onus is on our opponent to object; and, if we have indeed established all the foundational facts, we should have no difficulty in explaining why any such objection ought to be overruled.

The approach above can be taken when the foundational facts alone determine whether or not an item of evidence is admissible. With hearsay, for example, once the elements of an exception are established, the evidence is admissible. The approach above can not be taken, however, when proof of the foundational facts is only a condition precedent to the operation of a judicial discretion, such as the public policy discretion, the fairness discretion, or the discretion to exclude evidence on the grounds that it is more prejudicial than probative (in the uniform evidence legislation, these discretions are to be found in, respectively, ss 138, 90, and 135 and 137). Discretions such as these ultimately require the trial judge to make a value judgment. Proof of the foundational facts – such as illegality in the obtaining of evidence – does not lead to automatic exclusion. In such situations we may have to give greater thought to the way in which we go about establishing the foundational facts so as to give them a "colour" that will influence the trial judge to form the value judgment that favours our case. We will also have to prepare submissions that persuade the trial judge to exercise his or her discretion in our favour.

Objecting

[8.80] If, on the other hand, we are the party who is seeking to have an item of evidence excluded, then our approach is necessarily different. Presumably we will have been paying close attention as our opponent attempted to lay the foundation. We will have made an assessment as to whether that foundation has been laid. If a proper foundation has been laid, then an objection is pointless. If a proper foundation has not been laid, we should ask ourselves whether this was simply an oversight on the part of our opponent, which he or she could probably rectify if asked to do so. If so, then there is little to be gained from making an objection. But if we believe that our opponent is unlikely to be able to prove the foundational facts, or if we suspect that our opponent has failed to carry out a proper admissibility analysis and may not know what the foundational facts are, then it may be worth making an objection.

Corroboration and judicial warnings

[8.90] If we are unable to have an item of evidence excluded, we may be able to persuade the judge to give some sort of warning in relation to it. There are several categories of evidence in which the court is required to give a warning, but usually, before such a warning will be given, certain foundational facts will have to be established. These may be as obvious to the court as the fact that the witness has given identification evidence (although even this is not always straightforward: see, for example, *R v Benz* (1989) 168 CLR 110). Alternatively, the foundational facts may have to be established through the cross-examination of an opponent's witness as, for example, where we, when acting for the defence in a criminal trial, wish to have one of the prosecution's witnesses treated as an accomplice.

In Australia, and in particular under s 165 of the uniform evidence legislation, the most common kind of warning that the judge is required to give is in respect of the unreliability of a particular type, or source, of evidence. Such warnings are intended to be taken into account by the tribunal of fact in the credibility stage of reasoning, rather than in the relevance stage – that is, in the stage where the tribunal decides whether or not to accept the testimony of a witness, rather than in the stage where the tribunal decides what inferences to draw from the facts established by the witness's testimony. At common law, a court may be required to give a "corroboration" warning – that is, a warning that it may be unsafe to act on a particular type of testimony if that testimony is not corroborated; and very occasionally, the tribunal of fact is not permitted to act on a particular type of testimony unless it is corroborated. Under the uniform evidence legislation, by contrast, s 164 abolishes all corroboration requirements apart from those that apply in prosecutions for perjury. Whenever corroboration, or a corroboration warning, is required, the court will have to identify all the evidence that is capable of providing corroboration.

In Chapter 6, evidence was said to be corroborative when two or more sources report the same event or item of evidence. In the law of evidence, "corroboration" has a broader meaning, and includes both true corroboration, as defined in Chapter 6, and convergent evidence. The key requirements are that the "corroborating" evidence must be independent of the testimony of the witness whose evidence requires corroboration, it must be consistent with that testimony and it must implicate the accused in the commission of the crime. Thus, corroboration can be provided by a witness testifying to the same effect as the witness whose testimony requires corroboration; or it can be provided by a body of circumstantial evidence that points to the same conclusion.

RULES THAT PROHIBIT PARTICULAR USES OF EVIDENCE

[8.100] The approach described above can not be applied to every issue that arises in the determination of admissibility. In particular, it is of little assistance when the operation of a rule of evidence turns on the manner in which an item of evidence is being used. This is because the use to which an item of evidence is being put is not a "fact" that can be established by the evidence of a witness. Rather, it is a question that turns on the way in which the item of evidence can be connected to the facts in issue. This is only partly determined by what the party attempting to adduce the evidence says it is using the evidence for. As Gleeson CJ observed during the course of argument in *Bull v The Queen* [1999] HCATrans 432:

> The way you test the purpose of evidence is not by psychoanalysing the Crown Prosecutor, it is by asking what instructions the jury will be given at the end of the evidence as to the use they may make of it. That is the meaning of the expression "the purpose of evidence". The test that seems to have been agreed upon by everybody in this case, although they applied it in a different way, is if this evidence is admitted,

what is the use that will be made of it, that is to say, what will a jury be told as to how they may reason concerning this evidence.

General approach

[8.110] If we are seeking to have admitted into evidence an item that appears to be subject to a use-based exclusionary rule, we have two main options:

1. concede that the use to which we are putting the evidence does fall within the scope of the exclusionary rule, but show that it also falls within the scope of an inclusionary exception to the rule; or
2. explain how the evidence is actually being used for some other purpose that takes it outside the scope of the exclusionary rule.

In general, it is no answer to the second option that the evidence might also be relevant for a purpose that does fall within the scope of the exclusionary rule – that is, for a prohibited use. Evidence is often relevant for more than one purpose. If an item of evidence is relevant for a "permitted" purpose, it is generally admissible for that purpose, notwithstanding that it may also be relevant for a prohibited purpose. The court will simply direct the jury (or itself) that the evidence is only to be used for the permitted purpose – this is called a "limited-use instruction". With some of the exclusionary rules under the uniform evidence legislation, by contrast, the fact that the evidence is relevant for a permitted purpose may then make it admissible for the prohibited purpose: see ss 60, 77 and 101A which apply, respectively, to hearsay, opinion and credibility evidence.

If, on the other hand, we are seeking to have such an item of evidence excluded, then it may be necessary to:

- demonstrate that the evidence is "really" being used for a prohibited purpose, and any permitted purpose is just a "smokescreen" for that use (in making such an argument it is worth recalling the observations of Gleeson CJ above about the "purpose" of evidence); and
- show that the evidence is not admissible under any exception to the exclusionary rule; or
- concede that the evidence is relevant for both permitted and prohibited purposes, but argue that a limited-use instruction is likely to be ineffective because the prohibited use is so prejudicial or compelling that the tribunal of fact is unlikely to be able to disregard it.

In order to make any of these arguments, we need to be able to make two kinds of arguments:

1. arguments about what uses are permitted and what uses are prohibited by the various exclusionary rules; and

2. arguments about the way in which evidence is being used which show that it falls either inside or outside the scope of those rules.

The second kind of argument – arguments about the way in which evidence is being used – are merely specific examples of arguments about relevance that were extensively discussed in the previous chapter. The main focus of this chapter, then, is on the first of these kinds of arguments. The particular aim of the chapter is to describe the structure of the inferences that are prohibited by the rules discussed – namely the hearsay rule, the rule against opinion evidence, and the tendency and coincidence rules.

The hearsay rule

[8.120] The essence of the hearsay rule is to prohibit the court from using statements made other than in the course of the proceedings to prove the truth of their contents. A classic definition was provided by the Privy Council in *Subramanian v Public Prosecutor* [1956] 1 WLR 965 at 970:

> Evidence of a statement made to a witness by a person who is not himself called as a witness may or may not be hearsay. It is hearsay and inadmissible when the object of the evidence is to establish the truth of what is contained in the statement. It is not hearsay and is admissible when it is proposed to establish by the evidence, not the truth of the statement, but the fact that it was made.

Section 59(1) of the uniform evidence legislation contains a slightly modified version of the common law rule, providing that:

> Evidence of a previous representation made by a person is not admissible to prove the existence of a fact that it can reasonably be supposed that the person intended to assert by the representation.

The rationale for the rule can be easily understood if we represent in chart form the reasoning involved in the use of hearsay. Figure 8.1 is based on an example in the explanatory notes to the uniform evidence legislation. Assume a sexual assault case where the complainant testifies that she was assaulted by a man with whom she left a nightclub. The only issue is one of identity – that is, the accused does not deny that the complainant was assaulted, or that the perpetrator was a man with whom she left a night club; he just denies that he was that man. Let us start with evidence that is not hearsay. A witness testifies that she saw the accused leaving the nightclub with the complainant. The charting of this evidence is shown in Figure 8.1.

In the example shown in Figure 8.1, the witness claims to have actually perceived the accused with her own senses; the court's decision about whether or not to accept that it was the accused will depend on its assessment of the witness's

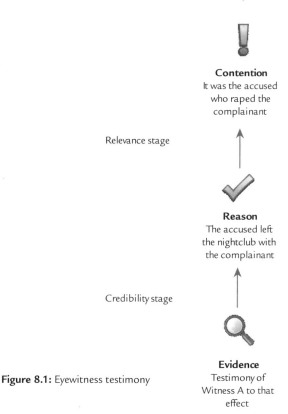

Contention
It was the accused
who raped the
complainant

Relevance stage

Reason
The accused left
the nightclub with
the complainant

Credibility stage

Evidence
Testimony of
Witness A to that
effect

Figure 8.1: Eyewitness testimony

credibility. The defence has a full opportunity to test the witness's credibility and to probe the witness's testimony for the possibility that she is mistaken or lying. Imagine instead, however, that the witness does not claim to have perceived the accused herself, and can only report to the court the fact that her friend told her that the friend saw the accused leaving the nightclub with the complainant. Now an additional step is required and this is shown in Figure 8.2.

This extra step concerns the credibility of the friend. The fact that the witness in court is reporting speech, rather than what she saw, presents no real difficulties for the assessment of the witness's credibility. But at the end of that assessment, the most the court can be satisfied of is that the witness is credible, and that the friend really did speak those words. Whether or not the friend's words are true, however, depends not on the credibility of the witness, but on the credibility of the friend. But in contrast to the witness, the credibility of the friend can not be tested in court, and it is therefore very difficult for the court to determine whether or not to accept that the friend really did perceive the accused leaving the nightclub with the complainant.

This is the reason for the hearsay rule. The probative value of out-of-court representations, such as that in the example above, depends on something that it is very difficult for the court to assess: the credibility of a human source who is not testifying in court, and who can not therefore be subjected to cross-examination. This means that the only possible "warrants" or "justifications" (in the sense that those terms were used in Chapter 7) for the court to take the extra step are for the court to *assume* that the friend is credible. Alternatively, the court will have to rely on some generalisation about the reliability of the class of representations to which the particular representation belongs (in fact, generalisations about the reliability of certain classes of representations do provide the rationale for most of the exceptions to the hearsay rule; but the fact that a representation might belong to a reliable class of representations does not alter its status as hearsay).

In hearsay analysis, the person who made the out-of-court statement is often referred to as the declarant; the uniform evidence legislation, on the other hand, refers to the "maker" of a "previous representation". Whatever language is used, hearsay typically has the structure that is shown in Figure 8.3.

This is an example of "first-hand" hearsay, where the maker of the previous representation has personal knowledge of the events he or she is describing. If, on the other hand, the maker of the previous representation was merely reporting what a third person had told them, then there would be a third credibility stage, relating to

Figure 8.2: A simple example of hearsay

the credibility of that third person. For each additional person between the witness in court and the person who actually perceived the events in question, an extra credibility stage is required. The more such stages there are, then obviously the less safe it is to rely on the evidence.

Of course, the hearsay rule is not limited to speech: it also includes written statements, business records, and assertive conduct (such as pointing). Not all testimony about out-of-court representations is hearsay, however. If the fact that the words were spoken provides the basis for an inference other than that the representation is true (or, to use the language of the uniform evidence legislation, if the representation is relevant and is being used to prove something other than the existence of a fact that it can reasonably be supposed the maker of the representation intended to assert by it), then there is no infringement of the hearsay rule in using the representation for that purpose. Evidence that is relevant for some other reason than to prove the truth of the representation is said to be "original" evidence. Structurally, original evidence is indistinguishable from any other type of evidence, as is shown in Figure 8.4.

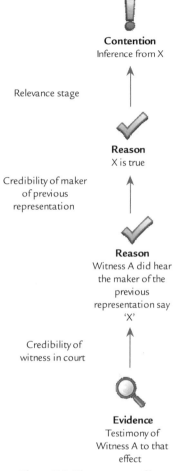

Contention
Inference from X

Relevance stage

Reason
X is true

Credibility of maker of previous representation

Reason
Witness A did hear the maker of the previous representation say 'X'

Credibility of witness in court

Evidence
Testimony of Witness A to that effect

Figure 8.3: The structure of hearsay

[8.130] Sometimes the speaking of "X" is itself a material fact, in which case the evidence is direct and there is no relevance stage. This is the case where the words are "performative" – that is, the speaking of the words has legal consequences. For example, the fact that a person said "I do" at the appropriate point in a marriage ceremony is part of the act of marriage; the same is true of words of gift, the words of offer and acceptance that form a contract, and defamatory words. In all these cases, the speaking of the words is a material fact and no hearsay issues arise.

At other times, an inference can be drawn from the fact that "X" was said, in which case the evidence is circumstantial and there are both credibility and relevance stages. Because it is the fact that "X" was said, rather than "X" itself, which provides the foundation for the inference; however, there is only a single credibility stage as there is no need for the court to consider the credibility of the declarant. We do not need to inquire into whether the speaker might have been mistaken or lying. The only person whose credibility is in issue is the witness in court, the same as for any other testimony. In *Subramaniam*, for example, the accused was charged with being in possession of ammunition during the Malayan Emergency. His defence was one of duress. He wanted to give evidence of what the insurgents had said to him; in particular, he wanted to describe the threats he said they had made to him. If he was found to be a credible witness, then this evidence provided a foundation for an inference about his state of mind, regardless of whether or not the insurgents had "meant" it.

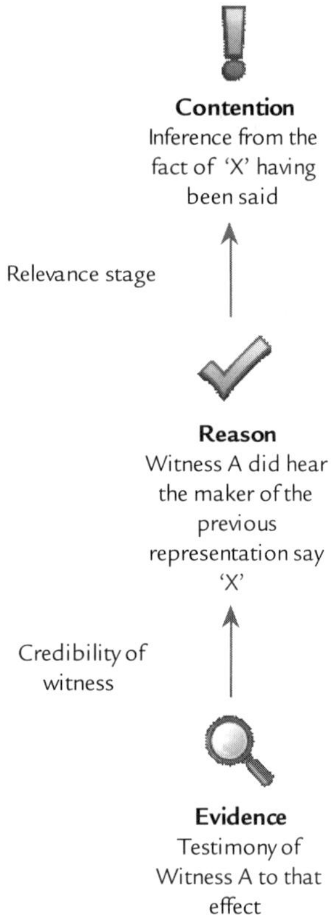

In some jurisdictions – in Australia it is those in which the uniform evidence

Contention
Inference from the fact of 'X' having been said

Relevance stage

Reason
Witness A did hear the maker of the previous representation say 'X'

Credibility of witness

Evidence
Testimony of Witness A to that effect

Figure 8.4: Original evidence

legislation applies – it is only hearsay to use a previous representation to prove the existence of a fact that it can reasonably be supposed the person intended to assert by the representation. In others – in Australia it is those in which the common law still applies – the hearsay rule also extends to "implied assertions". An out-of-court representation is being used as an implied assertion when it is used to prove the truth of a belief that can be inferred from the declarant's statement or conduct. Figure 8.5 illustrates the structure of an implied assertion.

The inference that the declarant held a particular belief is no doubt based on a generalisation to the effect that a person who says or does "Y" ordinarily (usually, often etc) believes "X". In Baron Parke's famous example of the sea captain in *Wright*

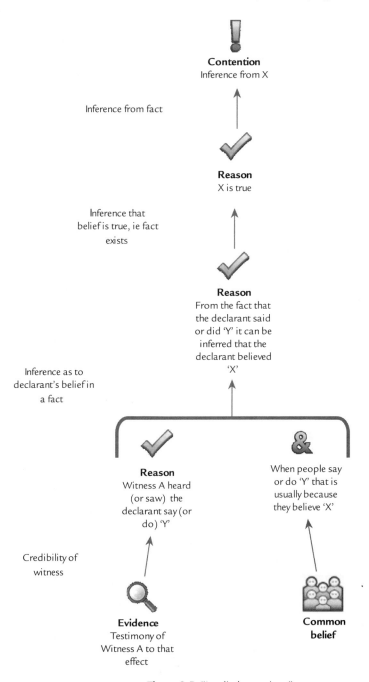

Inference from fact

Contention
Inference from X

Reason
X is true

Inference that
belief is true, ie fact
exists

Reason
From the fact that
the declarant said
or did 'Y' it can be
inferred that the
declarant believed
'X'

Inference as to
declarant's belief in
a fact

Reason
Witness A heard
(or saw) the
declarant say (or
do) 'Y'

When people say
or do 'Y' that is
usually because
they believe 'X'

Credibility of
witness

Evidence
Testimony of
Witness A to that
effect

**Common
belief**

Figure 8.5: "Implied assertions"

v Tatham (1837) 7 Ad & El 313; 112 ER 488, for instance, the captain of a ship that sank at sea has been seen by a witness to carefully inspect the ship before embarking on it with his entire family. From his conduct we might infer that he believed the ship to be seaworthy. Baron Parke said that it would be hearsay, however, to use that belief to prove that the ship was seaworthy, just as it would have been hearsay if the captain had expressly asserted that the ship was seaworthy.

[8.140] In Australia at least, it is always permissible to draw an inference about a person's state of mind from his or her statements or conduct. Sometimes this is justified on the basis that there is a special exception to the hearsay rule for statements about a person's contemporaneous state of mind (as in s 66A of the uniform evidence legislation); but it has also been justified on the basis that a person's statements and conduct are merely circumstantial evidence of their state of mind. No matter, inferences as to state of mind are permitted. Because of this, it is not hearsay, either at common law, or under the uniform evidence legislation:

- to draw an inference about a person's action from their intentions – that is, the fact that a person intended to do an act is a circumstance from which it can be inferred that they did do the act: see, for example, *Walton v The Queen* (1989) 166 CLR 283;
- to draw an inference about the state of a person's knowledge from their statements and conducts when their knowledge is either a fact in issue or a fact from which a relevant inference can be drawn. An example of the former is provided by evidence showing that a person knew they were insolvent. An example of the latter is provided by "esoteric" knowledge, such as knowledge that only the perpetrator of a crime could have: see, for example, *R v Matthews* (1990) 58 SASR 19. In both these situations, the objective state of facts is proved by other means;
- to draw an inference about how one person is likely to have behaved towards another on the basis of their beliefs about, or fear of, that person. For example, a woman who was afraid of her ex-husband is unlikely to have invited him around to shoot stray cats, regardless of whether or not her fear of him was well-founded: see *R v Baker* [1989] 1 NZLR 738; and
- to draw an inference that a particular type of business is being conducted from the making of the kinds of inquiries one would expect such a business to generate: see, for example, *McGregor v Stokes* [1952] VLR 347 (illegal betting); and *R v Firman* (1989) 52 SASR 391 (drug dealing) but compare *R v Kearley* [1992] 2 AC 228.

Most of the above are examples of circumstantial reasoning where one factual proposition is inferred from another on the basis of a generalisation that connects the two factual propositions. Hearsay, on the other hand, involves treating an out-of-court representation as equivalent to testimony, which means relying on it for its truth. The only way in which we can justify relying on the truth of an out-of-court statement is to assume the credibility of the person making the statement, or to rely on a generalisation to the effect that statements of the class to which the statement in question belongs are usually reliable. As has already been noted, generalisations of this kind may have led to the recognition of an exception to the hearsay rule, but they do not alter the status of the statement as hearsay.

The examples above also highlight an important feature of "hearsay" evidence: it is often relevant for more than one purpose. Provided that we can identify a chain of reasoning that connects the evidence to the facts in issue and does not involve a second credibility stage, then the evidence should be admissible for that purpose. This will be the case when the speaking of the words is either a material fact or fact in issue, or where a relevant inference can be drawn from the fact that the words were spoken.

Opinion evidence

[8.150] Opinion evidence is essentially evidence to the effect that a witness has inferred or would infer the existence of one fact from another, and that the court should do the same. Evidence of an opinion that a person holds is generally not admissible for the purpose of proving "the existence of a fact about the existence of which the opinion was expressed" (to use the language of s 76 of the uniform evidence legislation). If the opinion is relevant for some other purpose, however, then it can be used for that purpose (assuming that it does not fall foul of any other exclusionary rule). The fact that a person holds particular opinions might, for example, be relevant to his or her credibility as a witness.

The first barrier to the admissibility of opinion evidence, however, is that which applies to all evidence: the opinion must be relevant. A person's opinion that a fact exists will only be relevant if the fact that the person holds that opinion is capable of rationally affecting the tribunal of fact's assessment of the probability of that fact's existence: see *Smith v The Queen* (2001) 206 CLR 650; [2001] HCA 50. In general, this will only be the case if the witness has special expertise or knowledge about the drawing of such inferences, and if the tribunal of fact is likely to benefit from the assistance of the expert in deciding whether or not to draw the inference in question. Structurally, however, opinion evidence is fairly simple. As Walton (1997, p 210) points out, while arguments based on expert opinion can take many forms, the most basic is the following:

> *E* is an expert in domain *D*.
> *E* asserts that *A* is known to be true.
> *A* is within *D*.
> Therefore *A* may plausibly be taken to be true.

Figure 8.6 shows how we might represent this kind of argument in chart form.

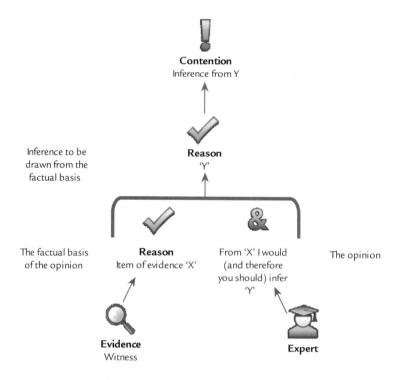

Figure 8.6: The structure of opinion evidence

Figure 8.6 is intended to highlight some additional aspects of opinion evidence that are not brought out by Walton's argument scheme:

1. There is a difference between the facts that form the basis of the opinion, and the opinion. All opinions must be based on facts. Those facts might be the results of a test carried out by the expert, whose opinion we are considering, or by another expert. They might be facts observed by the expert, or by another expert. Or they might be facts observed by a non-expert witness. The rules of evidence that regulate the admission of expert opinion evidence do not apply to the facts on which those opinions are based (although other rules of evidence may).

2. If the facts that form the basis of an opinion are not proved, then the opinion is essentially worthless. Imagine Figure 8.6, for example, with the factual basis of the opinion removed. No court could be persuaded to find "Y" on the basis of "X" if "X" is never satisfactorily proved.

3. The expert's opinion is not only based on the facts specific to the case; it must also be based on facts of general application that form part of the expert's

specialised expertise or knowledge. In the previous chapter, Figure 7.6 included an example of such general facts in the form of a generalisation justifying the drawing of an inference.

In general, if wishing to contest the opinion of an expert being called by our opponent, we can either contest the factual basis of the opinion, or we can contest the opinion itself. If the factual basis of the opinion is disputed, then we should be able to get the witness to agree in cross-examination that if the facts were as we contend, then his or her opinion would be different. If it is the opinion that we are contesting, on the other hand, then we will probably need to call our own expert witness. Walton (1997, p 223) suggests that there are six critical questions we can ask about experts:

1.   *Expertise* question: How credible is *E* as an expert source?
2.   *Field* question: Is *E* an expert in the field that *A* is in?
3.   *Opinion* question: What did *E* assert that implies *A*?
4.   *Trustworthiness* question: Is *E* personally reliable as a source?
5.   *Consistency* question: Is *A* consistent with what other experts assert?
6.   *Backup evidence* question: Is *E*'s assertion based on evidence?

These are not only useful questions to consider in preparing our examination and cross-examination of expert witnesses they also have a degree of correspondence with the rules of evidence that regulate the admission of expert evidence. The expert's possession of special expertise or knowledge is obviously the main foundational fact for expert opinion evidence; but it is not sufficient to prove some expertise at large. The expert witness must also be shown to be an expert in the field to which the issue about which they have been called to give evidence belongs. This is an example of questions of source credibility being used to determine admissibility and is thus an exception to the general rule – referred to in the previous chapter – that in a common law trial questions of source credibility are generally only matters of weight for the tribunal of fact to assess.

Tendency and coincidence evidence

[8.160] Like the hearsay and opinion rules, the uniform evidence legislation rules applying to tendency and coincidence evidence only prohibit particular uses of evidence: see ss 97, 98 and 101. Although the precise scope of the common law rules applying to propensity and similar fact evidence, which those rules replace, is arguably less clear, the discussion in this text will proceed on the basis that the common law rules also only apply when evidence is being used in a particular way. Two uses in particular are prohibited by the rules: the tendency or propensity use, and the coincidence or similar fact use.

The essence of the tendency or propensity use is to use the fact that a person has acted in a particular way on certain occasions as the basis for an inference that he or she acted in the same or in a similar way on the occasion that is the subject of the proceedings. Broken down into its constituent steps, a tendency chain of reasoning generally has the basic structure that is shown in Figure 8.7, in which the tendency is that of an accused person in criminal proceedings. Where the defence is one of identity, a court will sometimes allow evidence to be adduced about the relative unusualness of the particular tendency in order to strengthen the inference that it was the accused, rather than someone else, who acted in the particular way on the occasion that was the subject of the charge: see, for example, *R v Ellis* (2003) 58 NSWLR 700; [2003] NSWCCA 319.

Evidence with the structure charted in Figure 8.7 undoubtedly falls within the scope of the exclusionary rule in s 97, and is inadmissible unless it is of such high probative value that it can satisfy the tests in ss 97(1)(b) and 101(2). The probative value of a chain of inferences like that in Figure 8.7 depends on the persuasiveness of each of the three steps involved:

1. The credibility of the evidence of the other conduct – is it admitted by the accused? Was the accused convicted in relation to that conduct? Or is it merely a set of unproved allegations? Is there a possibility that the witnesses might have colluded in concocting the evidence?

2. The persuasiveness of the inference from the other conduct to the conclusion that the accused has a tendency to act in that way – this will depend on matters such as the number of other occasions in which the accused engaged in the conduct, the unusualness of the conduct, and so on. If there is a substantial break in time between the other conduct and the occasion that is the subject of the charge, an additional step will be required – that is, an inference of continuity. An inference of continuity is an inference from the fact that the accused had the particular tendency at the time of the other conduct, to the conclusion that the accused still (or already: see *Pfennig v The Queen* (1995) 182 CLR 461) had the tendency at the time of the occasion that is the subject of the charge.

3. The persuasiveness of the inference from the tendency to the conclusion that the accused acted in accordance with that tendency on the occasion that is the subject of the charge. The persuasiveness of this inference will also depend on a number of factors, including the distinctiveness of the tendency and the degree to which the occasion the subject of the charge conforms to that tendency. The strength of this final step will also depend on the existence and persuasiveness of any other evidence suggesting that the accused committed the crime in question.

[8.170] **Coincidence** reasoning has a different structure. We can distinguish between two common types of coincidence reasoning. The first is where the evidence is used to prove that a series of events that could be accidents or chance

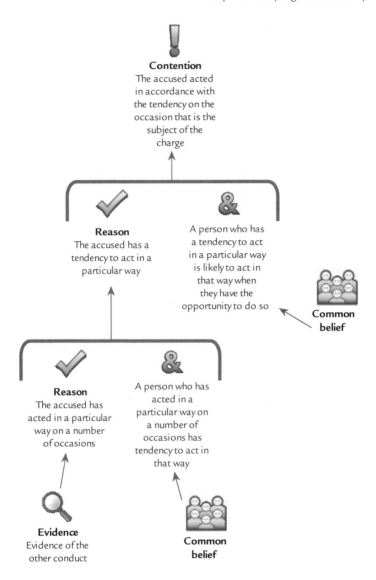

Figure 8.7: The structure of tendency evidence

occurrences, or that could be crimes, are in fact crimes. Examples of this type of coincidence reasoning are provided by *Makin v Attorney-General (NSW)* [1894] AC 57 (the "babies in the backyard" case); *R v Smith* (1915) 11 Cr App R 229 (the "brides in the bath" case); and *Perry v The Queen* (1982) 150 CLR 580. This type of coincidence reasoning generally has the structure that is shown in Figure 8.8

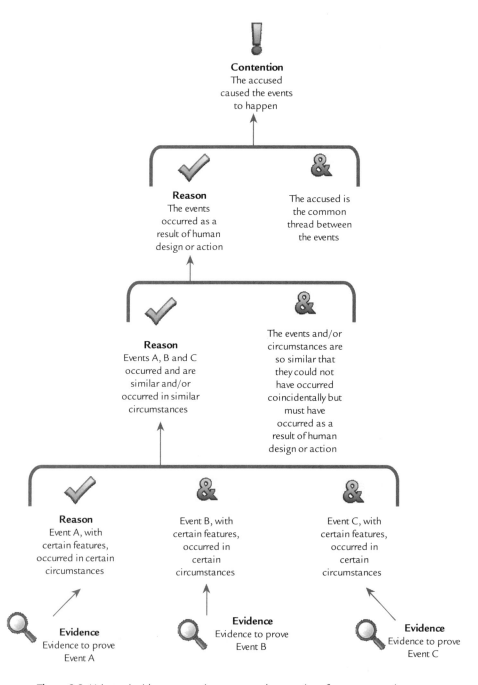

Figure 8.8: Using coincidence reasoning to prove that a series of events were crimes

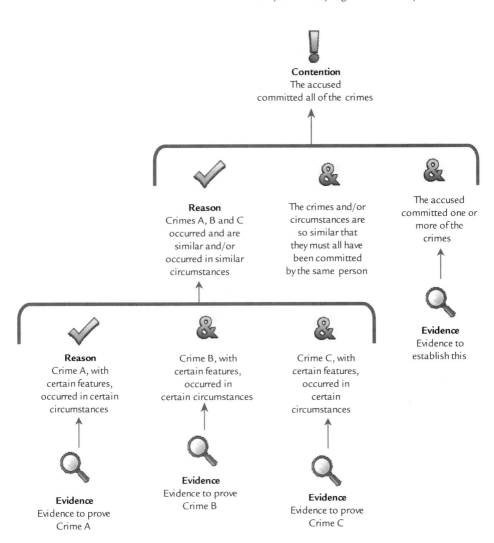

Figure 8.9: Using coincidence reasoning to prove that a series of crimes was committed by the accused

(we can assume that if the accused did cause the events to happen they would be crimes).

The second common type of coincidence reasoning is used to prove that a series of events – that were undoubtedly crimes – were committed by the same person, namely the accused. This is useful when there is evidence to identify the accused as the perpetrator of one or more of the crimes, but a paucity of evidence to identify the accused as the perpetrator of the other crimes. Figure 8.9 is an example of this type of reasoning as provided by *Sutton v The Queen* (1984) 152 CLR 528.

The probative value of both these types of coincidence reasoning ultimately rests on the persuasiveness of the generalisation that is used as the basis for eliminating (in the first type of reasoning) the possibility of chance occurrence and (in the second) the possibility of there being more than one criminal. The persuasiveness of those generalisations depends, in turn, on the degree to which the events possess such singular, similar, or unifying features that the alternative possibility strikes the tribunal of fact as being "too much of a coincidence": see Hamer (2003). In some cases, as backing evidence for the generalisations relied on, the court will permit the adducing of evidence on such matters as the degree of unusualness of a particular modus operandi: again, see *R v Ellis* (2003) 58 NSWLR 700; [2003] NSWCCA 319.

Summary

[8.180] The general approach to admissibility described in the first part of this chapter involves the following steps:

- identify the evidence in relation to which questions of admissibility may arise;
- identify the purpose for which the evidence is being led;
- identify the foundational facts that will be used to determine the admissibility of the evidence; and
- identify the means of proving those foundational facts.

Then at trial:

- prove the foundational facts; and
- adduce the evidence.

This approach can not be applied to rules that instead, or in addition, turn on the issue of how an item of evidence is being used. The second part of the chapter therefore attempts to identify the structure of the inferences prohibited by:

- the hearsay rule;
- the rule against opinion evidence; and
- the tendency and coincidence rules.

Pulling it all together for trial

9

Introduction

[9.10] This chapter is about pulling all the threads of our previous analysis together into a form that we can use to run the trial. This form is the **Trial Book**, and the compilation of the Trial Book is the culmination of all of the analysis we have done. Before we can compile the Trial Book, however, there are a number of final steps we need to take in order to complete our analysis. These include:

- selecting and ordering witnesses;
- selecting themes and labels;
- drafting our opening address;
- planning the examination of our own witnesses;
- planning the cross-examination of our opponent's witnesses; and
- drafting our closing address.

Each of these steps is discussed in detail at [9.30]–[9.80]. Before turning to these steps, however, it is worth reiterating a point made at the end of Chapter 2. The focus of this text is on identifying our aims for the trial: the arguments we want to be able to make in our closing address, the evidence we need to adduce in order to be able to make those arguments, and so on. This text does not, however, purport to deal with the actual trial techniques that we need to apply in order to achieve these aims: how to examine and cross-examine witnesses, how to structure our opening and closing addresses in order to maximise their impact, and so on. Trial techniques are already well covered in existing advocacy texts, a number of which are referred to in the Notes for this chapter. This text is not intended to replace such texts, but to complement them by covering in depth something that is absolutely crucial to the effective application of trial techniques but which tends to be dealt with fairly briefly by advocacy texts – that is, methods for analysing evidence in order to prepare a matter for trial.

It is this chapter, however, that effectively represents the point of transition or overlap between the subject matter of this book and the subject matter of advocacy texts. From the point of view of analysing the evidence in order to prepare for trial – the subject matter of this book – this chapter contains the final steps needed to "complete" the analysis. From the point of view of trial presentation, however, the subject matter of this chapter is really just the beginning. The aim of this chapter, then, is to act as a "bridge" between trial preparation and trial presentation, between the subject matter of this book and the subject matter of advocacy texts. This chapter does not, however, aim to deal with this overlapping subject matter in the same detail with which it is dealt in advocacy texts: there is no point in "reinventing the wheel" and redoing that which advocacy texts already do well. For that reason, this chapter is written in a more concise, point-form style than the previous chapters.

Summary of the method

[9.20] As was stated above, this chapter is about pulling all the "threads" of our analysis together into a form that we can use to run the trial. Those "threads" are the various analytical steps described in the previous chapters. These steps include:

- defining our objectives;
- organising the documents;
- identifying the tasks we need to complete in order to prepare for trial;
- creating an "inventory" of evidence by sorting all the evidence into some logical order or scheme (usually a chronology);
- carrying out any further investigation;
- selecting a theory of the case in both its aspects, namely the legal case and the factual theory;
- completing any necessary research into the legal case;
- identifying the elements of the legal case ("the facts in issue") and the factual theory ("the material facts") that we must prove in order to succeed in the trial;
- identifying the arguments we will use in order to persuade the court to accept our theory of the case;

- identifying the evidence we will need to adduce in order to be able to make those arguments; and
- carrying out any admissibility analysis.

Selecting and ordering witnesses

[9.30] When we started our analysis we probably had a bundle of witness statements and a pile of documents. Through the methods set out in Chapters 3 and 4 we will have extracted all the information available to us and placed it in chronological (or some other meaningful) order. In Part B we organised the evidence according to the objects of proof – that is, the facts in issue and the material facts. Through this process we should have moulded all the disparate pieces of evidence into one coherent narrative. This narrative or factual theory provides the basis for our opening and closing addresses; but our factual theory should also guide our presentation of the evidence.

Of course, evidence must be adduced witness by witness, document by document, exhibit by exhibit. We can not chop and change between witnesses in order to present all the evidence in absolute chronological order; nor can we order all the evidence according to the issues to which it relates. Nevertheless, in ordering our witnesses, and in planning our witness examinations, we need to bear in mind the fact that we are attempting to present a coherent narrative. Therefore, we should choose the order of evidence that will best enable the tribunal of fact to understand the evidence as it unfolds and assist the tribunal of fact to grasp the theory we are presenting. To the extent that we can lead the evidence in chronological order, we should do so. For example, in a personal injury case it generally makes more sense to call the witnesses to the accident that caused the injury before calling the witnesses who will testify about the effects of the injury.

Before we can decide on the final order of our witnesses, however, we need to decide which witnesses we will call. If a potential witness is the only person capable of giving evidence that is necessary to establish a material fact, then obviously we will have no choice but to call them. However, usually we do have some choices. Our analysis may have revealed that there are a number of witnesses capable of proving the same fact. Of course, if the fact is hotly disputed by our opponent, we may want to call all these witnesses; but usually there is a point at which corroboration becomes repetitive and even counter-productive. So a choice may have to be made, and in making that choice we have to recognise the reality that some people do make better witnesses than others. If we have met all the potential witnesses – and we should have – then we should be in a position to identify those who are most likely to best advance our case.

Selecting themes and labels

[9.40] The theme is concerned with courtroom presentation of our factual theory. According to Anderson and Twining (1991, p 167), the theme "is a feature of the story that is selected for emphasis on the basis of the persuasive effect that the advocate wishes to make on the trier of fact". Elsewhere, Twining (1990, p 226) has described the theme as "any element of the theory that is sufficiently important to deserve emphasis by repetition". Bennett (1986), in a passage quoted by Anderson, Schum and Twining (2005, p 168), suggests that the "theory should be that explanation of the facts which shows logic requires your side to win, and the theme should be that explanation of the facts which shows the moral force is on your side". Mauet and McCrimmon (2011, p 11) define a theme as "a memorable word or phrase that summarises your position on a critical issue".

Similarly, Imwinkelried (1986, pp 63ff) defines a theme as "the label for the attorney's strongest argument on the pivotal element of the theory". It might be the best piece of evidence on the key area of dispute – for instance, in a case where the defence is one of identity, a pithy encapsulation of the reason why the eyewitness's testimony should be accepted, or a label for the key piece of forensic evidence. As he notes, a suitably pithy label or expression for the key argument or the key piece of evidence can be repeated and played on throughout the trial. However we define it, it is always important when preparing for trial to try to identify a theme that we can use to encapsulate the essence of our arguments.

Mauet and McCrimmon (2011, p 12) also suggest that we should select "labels" for use in our trial presentation. They define "labels" as "the tags you put on people and events during the trial". For example, one of our aims in using labels is to personalise our client, and to depersonalise the opposing party. To appreciate the importance of choosing the right label in order to affect how people perceive things, we need only remind ourselves of the kind of language and labels used by the belligerents in war. In order to choose the correct labels, we need to ask ourselves, "What emotional or visual effect are we trying to achieve"; and "What word or words will help us to achieve that effect?"

Drafting the opening address

[9.50] The opening address is our opportunity to outline the issues and to provide the tribunal of fact with a framework within which it can structure its own analysis of the evidence. In particular, we can use the opening address as a means of introducing the tribunal of fact to the narrative, the factual theory we are attempting to present, and to our themes. This will help them to understand the significance of the evidence as it is presented, to appreciate where it fits in the overall structure of our factual theory and to see things from our point of view. Thus, the opening address can be likened to a road map: we can use it to tell the tribunal of fact where we are going and how we are going to get there. Excellent and detailed advice about the specific content and structure of an opening address can be found in Mauet and McCrimmon (2011), Chapter 3; Curthoys and Kendall (2006), Chapter 6; Glissan (2011), Chapter 3; and Stuesser (2011), Chapter 6. In particular, we should remember that the opening address is not argumentative; and that we must never promise more than we can actually deliver.

Planning the examination of our witnesses

[9.60] In order to decide what information and documents we have to put into our Trial Book for each of our potential witnesses, we need to ask and answer a number of questions. The answers to most of them should be provided by our previous analysis:

- Do we **need to call** this witness?
- What **factual propositions** are we hoping to establish through the evidence of this witness? What evidence are we hoping the witness will give in order to establish those propositions? How do we propose to elicit that evidence?
- If the witness is being called as an **expert**, how will we establish the foundation for the witness's testimony?
- Is there any way in which we can **enhance the credibility** of our witness and his or her evidence?
- Are there any **negatives** about this witness's evidence or credibility that we should deal with during examination-in-chief rather than leaving for our opponent to raise for the first time in cross-examination?
- Is there any value in putting aspects of our **opponent's theory** or likely theory to the witness for comment?
- Are there any aspects of the witness's evidence in relation to which we anticipate our opponent may make an **objection**? How will we deal with any such objections?
- Are there any items of **documentary or real evidence** that we wish to tender through this witness? What is the **basis** for the admission into evidence of those items of evidence? What **foundational facts** must be established before the evidence can be admitted on that basis? How will we go about establishing those foundational facts?
- In what **sequence** should we try to elicit all this evidence in order to maximise its impact on the court?

Once we have answered these questions, we can prepare a summary or guide to the witness's examination-in-chief. This may involve writing down every single question we think we need to ask the witness. Alternatively, we may just summarise the areas we need to cover, factual propositions we need to establish and documents we need to tender, through the evidence of the witness.

Planning the cross-examination of our opponent's witnesses

[9.70] Our previous analysis should also enable us to answer the following questions in relation to each of our opponent's potential witnesses:

- Is this witness's evidence likely to be **unfavourable to our case**? If not, then depending on the answer to the next two questions, we may not need to cross-examine the witness.
- Is there any evidence **favourable** to our case that we may be able to elicit from this witness?
- Are there any items of **real or documentary evidence** helpful to our case that we could seek to tender through this witness? What is the basis for the admission into evidence of those items of evidence? What foundational facts must be established before the evidence can be admitted on that basis? How will we go about establishing those foundational facts?
- If the witness's evidence is likely to be unfavourable to our case, is there any basis on which we might reasonably **object** to that evidence? (Of course, this question is actually about planning for the witness's examination-in-chief, rather than for our cross-examination of the witness.) If so, what would be the basis of such an objection?
- If the witness's evidence is unfavourable because it **contradicts** or is logically inconsistent with the testimony of one or more of our witnesses, then presumably our theory must be that the witness is either mistaken or lying. What propositions can we put to the witness in order to establish a foundation for this possibility?
- What propositions favouring our case are we likely to be able to **force the witness to agree** with? How can we do this?
- Does the evidence we have led, or will subsequently lead, as part of our own case, contradict or cast doubt on the testimony of the witness? If so, then **the rule in *Browne v Dunn*** (the "puttage" rule) requires us to put those aspects of our case to the witness, and we must consider the best way of doing this.
- If we are **attacking the credibility** of the witness, will we be "bound" by their answers or will we be allowed to lead evidence to prove the truth of an allegation that the witness has denied? (The answer is determined by the "collateral issues" or "finality" rule; the uniform evidence legislation's version of this rule and its exceptions are found in ss 102 and 106 of the uniform evidence legislation.)
- If, on the other hand, our factual theory concedes the truth of certain aspects of the witness's evidence, but seeks to offer an **alternative explanation** for them, then we may not need to cross-examine the witness on those aspects of their evidence.

- Bearing in mind that our cross-examination may lose its impact if we attempt to make too many points, what are the **most important points** to make? Which points might we safely omit? What is the **best order** in which to approach the topics we have selected for cross-examination?

Of course, any cross-examination plan is inevitably more provisional than a plan for the examination-in-chief of a witness. This is because our cross-examination plans may have to be revised in light of the actual evidence given by the witness in his or her examination-in-chief. We need to listen carefully to the examination-in-chief so that we are clear about the evidence the witness has actually given, as opposed to the evidence we anticipated that he or she would give. That said, we should nevertheless prepare a summary or guide to the cross-examination, listing the areas we need to cover, factual propositions to which we need to get the witness's agreement, and so on.

Drafting the closing address

[9.80] In a sense the whole of this book has been leading up to the closing address. In particular, the primary aim of the methods discussed in Part B was to enable us to identify the evidence we would need to lead in order to be able to make the best possible closing address. Of course, we can only finalise our closing address once the evidence is actually in; but through the analysis we have carried out as part of our preparation for trial we should have worked out the broad outline of those arguments. In contrast to the opening address, the closing address is an argument, but it is an argument based on evidence. In the closing address we attempt to explain to the court why the evidence supports our theory of the case rather than that of our opponent.

There is, however, a very important difference between any map we have created of our theory of the case and the closing address: whereas the case map is organised according to the logical structure of our argument, the primary aim of the closing address is to persuade. Of course an illogical closing address is unlikely to be very persuasive, but this does not mean that the most persuasive form the closing address can take will simply be to step through the various arguments according to their logical structure (see, for example, the difference between the case map in the Appendix and the description of the closing address in that case). Excellent advice about the structure and contents of a persuasive closing address can be found in Mauet and McCrimmon (2011), Chapter 7; Curthoys and Kendall (2006), Chapter 10; Hampel, Brimer and Kune (2008), Chapter 7; Glissan (2011), Chapter 8; and Stuesser (2011), Chapter 7. If we have prepared our matter in the manner suggested by this text, then we should have no difficulty in complying with that advice.

Compiling the Trial Book

[9.90] The end result of all our analysis is a "document" that is often called the "Trial Book", although in practice it is more likely to take the form of a ring binder with a series of dividers, than a book. The point of significance, though, is that the Trial Book contains all the information we need to conduct the trial in an easily accessible format. As Stuesser (2011, p 31) suggests, the test of a well-prepared trial book is "whether another counsel, who is unfamiliar with the case, could take the matter to trial using that book alone". Mauet and McCrimmon (2011, pp 3-9), Stuesser (2011), Chapter 4, and Anderson, Schum and Twining (2005, pp 317-324) all contain excellent and detailed discussions about the preparation of a Trial Book. What follows is more abbreviated.

As with all the methods discussed in this book, there is no single, correct way of preparing the Trial Book. That said, if we have done our jobs properly, the Trial Book is likely to contain all the following information and documents:

- The **court documents**, in chronological order. These should be accompanied by an **analysis of the pleadings** indicating the attitude of all the parties to each of the pleadings (this can be done in a table format).
- Any relevant **court orders**. If there is an issue as to compliance with the court orders, we should include all documents relevant to that issue, an outline of our submissions on this point and (ideally) a procedural chronology.
- Any documents containing our **previous analysis** of the case, such as chronologies, factual summaries, evidence charts or outlines, and so on.
- Our **opening** address.
- A section for each of **our witnesses**. This should contain the following information:
  — name, address, employment and contact details;
  — who they are in relation to the proceedings – for example "the injured worker" or "the father of the injured worker";
  — an outline of the key points of evidence to be adduced from the witness (this outline should include space to write down the details of the answers provided by the witness);
  — copies of any subpoenas served on the witness, together with details of service;
  — copies of all previous statements made by the witness, including details of when and to whom those statements were made;
  — details or copies of all other information or documents relevant to the credibility of the witness;
  — copies of, or cross-references to, all items of documentary evidence that the witness will be asked to authenticate;
  — copies of, or cross-references to, all items of real evidence that the witness will be asked to authenticate.

- A section for each of our **opponent's likely witnesses**. This should contain all the same information as that provided for our own witnesses.
- Where the **substantive law** is unclear, an outline of our **submissions** on the points in question, together with copies of all relevant legal **authorities** (usually we need a copy for ourselves, a copy for our opponent and a copy for the court).
- Where there is likely to be a dispute about the **admissibility** of one or more items of evidence, an outline of our **submissions** on the issue, together with copies of all relevant legal **authorities** (again, we will need at least three copies of these).
- A draft of our **closing** address.

Many jurisdictions now require the preparation of a **Court Book** by the parties before the commencement of the trial. This is likely to contain all relevant court documents and orders, together with copies of any documentary evidence likely to be tendered or referred to during the trial. Each of the parties will have a copy of the Court Book, as will the court itself; a copy should also be prepared for the use of witnesses. The Court Book is likely to contain many of the documents referred to above. Instead of reproducing them in the Trial Book, we might simply refer to the document by its Court Book number or page (for example, "Witness A will authenticate the following documents in the Court Book: ...").

We should also ensure that our copy of the Court Book is cross-referenced to our Trial Book: for example, we might add an extra column to our copy of the Court Book index, in which we can put the initials of the witness who will be used to authenticate a particular item of evidence. It is also a good idea to add a column to write in the exhibit number of the document, once it is accepted into evidence.

The end and the beginning

[9.100] With all of our analysis completed, we should now be ready to walk into court and start the trial.

Notes

Note to Evidence teachers

[10.10]   One of the purposes of writing the first edition of this text was to facilitate a shift towards a "proof-oriented" approach to the teaching of the Evidence and Proof courses at Melbourne Law School. The advantages of such an approach are discussed at length in Twining (1984), Palmer (2002 and 2011) and Twining (2007), but can briefly be summarised as follows:

- The proof-oriented approach requires students to develop skills in factual analysis, including reasoning skills: such skills are crucial in legal practice, are transferable and are not usually taught anywhere else in the law school curriculum.
- The development of skills in factual analysis can also sharpen critiques of the common law approach to fact finding and the rules of evidence – for example, the kind of critical approach described by Mack (2000) and taken by Boyle (2007) requires a detailed analysis of evidence along the lines discussed in Chapter 7 of this text. A detailed factual analysis is also essential to the kind of

analysis of judicial reasoning in respect of the application of exclusionary rules engaged in by Redmayne (2007).

- The proof-oriented approach to evidence locates the rules of evidence in the context in which they actually operate – that is, in the context of legal proceedings in which the parties are attempting to prove or disprove a case.
- Because the operation of many of the exclusionary rules turns on the way in which the evidence is being used, the emphasis in the proof-oriented approach on understanding the use that is being made of a particular item of evidence as part of an overall case also makes it easier for students to understand and apply those exclusionary rules.

The teachers of Evidence and Proof at Melbourne Law School (primarily Dr Jeremy Gans and myself) have now been taking a proof-oriented approach to the teaching of evidence for a decade and can concur with Twining (2007, p 79, note 61) in declaring: "It works." For that reason, it is a little dispiriting that in the 30 years since Twining first delivered his paper on "Taking Facts Seriously" in 1980 (reprinted as Twining (1984)), the paper has become "quite well known but has made almost no impact": Twining (2007, p 65; and see also Roberts (2007), p 25). Indeed, even reading the work of an ostensible ally of Twining, such as Roberts (2007), can be a frustrating experience for an advocate of the proof-oriented approach: while I agree with Roberts (2007, p 26) "that one does not have to be a Wigmorean chart methodist to take facts seriously", taking facts seriously, as Twining (2007, pp 77-83) points out, surely does at the very least require one to go beyond teaching students *about* factual analysis and reasoning, and to actually provide them with an opportunity to learn *how* to do it.

It does, nevertheless, seem to me that the counter-view to Roberts – that one *does* have to be a Wigmorean chart methodist to take facts seriously – has unnecessarily hindered the cause of factual analysis, particularly in an age of easy-to-use argument mapping software that has, in my respectful view, rendered Wigmore's actual charting methods redundant. This is because, whether or not Wigmore's charting methods have any pedagogical advantages over the use of argument mapping software (and I personally doubt that they do), arguing the case for factual analysis and visual argument mapping by reference to Wigmore's rather peculiar and antiquated charting methods seems – like arguing for the pleasure and convenience of car travel by offering someone a ride in a Model T Ford – as likely to alienate and alarm potential converts as to attract them. It is partly for this reason that the Appendix to this second edition of *Proof* contains a much more detailed discussion of software-based charting.

[10.20] In terms of course structure and content, for an evidence teacher wishing to adopt a proof-oriented approach, one need not reinvent the wheel as there are already several models on offer. These include descriptions of the Melbourne courses, which can be found in Palmer (2002 and 2011). A major difference between the current versions of the course and the one described in the 2002 article is that at the time of writing that article, a unit on "analysing individual items of evidence" preceded a unit on "organising complex masses of evidence". In the writing of the first edition of this text, however, I came to the view that it is better to teach students macro-analysis (Chapters 5 and 6) before micro-analysis (Chapter 7). In other words, to start with the big picture and then go into the details, if necessary, rather than starting with the details and trying to build up the big picture from those details. A brief description of the Evidence and Proof course that Twining teaches as part of the London LLM course can be found in Twining (2007, pp 81-82, note 65); and Ligertwood (2007, pp 253-259) contains a much more detailed description of the Evidence/Advocacy courses taught at the University of Adelaide.

Any shift towards a proof-oriented approach is also likely to require a shift in the method of assessment away from the traditional three-hour examination focusing on the application of exclusionary rules and policy issues in the law of evidence. The assessment at Melbourne, for example, now takes the form of a three- or four-day take-home examination in which students are required to prepare an Advice on Evidence based on an actual brief of evidence. The briefs are all criminal prosecutions (because this provides a better basis for the part of the assessment that is concerned with the law of evidence and admissibility) and students are usually asked to adopt the standpoint of the prosecutor. The briefs usually contain a diverse body of evidence, such as witness statements, records of interview, expert reports and telephone records. Students are required to submit an Advice on Evidence that performs the following tasks:

1. Sets out the factual theory upon which they will rely.
2. Identifies the real issues in the case.
3. Explains how they will go about proving the factual propositions that are likely to be the subject of genuine dispute in the trial. This is the "case map" and students can express their arguments in the form of prose, charts, outlines or in some combination of these.
4. Analyses the admissibility of any items of evidence in relation to which objection might reasonably be anticipated.
5. Indicates, in light of the above, the likelihood of conviction.

Approximately 50% of the marks for the subject are allocated to the case analysis part of the Advice, with the other 50% being allocated to the admissibility analysis. Similar assessment is set in the LLM subject Proof in Litigation, except that the focus there is exclusively on the case analysis, with no admissibility analysis being required. Several examples of the briefs of evidence used as the basis for assessment in these subjects, together with numerous sample answers, can be accessed by clicking on the "**sample analyses**" link at the following website:

www.evidence.com.au

PART A: FIRST STEPS

Chapter 2: Preliminaries

[10.30] There is very little in the way of critical or analytical literature on the subject material of this chapter: see Morris (1991), however, for a helpful discussion of how to organise material for inclusion in a brief. In terms of electronic document management and discovery, see Mason (2012) and Stanfield (2009).

Chapter 3: Chronologies

[10.40] As with the previous chapter, there is very little in the way of critical literature on the subject of how to prepare chronologies. Tillers and Schum (1991) do include chronologies as one of several possible methods for marshalling evidence during preliminary fact investigation, but do not "privilege" it in the way that I have in this text. Some extremely helpful articles by Krehel on the preparation of chronologies, as well as software specifically designed to assist in the creation of chronologies, can be downloaded from www.casesoft.com. Most advocacy texts, however, pay relatively little attention to the preparation of chronologies. Perhaps it is assumed that all litigators will be aware that preparing a chronology is something that they should do, and that they will know how to go about doing it.

On a more technical note, a chronology is always a work in progress, new information being added as it comes to light. For this reason it is usually wise to create a chronology in electronic form – a table in a word-processed document provides one simple method; alternatively, a spreadsheet could be used. In both cases, separate columns should be allocated for each of the categories of information it is necessary to record. If the chronology is created electronically, additional events can be inserted, and then the chronology can be sorted by date.

Further, it may be necessary to print out different versions of our chronology at different times. For example, a chronology to be handed up to a court must be limited to uncontentious material; but if our own chronology is limited in this way then it will have left out much information of importance. Therefore, a chronology needs to be capable of being edited so that different versions can be produced for different purposes.

Krehel is adamant that there are enormous advantages in using database rather than word-processing software to create a chronology. Microsoft Access, for example, is commonly bundled as part of Microsoft Office although, as Krehel points out, it does have its drawbacks. According to Krehel, the main advantage is that database software allows us to be selective about which parts of the database we print. For example, if we have a field that we use to indicate whether or not a fact is disputed, we can choose to print out only the undisputed facts; or we could print out all of those records for which the source of the fact in question is a particular witness or document.

Chapter 4: Investigation

[10.50] This chapter drew very heavily on an article by Tillers and Schum (1991), entitled "A Theory of Preliminary Fact Investigation". Other helpful discussions of fact investigation and evidence marshalling include Binder and Bergman (1984); Schum and Tillers (1991); Schum (1994), in particular Chapter 9, "Discovery and the Generation of Evidence"; Anderson, Schum and Twining (2005), Chapter 2, "Fact Investigation and the Nature of Evidence"; Abimbola (2002); and, for a very practical, example-driven approach, Vincent (1984). The chapter made the point that investigation is in part about the reading of the "clues" or "signs" that we find in the world. There is a parallel here between law and semiotics, which can be described as the science of the study of signs. The whole topic of investigation is dealt with in a fascinating manner from a semiotics perspective by the various papers collected in Eco and Sebeok (1983).

PART B: THEORY AND PROOF

Chapter 5: Case theory

[10.60] There is a considerable body of literature about case theory, perhaps the bulk of which has been written by advocacy teachers in the United States. Among the best of these are Imwinkelried (1986); Lubet (1990) and (2013); and Ohlbaum (1993). Useful Australian discussions of case theory are contained in Glissan (2011), Chapter 2, "Preparation and Case Analysis" ; and Hampel, Brimer and Kune (2008), Chapter 2, "Preparation and Analysis". Chapter 5 of the present text draws on several of these, as well as the more analytically precise discussion of case theory in Anderson, Schum and Twining (2005), Chapter 4, "Methods of Analysis"; and Berger, Mitchell and Clark (2013), Chapter 2, "Formulating the Case Theory".

The distinctions drawn in the chapter are probably closer to those drawn by Berger, Mitchell and Clark than to those drawn by Anderson, Schum and Twining. Where this text distinguishes between the "(legal) case" and the "(factual) theory", Anderson, Schum and Twining (2005, pp 153-155) talk about the "theory" and the "story", and Berger, Mitchell and Clark (2013), Chapter 2, refer to the "legal theory" and the "factual theory". The splitting in this text of case theory into "case" and "theory" (or "legal case" and "factual theory") is intended to emphasise the fact that, while case and theory are distinct, if intertwined, both are necessary and, together, jointly constitute the case theory. Anderson, Schum and

Twining's use of the term "story", by contrast, seems – at least to this author – to suggest that the story is something distinct and separate from the case theory.

The role that narrative plays in the tribunal of fact's decision-making process has been the subject of study by psychologists, most notably Pennington and Hastie (1991). See also Friedman (1992); Lempert (1991); and Twining (1990), Chapter 7, "Lawyers' Stories". The point of the discussion in the text is really to emphasise what may seem obvious – that the tribunal of fact is more likely to accept a factual theory if it is able to fit it into the structure of a coherent narrative. One of the advocate's main tasks, then, is to select and present evidence in such a way as to maximise the chances of this occurring. This may mean omitting or de-emphasising certain aspects of the evidence, highlighting others, or ordering the evidence in a particular way.

The discussion in the section on objects of proof was inspired by Wigmore (1937), Part II, "Circumstantial Evidence". Wigmore attempted to classify all objects of proof – or, as he called them, "probanda" – into four main types: the doing of a human act; a human trait or condition; an event, condition, cause, or effect of external nature; and identity. He then classified the various types of circumstantial evidence that could be used to prove each of these four classes of probanda, dividing them according to whether they pointed forward in time to the event in question ("prospectant" evidence); pointed back in time to the event in question ("retrospectant"); or accompanied the event in question ("concomitant"). Wigmore's classification of evidence in cases where the probanda is "the doing of a human act" was set out at [4.110], under the heading "Marshalling for 'clues'". It was simply not possible to attempt to emulate Wigmore's classification system in a work of this scope.

Instead, the section discusses, very briefly, some of the issues that arise in relation to causation. More detailed discussions of causation are to be found in Hamer (1999) and Borgelt and Kruse (1997). There is also a burgeoning body of case law about the use of expert evidence to establish causal links – for example, in cases where the precise aetiology of a particular individual's illness may be unknown, but broad epidemiological evidence suggests that the defendant's negligence increased the statistical chances of the plaintiff developing the illness. In Australia, see, for example, *Seltsam Pty Ltd v McGuinness; James Hardie Pty Ltd v McGuinness* (2000) 49 NSWLR 262.

Chapter 6: Proving the theory

[10.70] The main concern of Chapter 6 was to find a method of analysing evidence that could be used by lawyers preparing for trial. The initial inspiration had been the charting methods developed by Wigmore (1937), Part V, "Mixed Masses of Evidence, in Trials, for Analysis". These methods had never really caught on in law, but were revived, in a simplified and modified form, by Anderson and Twining

(1991). They had also been discovered by scholars outside the law, in the fields of systems engineering and artificial intelligence: see Schum (1994, pp 156-169) and Prakken, Reed and Walton (2003). In technical terms, Wigmorean charts are "directed acyclic graphs whose nodes indicate propositions and whose arcs represent fuzzy probabilistic linkages among these nodes": Schum (1994, p 169).

One of the problems with Wigmore's own charts is the complexity and breadth of the symbolic language. Anderson and Twining (1991, p 145) overcame this problem by developing a simplified palette of symbols. Another problem – this time not addressed by Anderson and Twining, nor by Anderson, Schum and Twining (2005) in the second edition of their text – is the fact that the propositions and evidence are not included in the body of the chart, but are listed separately in a "key list". This problem is easily overcome, however, through the use of argument mapping or flowcharting software that allows the incorporation of the evidence and other factual propositions within the body of the chart: see van Gelder (2007) (as well as the other articles published in the same volume of the journal *Law, Probability and Risk*). The charts in this text, for example, were prepared using bCisive; but there are many other programs that could have been used, including the precursor of bCisive, **Rationale**. Links to suitable software can be accessed via the website associated with this text, www.evidence.com.au.

Another, perhaps more fundamental objection, is that because of their rigour and precision, Wigmorean charting methods are too time-consuming to be of any use to practitioners. Anderson and Twining (1991, p 118), for example, concede that "the chart method in its purest form may be too laborious for everyday use by practitioners", but nevertheless claim that Wigmorean analysis has a role to play in the actual preparation of real trials: see Anderson, Schum and Twining (2005), Chapter 12, Part A, "The Trial Lawyer's Standpoint: A Wigmorean Lawyer Prepares for Trial". That I have written this text is obviously evidence that I concur with their view. However, the analytical method described in this text is intended to be easier to master and apply, and therefore more suitable for practitioners engaged in the conduct of actual litigation (as well as for students) than Wigmorean charting: see Twining (2007, p 81, note 64).

[10.80] Wigmore developed his method by analysing decided cases, and most published examples of Wigmorean analysis since Wigmore have also involved decided cases,[1] including the analysis contained in the Appendix to this text. In analysing decided cases, our standpoint is obviously historical, looking backwards

---

1   Wigmore (1937) analysed two decided cases: *Commonwealth v Umilian* and *Hatchett v Commonwealth*. Other published analyses of decided cases include Kadane and Schum's analysis of the Sacco and Vanzetti trial (1996); Robertson's analysis of the Arthur Allan Thomas trial in New Zealand (1990); and Twining's analysis of the Bywaters and Thompson case, in Twining (1990), Chapter 8, "Anatomy of a *Cause Célèbre*: The Case of Edith Thompson", and Anderson, Schum and Twining (2005), Chapter 7, "Analyzing the Decided Case: Anatomy of a *Cause Célèbre*".

in time to a trial that has been completed: compare Anderson, Schum and Twining (2005, p 130). The standpoint of the litigator, by contrast, is forward-looking – to a trial for which the lawyer is preparing. As Anderson, Schum and Twining (2005, pp 124-125) emphasise, standpoint is always important, and this difference in standpoint is of crucial importance.

The first and most fundamental difference between these two standpoints concerns the reasons for carrying out the analysis. Wigmore suggested that the objective of carrying out an analysis was "to determine rationally the net persuasive effect of a mixed mass of evidence": Wigmore (1913), quoted in Anderson and Twining (1991, p 108). This "evaluative" objective (see Anderson and Twining (1991, p 120)) is implicit in any attempt to determine whether a case was rightly decided on the evidence, whether that evaluation is being carried out by an academic critic of a decision or by an appellate lawyer attempting to persuade the appeal court that the trial court's verdict was "unsafe and unsatisfactory". Wigmorean analysis might also be used to expose defects or errors in the way that the trial court did or did not reason from and about the evidence.

For the litigator, the evaluative objective of determining the net persuasive effect of the evidence would be necessary in order to advise a client about his or her prospects of success if a matter were to proceed to trial. If the matter *is* proceeding to trial, however, then the litigator will have "advocacy" objectives (see Anderson and Twining (1991, p 120)), the most important of which is to "maximize the probability that [the litigator's] theory of the case will be accepted and to minimize the risk that opposing counsel will achieve their objectives": Anderson, Schum and Twining (2005, p 316). The means of persuading a court to accept a theory of case are twofold: first, evidence; and second, the arguments that can be constructed out of that evidence.

For the litigator, then, the fundamental objectives in carrying out any Wigmorean analysis are to construct the arguments that he or she wishes to present in closing, and to identify the evidence that will need to have been presented in order for those arguments to be made. This is because a closing address is an argument based on the evidence presented at trial, and if the evidence has not been presented, then the argument can not be made. What evidence will have to have been adduced from the lawyer's own witnesses? What concessions will he or she need to have obtained during cross-examination of his or her opponent's witnesses? What evidence is the lawyer's opponent likely to adduce, and how can that evidence be dealt with? What explanations can the lawyer offer for any unfavourable evidence, and what evidence can he or she lead to support those explanations? What evidence is available to rebut or eliminate his or her opponent's theory of the case? Wigmorean analysis provides a means of answering all these questions, and in doing so its purpose is not only to analyse the data that has been or could be admitted into evidence, but to identify the data that must be admitted if certain arguments are to be made in closing.

[10.90] This difference in objective between the legal historian and the litigator is related to a second and equally fundamental difference. The legal historian's knowledge of the evidence is complete. All of the investigation has been done, the trial is over, the witnesses have given their evidence, and have been cross-examined, and the evidential rulings have been made. The litigator's position is very different. Although Anderson, Schum and Twining assert that, prior to trial the "lawyers each have a defined and relatively settled body of evidential data ... the available chips are all on the table",[2] this does not accord with my own experience as a litigator in Australia.

In the United States, the parties are often able to take depositions from all witnesses, including the opposing party. Through the taking of depositions, the parties are therefore able to find out in advance what the evidence is; obtain important admissions; and if the witnesses stray from their depositions, the depositions can be used as the basis for cross-examination. Thus, "discovery" includes access to all of one's opponent's evidence, witnesses as well as documents. The rules of civil procedure in Australia do not contain any comparable mechanisms.

Indeed, it is not uncommon in civil proceedings in Australia for the parties to go to trial not knowing precisely which witnesses the other side will call; and even if we can identify the likely witnesses, there is no mechanism to compel them to answer our questions before the trial, or to force our opponent to provide copies of any statements they may have made, as these will often be protected by legal professional privilege. Even on the very eve of the trial, then, knowledge of the evidence may be incomplete. Moreover, it is often impossible to predict what will happen during the course of the trial: how will our own witnesses fare under cross-examination; what concessions will we able to force from our opponent's witnesses; what evidence will be excluded, and what evidence will be admitted? Therefore, it is only at the close of both cases that the state of the evidence is truly known; and it is therefore only at that stage that a thorough and rigorous Wigmorean chart could be prepared. But by that stage a litigator should be too busy finalising closing arguments to carry out a proper Wigmorean analysis.

Another important difference in the state of the evidence as it is received by the litigator and by the legal historian, is that when the legal historian receives the evidence it has already been subjected to a degree of ordering and selection by others: trial counsel have decided what evidence to lead and have made their closing addresses; the judge has directed the jury; and an appellate court may

---

2   Anderson, Schum and Twining (2005, pp 315-316); this statement is, however, fairly heavily qualified in a footnote that concedes that the theory – that "through meticulous investigation and use of discovery mechanisms, both lawyers should have a firm idea of the data available for presentation" – "can never be fully realized and sometimes not even approached".

also have examined the case and handed down its own decision. All these persons will have had to construct a narrative out of the raw data, drawing together the disparate strands of evidence given by a variety of witnesses into a more or less coherent whole. Clearly, this is not how things stand when the litigator receives the evidence: the litigator has to do his or her own ordering of the raw data. Moreover, this ordering is likely to be an ongoing process, as investigation, discovery and other forms of pre-trial preparation produce additional evidence. Once the evidence is ordered in some way – for example, by being placed in a chronology – then the litigator must select the evidence that he or she perceives to be of relevance to the case: compare Anderson, Schum and Twining (2005, p 130).

These differences suggest several things:

1. Before any Wigmorean analysis can be carried out, a great deal of preliminary evidential analysis must first be completed. The currently available evidence must be reviewed, ordered and from it the relevant evidence must be selected. That is why this text devotes three chapters to the preliminary analysis of evidence.

2. When a Wigmorean analysis is carried out, the product will necessarily be looser, and more tentative, than the kind of analysis that can be completed by the legal historian. In particular, it will not be possible to include evidential propositions derived from actual testimony until the close of evidence, and by then it will usually be too late to carry out such an analysis. Many of the evidential propositions included in the analysis will therefore have to be based on the testimony that the litigator anticipates will be given (as indicated, for example, by any witness statements).

3. Due to the constraints of time under which it is completed, the analysis will generally need to be "quick and dirty".[3] The analysis may still be of use to the litigator, even if the correct classification of an item of evidence or the precise nature of the relationship between evidential propositions is not always achieved. Indeed, getting things exactly right is likely to be of less importance to the litigator than to the legal historian because, for the litigator, the chart is not an end in itself – it can not, for example, be handed up to the court as a substitute for a closing argument. Rather, it is a means of enabling the litigator to construct the most persuasive closing argument possible, and to identify the evidential foundations that will need to be laid during the trial in order to make that argument. As long as those objectives are achieved, a bit of sloppiness in the analysis is unlikely to matter.

---

3   A phrase used by Prakken in oral presentation at the Conference on *Inference, Culture and Ordinary Thinking in Dispute Resolution* (Cardozo School of Law, New York City, 27-29 April 2003) and for which he subsequently provided the following source: Schlechta K, "Remarks about nonmonotonic logics and dynamic reasoning" (unpublished notes (2000)), formerly available at http://www.cmi.univ-mrs.fr/ks/remarks.html.

For these reasons, the chapter aims to provide a "quick and dirty" method of analysis that is not overly prescriptive and which downplays questions of classification in favour of an approach that emphasises the construction of arguments. It is also for these reasons that the text tries to give equal weight, if not space, to two other methods of "outputting" one's analysis: prose and outlines. The outlining method was never discussed by Wigmore, but Binder and Bergman's text on fact investigation contains a very sophisticated discussion of outlines, identifying a variety of different kinds of outlines that can be prepared: see, in particular, Chapter 3, "Analysis: The Prerequisite to Inquiry"; Chapter 4, "Story Outlines"; and Chapter 5, "The Substantive Structure for the Evidence-marshalling Outlines". See also Anderson, Schum and Twining (2005), Chapter 6, "Outlines, Chronologies, and Narrative".

Wigmore did describe a version of the "prose method", which he labelled the "narrative method". As usual, his approach to method was much more prescriptive than that taken in this text. The prescriptions he laid down also tended to reveal his own standpoint as a legal historian, rather than as an advocate. For these reasons, I have really not drawn on Wigmore's narrative method, but have instead suggested that a litigator think in terms of closing arguments that can be structured in any number of ways.

Chapter 7: Arguing from and about evidence

[10.100] The writing of this and the previous chapter were informed, perhaps to an inordinate degree, by the works of Schum, in particular *Evidential Foundations of Probabilistic Assessment* (1994), and *Evidence and Inference for the Intelligence Analyst* (1987). Much of the conceptual terminology used in this and the previous chapter can, for example, be traced to Schum, including all the following terms: "harmonious", "dissonant", "corroborative", "convergent", "conflicting", "contradictory", "ancillary", "inherent and derived relevance" and "inferential force". For readers interested in knowing more about any aspect of evidence, there is, in this author's opinion at any rate, no better place to start than Schum (1994). Tillers' revision of Wigmore (1983) also contains an extremely helpful discussion of the topic of catenate inferences, and the drawing of inferences generally.

The original draft of this chapter took a much more taxonomical approach – that is, classifying evidence according to its source and relationship to the facts in issue. This was based on a taxonomy contained in Schum (1994, p 115). In explaining his taxonomy, Schum (1987, Volume II, pp 8-9) points out that Wigmore's tripartite classification of evidence as testimonial, circumstantial or real is incomplete and cuts across different dimensions or aspects of evidence. An evidential taxonomy is, however, of more use to logicians than it is to litigators, who are not so much concerned with how to classify evidence as with how to use it as the basis for an argument. For those who are interested in a little more analytical precision, however, Schum (1994) provides the best starting point.

Credibility evidence

[10.110] With some hesitation, I chose not to follow Schum's approach to credibility and credibility evidence. According to Schum (1994, pp 100-104), the credibility stage of reasoning can actually be broken down into three distinct steps that he calls, respectively, "veracity", "objectivity" and "observational sensitivity". Veracity is concerned with the truthfulness or sincerity of the witness – for example, is the witness attempting to tell the truth; do they believe their own testimony? Just because a person is being honest, however, does not mean that what they say is true: it just means that they themselves believe it.

The next step concerns the witness's "objectivity" – that is, is their belief consistent with the information they received from their senses? As Schum points out, people's beliefs do not always correspond with their sensory perceptions – sometimes a person's preconceptions, expectations or wishes override the data provided by their senses, so that their belief is not actually founded in, or consistent with, their sensory perceptions. The final step relates to what Schum calls their "observational sensitivity". This step is concerned with the accuracy of the person's sensory perceptions. According to Schum (1994, p 107), all credibility-related evidence can be grouped as follows under one or more of these three categories:

Veracity
- Conviction of crimes related to dishonesty
- Other misconduct related to dishonesty
- Character evidence regarding honesty
- Influence/corruption among witnesses
- Testimonial bias
- Demeanour and bearing
- Polygraph, "truth" serums, psychological tests

Objectivity
- Expectancies
- Objectivity bias
- Memory-related factors

Observational sensitivity
- Sensory defects
- General physical condition
- Conditions of observation
- Quality/duration of observation
- Expertise/allocation of attention
- Sensory bias

Each of the types of evidence above is "specific" in the sense that it is relevant to one, and only one, of the three categories. Other types of credibility evidence are less specific in the sense that they may be relevant to more than one of the categories. Schum suggests that:

- "observational instructions and objectives" (for example, instructions given to an expert) can be relevant to both observational sensitivity and objectivity;

- "stakes, motives, interest" and "self-contradiction" can be relevant to both objectivity and veracity; and
- "contradictory" and "conflicting" testimony from other witnesses, and "prior inconsistent statements", can be relevant to all three of the categories.

While I like the analytical precision of Schum's approach, in the end I decided that the advantages of this precision did not outweigh the disadvantages of trying to make litigators think about credibility in ways that are unfamiliar to them.

For some expressions of judicial reservation about the usefulness to an assessment of credibility of matters such as demeanour, see Davies (2002) and McLellan (2006).

The structure and ingredients of arguments

[10.120] There is a large body of work on the structure and ingredients of arguments: see, for example, Prakken, Reed and Walton (2003); Prakken (2004); Walton (2002), (1996a) and (1996b); and Pollock (1987), (1995) and (1998). Anderson (1999) and Twining (1999) have both written about the role of generalisations in legal reasoning, with Anderson identifying five different kinds of generalisations: scientific, expert-based, general knowledge, experience-based and belief-based. Their articles now form the basis of Anderson, Schum and Twining (2005), Chapter 10, "Necessary But Dangerous: Generalizations and Stories in Argumentation About Facts".

Another source is Toulmin's work on the uses of arguments. According to Toulmin (2003; see also Toulmin, Reike and Janik (1984)), the ingredients of an argument are:

- Data, D, which leads to a –
- Claim, C, which may be qualified by a –
- Modal Qualifier, Q, and which is justified by a –
- Warrant, W, which is supported by –
- Backing, B, but which may be subject (the Claim, that is) to –
- Conditions of exception or rebuttal, R.

This can be represented in diagrammatic form as follows:

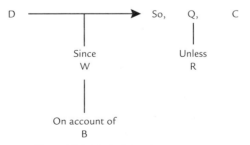

Figure 10.1: Toulmin's argument pattern

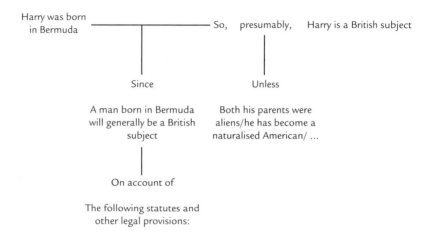

Figure 10.2: One of Toulmin's examples

These ingredients have obvious parallels with the ingredients described in Chapters 6 and 7 of this text. Data, D, is equivalent to an item of evidence; a claim, C, is an inferred factual proposition, a main argument, or a material fact; a warrant, W, is a generalisation; rebuttal, R, is an alternative explanation; backing, B, is evidence used to establish the truth of a generalisation: as was noted in the text, in a common law trial backing evidence is usually only adduced to support the generalisations relied on by experts. Additional ingredients mentioned in Chapters 6 and 7 included evidence to support or to eliminate an alternative explanation.

It is therefore possible to think of the evidence charts discussed in Chapters 6 and 7 as a series of nested Toulmin diagrams. Each claim – whether it be an inferred factual proposition, a main argument, or a material fact – may be supported by more than one item of evidence or datum. Where more than one inference is required to connect an item of evidence to a material fact, then an inferred factual proposition or main argument may be both the "claim" in the "diagram" below it, and the "data" in the one above it.

The assessment of probabilities and the nature of proof in a common law trial

[10.130] Chapter 7 does not deal with the question of the *nature* of proof in a common law trial, although it is perhaps implicit in what is said that the text takes the view that proof is more concerned with persuasion than with the discovery of some objective "truth". To answer the question contained in the title of Cohen (1991), the text is more consistent with the tribunal of fact's verdict representing what it "accepts" to be true on the basis of the evidence, rather than what it necessarily "believes" to be true. Other useful discussions of the nature of proof in a common law trial, and the state of mind required of the tribunal of fact, are to be found in Allen (1991a) and (1991b); Cohen (1977); Eggleston (1983); Hodgson (1995); Nesson (1985) and (1986); and Thomson (1986). Among other things, several of these articles address well-known chestnuts of proof, such as the problem of the "blue bus".

It will be immediately apparent to any reader familiar with the "New Evidence Scholarship" (for the meaning of this term, see Lempert (1986); Jackson (1996); and Anderson (1991)) that this book omits any discussion of methods for the actual *calculation of probabilities* in litigation. The reason for this is that I am not convinced that a litigator preparing a matter for trial needs to be familiar with the debates about the assessment of probabilities that have been such a feature of the New Evidence Scholarship. The task of assessing probabilities does not actually fall to the lawyers presenting a case, but to the tribunal of fact; and I doubt very much whether lawyers presenting a case are likely to increase the effectiveness of their advocacy by couching their arguments in terms of, for example, Bayes' Theorem.

Goldman (1999, pp 115-123, and see also 2002), may well be right to assert that the assessment of evidence in accordance with Bayes' Theorem is likely to bring the tribunal of fact close to the truth, provided that the probabilities that are fed into the theorem are objectively accurate. But, as Redmayne (2003) points out, this is a very serious qualification. In most cases of interest to courts, accurate, objective probabilities are simply unavailable. Without a numerical probability for a given event, an actual Bayesian calculation can not be carried out, no matter how readily we might be able to model such a calculation. This is not the place to explore the implications of this particular problem. Nevertheless, for those interested in becoming familiar with these debates, the best place to start is, as always, Schum (1994), and the extensive bibliography therein. Further useful discussion can be found in the articles referred to in the previous paragraphs.

PART C: FINAL PREPARATIONS

Chapter 8: Analysing for admissibility

[10.140] A common criticism made by evidence lawyers of our colleagues in substantive law fields is that they often tend to treat the facts as if they are just that, "facts", which are given or agreed on at the outset of litigation. What is treated as being worthy of interest, then, is the *legal* uncertainty consequential to those facts. Evidence lawyers rightly object that it is the "facts", not the law, that give rise to the greater uncertainty – a truth concealed by the academic focus on appellate decisions – and that the focus on the application of substantive law to "given" facts ill prepares students for the world of legal practice in which the facts are never a "given": see, for example, Palmer (2002); Twining (1990), Chapter 2, "Taking Facts Seriously"; and Twining (2007).

In writing this chapter it became apparent that evidence lawyers (including myself) often fall into the same trap when it comes to the application of the rules of evidence to particular items of evidence – that is, the trap of assuming that the features of that item of evidence on which admissibility turns are given and immutable, rather than being themselves the objects of proof and the subjects of controversy. No doubt we do so for the same reason that our colleagues in substantive law fields assume that the facts themselves are a given – that is, because we are used to reading judgments in which the court describes the features of an item of evidence before applying the rules of evidence to that item.

The approach to the application of the law of evidence described in this chapter is, therefore, fundamentally different from that taken in the evidence texts with which this author is familiar (including the author's own evidence texts). It advocates treating "foundational" facts – that is, the facts upon which the admissibility of an item of evidence is likely to turn – as objects of proof in the trial, to be approached in the same way as any of the other objects of proof. Part of this involves identifying the foundational facts – we do this by referring to texts on the law of evidence. There are several useful Australian textbooks and casebooks on the law of evidence, as well as annotations of the uniform evidence legislation, including Gans and Palmer (2014); Odgers (2014); Anderson, Williams and Clegg (2009); Hunter, Cameron and Henning (2005); Heydon (2013); and Ligertwood (2010). Other helpful texts are listed in the Bibliography.

In terms of the practicalities of actually laying a foundation, Mauet and McCrimmon (2011) is arguably even more helpful, containing detailed illustrations of methods for laying the foundations for a wide variety of types of evidence, ranging from business records to character evidence.

Chapter 8 also discusses some specific exclusionary rules; for more detailed discussion of these rules, see Gans and Palmer (2014). For articles taking an approach to the hearsay rule that is more or less compatible with that taken in the chapter, see Palmer (1995a), Schum (1992) and Tillers and Schum (1992). For compatible discussions of the common law precursors to the tendency and coincidence rules, see Hamer (2003) and Palmer (1994), (1995b) and (1999).

Chapter 9: Pulling it all together for trial

[10.150] As was noted in Chapter 9, this text does not purport to cover all the ground covered by existing advocacy texts. In Australia there are a number of good texts dealing with trial technique, including Mauet and McCrimmon (2011); Curthoys and Kendall (2006); Glissan (2011); Hampel, Brimer and Kune (2008); Stuesser (2011); and Ross (2007). Other texts are listed in the Bibliography.

Appendix: A sample analysis

Introduction

[11.10] This Appendix contains a partial analysis of the prosecution case against David Eastman for the murder of Colin Winchester. The Appendix is broken into the following parts:

- The evidence: this includes some background facts and an annotated article from the *Canberra Times*, published the day after Eastman's conviction, which between them provide a broad outline of the evidence in the case, together with a brief description of the prosecutor's closing address.
- An analysis of the evidence, including a set of charts mapping the case, as well as examples of the case map in both prose and outline form.
- A discussion, including examples, of six of the mistakes most commonly made when charting evidence.

Given that this sample analysis is of a decided case, an analysis, ordering and mapping of the evidence has already been carried out both by the parties and by the courts. There has been extensive investigation, for example, and a chronological narrative has been developed. For that reason, the analysis that follows includes neither a chronology, nor a statement of the factual theory on which the prosecution relied (this can be inferred from the *Canberra Times* article). Moreover, the evidence in this case, like any decided case, has all been adduced, so the body of evidence being analysed is final, complete and stable. The analysis set out in this Appendix is necessarily different, therefore, from that required of a litigator preparing for trial. The advantages of working from a decided case, however, are that the evidence can be presented in a much more compact format than in a brief of evidence (in the Eastman case, for example, the brief must have comprised thousands, if not millions, of pages); and a further advantage of working from a piece of journalism is that it enables us to identify some of the things that are distinctive about the way in which we organise evidence for the purposes of litigation. More complete analyses based on full briefs of evidence can be accessed by clicking on the "**sample analyses**" link at the following website:

www.evidence.com.au

THE EVIDENCE

[11.20] On 3 November 1995, David Harold Eastman was found guilty of the 1989 murder of AFP Assistant Commissioner, Colin Winchester: see, among other cases, *Eastman v The Queen* (1997) 76 FCR 9 and *Eastman v The Queen* (2000) 203 CLR 1; [2000] HCA 29. The following day, the *Canberra Times* published an article by Roderick Campbell, who had been reporting on the case from the time of the murder, headlined "Unravelling a Web of Hatred". The final section of the article, under the heading "The Coincidences", contained a brief description of the prosecutor's closing address.

Eastman's trial had lasted some six months, with the prosecution calling evidence from more than 200 witnesses. There were almost 7,000 pages of transcript and over 300 documentary and other exhibits. The article's description of the evidence against Eastman is, therefore, necessarily an overview which omits many of the details that would be necessary for a complete case map. For example, the article does not identify the source for most of the items of evidence that the prosecution relied on; and treats as simple facts propositions that actually had to be proved by complex and detailed bodies of evidence. The article also omits a number of important background facts or details that would have been known to its readers (the stories of both Winchester's murder and Eastman's trial were well known in Canberra) and that are essential to a proper understanding of the case. A more complete discussion of the evidence can be found in the Federal Court's judgment in Eastman's appeal from conviction. Part of this judgment has been extracted (in a slightly edited form) to provide the "Background facts" below at [11.30]; other details from the judgment have been added at the relevant point of the article itself by means of footnotes.

Eastman is a highly capable litigant in person, and following the refusal of his appeal against conviction has made numerous applications and appeals to the Federal Court, Supreme Court of the ACT, and High Court. In 2001 Eastman applied for a judicial inquiry into his conviction under s 475 of the *Crimes Act*

1900 (ACT), and on 7 August 2001 Miles CJ of the ACT Supreme Court granted the application, directing that an inquiry be held into the question of Eastman's fitness to plead during his trial. The question arose largely because of the way in which Eastman had behaved during his trial, repeatedly sacking his lawyers (such that he was often unrepresented), and abusing the judge and prosecutor (often in front of the jury). Miles J's decision to order an inquiry led to a number of further applications and appeals which delayed the commencement of the inquiry until 2004 (I appeared in that inquiry as junior counsel for Eastman). On 6 October 2005, Miles CJ handed down his report, finding that on the probabilities Eastman was fit to plead throughout his trial. Further applications and appeals followed.

On 29 April 2011 Eastman applied for a further judicial inquiry into his conviction. The application was eventually granted on 3 September 2012. This inquiry was to focus on the evidence, rather than on Eastman's mental state. The inquiry was conducted by the former Chief Justice of the Northern Territory, Brian Martin. Martin AJ delivered his report in May 2014. After reviewing the evidence, Martin AJ concluded that "While I am fairly certain [Eastman] is guilty of the murder of [Winchester], a nagging doubt remains". The doubt primarily arose from issues connected to the expert witness Barnes, whom Martin AJ found gave evidence that lacked a proper scientific basis, and whom Martin AJ described as being "far from independent and objective" such that he "regarded himself as a police witness and was biased accordingly". There were also numerous failures by the prosecution to disclose relevant material to the defence, including material "that would have been devastating to Mr Barnes' credibility". Martin AJ found that the combination of these flaws meant that Eastman did not receive a fair trial, was denied a fair chance of acquittal and that as a result a substantial miscarriage of justice had occurred. He therefore recommended that Eastman's conviction be quashed. Under Part 20 of the Crimes Act, the decision as to whether or not to accept Martin AJ's recommendation lay with the Full Court of the Supreme Court of the ACT. On 22 August 2014, the Supreme Court agreed that Eastman did not receive a trial according to law, quashed his conviction and ordered a retrial. Eastman was released on bail shortly afterwards. At the time of publication it is unclear whether any retrial will take place.

Background facts

[11.30] At the time of his death, Colin Winchester was an Assistant Commissioner in the Australian Federal Police (the AFP) and the highest ranking police officer serving in the Australian Capital Territory. Death occurred at about 9.15pm on 10 January 1989, as the deceased was alighting from his car near his home in Lawley Street, Deakin, a suburb of Canberra. Mr Winchester was in the habit of parking his car in his neighbour's driveway. His neighbour, a widow, found comfort in having a car on her premises, pointing to the presence of occupants in her house.

When found by his wife shortly after the murder, the deceased was in a slumped position behind the driving wheel of his car; the driver's door was open and his right leg was on the ground. The automatic transmission was in "park" and the car lights had been turned off. He had been shot twice at close range – once in the back of the head and once in the face on the right hand side. According to the medical evidence, the wound to the back of the deceased's head occurred first and was likely to have caused instant death.

Immediately before his death, Mr Winchester had visited his brother, Ken, in nearby Queanbeyan. This visit was not part of a normal routine or pattern and therefore it could not be suggested that the killer was earlier aware of the deceased's likely movements. Mr Ken Winchester said that he had not noticed any other vehicle about when his brother left to go home.

Mrs Winchester said that she heard the sound of her husband's car at about 9.15pm and that a short time later she heard noises she described as sounding "like sharp stones coming up on to the front of the window". She said that there were two distinct sounds – the second following immediately after the first. Obviously, they were the sounds of the two shots that killed the deceased. When Mr Winchester had not come into the house, Mrs Winchester went looking for him and it was then that she found his body. The Crown's case was that the shots had been fired from a .22 calibre weapon to which a silencer had been affixed and that supersonic ammunition (such as PMC Zapper) had been used. If that were correct, the use of the silencer would have muffled the sound of the shots that were fired but not that of the bullets breaking the sound barrier. This would also account for the manner in which Mrs Winchester described the sounds that she heard.

Police officers who attended at the scene of the crime searched the immediate area. Two PMC cartridge cases were found but no weapon was located. Indeed, the murder weapon has never been found. Microscopic examination of the two cartridge cases by a police witness, Superintendent Prior, led him to form the opinion that the murder weapon was a Ruger 10/22 rifle. That conclusion was not challenged by the defence.

The assistance of Mr Barnes from the Victorian Forensic Science Laboratory was sought by the investigating police officers as a matter of urgency. He arrived at the scene of the crime at about 3am on 11 January 1989 and commenced work in his field of expertise – the collection and interpretation of gunshot residue. Mr Barnes took stub samples from both entry wounds and from selected areas of the car. Later that morning, a police officer, Sergeant Nelipa, vacuumed the ground in the immediate area of the driver's door of the car. Eastman's car was later impounded and searched for gunshot residue on 18 January 1989. Both Mr Nelipa and Mr Barnes were involved in that search.

It was the case for the Crown that the murder weapon was a Ruger 10/22 rifle that had been purchased by Eastman from a Louis Klarenbeek, and that at the time of purchase the rifle was fitted with a silencer. Mr Klarenbeek was questioned by the police and gave them a statement, but he died before the trial commenced. During the trial, the defence adduced evidence through Detective Pattenden that he had spoken to Mr Klarenbeek on 28 January 1989 and that he had, on that day, shown him a photoboard containing several photographs, one of which was of David Eastman. Mr Pattenden said that Mr Klarenbeek said that he did not recognise any of the photographs.

The police traced the ownership of the Ruger back from Mr Klarenbeek to a Mr Noel King. Mr King had, in turn, purchased it from a Mr Caldwell. When Mr King sold the rifle to Mr Klarenbeek in October 1988 it was fitted with a telescopic sight and the barrel had been threaded so that a silencer could be fitted.

Mr Caldwell said that over a number of years he had spent his holidays on a particular Reserve where he and his companions had engaged in target practice and rabbit shooting. He took police to the location where, using metal detectors, the police located a number of spent .22 calibre cartridge cases. Ultimately, testing by Mr Prior revealed that nine of those cartridges resembled, very closely, the two cartridges that had been found at the scene of the crime. Mr Klarenbeek also handed police seven .22 calibre cartridge cases. He said he had recovered them from an area where he had test-fired the Ruger that he had purchased from Mr King. Four of those cartridges were identified by Mr Prior as having been fired by rifles other than a Ruger. His examination of the remaining three led him to conclude that two of them were Stirling brand and one was a CCI brand cartridge case. None of them was a PMC brand. In concentrating his examination on those three cartridge cases, Mr Prior ultimately formed the opinion that one of them had been fired from the same rifle that had fired one of the cartridge cases found at the scene of the crime. Evidence that Mr Klarenbeek had used Stirling and CCI brands when he test-fired the rifle had an additional significance in relation to the gunshot residue evidence.

Mr Prior's conclusions were independently supported by Mr Barnes, by Special Agent, Richard Crum, of the United States Federal Bureau of Investigation and by Chief Superintendent, Bernard Schecter, the head of the Investigations Department, Division of Identification and Forensic Science of the Israeli National Police. No attempt was made, either during the trial or on the appeal, to question the qualifications of Mr Crum or Mr Schecter. There can be no doubt, therefore, that the rifle used to kill Mr Winchester was the rifle that Mr Klarenbeek had acquired through Mr King from Mr Caldwell.

Mr Webb gave evidence that he had seen an advertisement for the sale of various firearms that had been placed in the *Canberra Times* by Mr Klarenbeek on Saturday, 31 December 1988. On arrival at Mr Klarenbeek's house in Queanbeyan that day he was shown several weapons, including a Ruger 10/22 rifle. He noticed that its barrel was threaded so that a silencer could be fitted and that it had a telescopic sight. There were three silencers on the table where Mr Klarenbeek was displaying items that he had for sale. Mr Webb said that as he was leaving Mr

Klarenbeek's premises another person arrived. It was necessary for Mr Webb to turn sideways so that the two men could pass on the pathway without colliding. He said he made eye contact, and the other person was not moving out of the way. He subsequently identified that person as Eastman. Mr Webb said that he returned to Mr Klarenbeek's house on Thursday, 5 January 1989 and purchased a Tof .22 rifle. He then noted that the Ruger 10/22 was no longer on display. He said that Mr Klarenbeek did not require him to produce any type of licence.

Shortly after the murder, following a television program in which the police appealed for information about Ruger rifles, Mr Webb contacted the police. He told them that he had seen one at Mr Klarenbeek's house but he made no mention of the man who had arrived as he was leaving, nor did he refer to him when he gave a written statement to the police six months later, on 28 August 1989. Much later in the year he saw, so he claimed, Eastman on television and recognised him as the man whom he had seen at Mr Klarenbeek's house. In evidence-in-chief he said that he had not mentioned the other man when he first spoke to the police as he did not recall the subject being raised. However, he admitted that in his statement of 28 August he had falsely stated that while he was at Mr Klarenbeek's house on 31 December 1988, "nobody else came to look at the rifle he had for sale ...". Mr Webb also repeated that statement when giving evidence on oath at the Inquest. He offered, as his explanation, that he did not want to get involved, that he had visited Mr Klarenbeek during his working hours without his employer's permission and that he was scared for himself and his family. He also assumed that Mr Klarenbeek would have been able to identify the person who had bought the Ruger 10/22 rifle. It was not until sometime late in 1992 that Mr Webb told the police that he had identified Eastman on television some three years or so earlier.

The Article: "UNRAVELLING A WEB OF HATRED"

[11.40]   The following is the text of the article published in the *Canberra Times* on 4 November 1995 concerning the key evidence presented in the case:

> *The prosecution case can be compartmentalised conveniently under the headings: motive, Eastman and firearms, the scientific evidence, the threats, sightings, and the tapes.*
>
> *The prosecutor, Michael Adams QC, sought to draw much of the material together in what he described as the "coincidental approach" to assessing evidence. His remarks on this point follow the relatively brief summation of the key evidence that follows.*
>
> **Motive**
>
> Although motive is not a necessary element of the crime of murder, the prosecution sought to demonstrate that Eastman's motive for killing Winchester had its roots in his hatred for those in the public service and the police, whom he thought responsible for the injustices he had suffered.

By late 1987, Eastman had been campaigning for a decade on several fronts against the public service.[1] He had had one or two successes but had yet to achieve his ultimate goal of reinstatement in the public service.

Then, on 17 December 1987, he became involved in a fracas with a neighbour, Andrew Russo, over the inconsequential issue of parking. Blows were exchanged and both men were injured. Russo took himself to hospital, while Eastman went to the police. A short time later, Eastman was charged. He was outraged, and became convinced that a police officer he had encountered in previous years, Trevor Coutts, had improperly influenced the investigation.

A week later Eastman wrote to his German penfriend, Irene Finke, that he wanted to kill Russo, Russo's witnesses and "the bastard police". In the same letter he wrote, "I sympathise with men who kill hundreds, thousands, millions", a remark the prosecution said demonstrated the depth of his hatred.

Throughout 1988, Eastman continued his fight to gain a medical clearance to rejoin the public service. He also embarked on a determined campaign to convince police that he had been wrongly charged and that it was Russo who had been the instigator of the fracas. The prosecution argued that Eastman was fearful that an assault conviction would seriously harm his employment prospects. Eastman denied this. He said he never thought a minor assault charge would pose much of a problem.

The Crown case was that the two threads – the hoped-for public service job and the Russo assault charge – merged in December 1988. On 16 December, a decision was made that Eastman was fit to re-enter the Service. On the same day, Eastman and Shadow Attorney-General, Neil Brown, met Winchester to further pursue the

---

1   Eastman had resigned from the public service in 1977, and had opted to take his superannuation in the form of a lump sum rather than a pension; this choice rendered him ineligible to rejoin the public service. Shortly thereafter Eastman changed his mind; the first step in his campaign to rejoin the public service was to reverse the decision to take his superannuation in the form of a lump sum. This first step in the campaign was achieved in 1984. In 1985, however, Eastman was ruled to be medically unfit for a return to the public service. On 4 November 1986, the Administrative Appeals Tribunal (AAT) also held that Eastman was medically unfit, and in its reasons for decision listed a number of acts of violent behaviour towards fellow employees and threats made to various people about which evidence had been led before the AAT by the Commissioner for Superannuation. By a letter dated 21 December 1988, Eastman was informed that he had succeeded in reversing the decision that he was medically unfit for work in the public service, subject to a condition that he was only fit to "perform duties of a clerical nature in a middle management position … involving self-paced projects and minimal contact with other people". This condition was based on Eastman's history of violent behaviour; or, as it was described in the reasons for the decision, "the difficulties [Eastman] has experienced in interpersonal relations". On 22 December 1988 Eastman appealed against the imposition of this condition (but was ultimately unsuccessful in this appeal).

Russo matter.[2] On 21 December, Eastman learned the outcome of both matters, one favourable, one not. The public service had theoretically accepted him; Winchester had turned him down.

Further representations were made by Brown to the then AFP Commissioner, Peter McAulay.

Eastman was due to appear in court on the assault charge on 12 January 1989.

The Crown asserted that Commissioner McAulay's advice that he would not intervene in the assault matter was received by Eastman on 10 January, the day of the murder.

Eastman disputed the suggestion that the outcome of the Winchester representations was crucial to him. He knew police could not drop the charge, and that only the Director of Public Prosecutions had the power to do so.

About a week before the murder, Eastman allegedly told Superintendent Mick Craft that the police "executive" was corrupt and had a lot to answer for. As he said this, he allegedly gestured towards Winchester's office.

Eastman and a friend, Bob Briton, asserted that the conversation with Craft took place in 1988, not early 1989. Both denied any gesturing or reference to police corruption.

Firearms

The Crown alleged that Winchester was shot with PMC-brand ammunition which was fired from a .22 calibre Ruger 10/22 semi-automatic rifle fitted with a silencer.

It was alleged that the murder weapon was sold by the late Louis Klarenbeek, of Queanbeyan, on or about 31 December 1988 to a man who had not wanted to buy a telescopic sight. The rifle had been threaded for a silencer and Klarenbeek had a number of these for sale at that time.

Eastman bought a Stirling rifle fitted with a telescopic sight from Geoffrey Bradshaw on 10 February 1988. He returned the gun, but not the sight, later in the day. He said he smashed the sight and threw it in a bin. At the time of the purchase, he had parked his car out of sight and gave Bradshaw a false name and address.

Three days later, he bought a Ruger rifle from James Lenaghan. He asked if he could buy it without a licence and again parked out of sight.[3] Some time later – Eastman said it was one or two months later – he placed the Ruger and 46 rounds of Stinger

---

2   Mr Brown testified that "my general impression of what he was saying was that he wanted to have this particular matter, that is to say this matter concerning the police, cleared up, I assume because it would enhance his prospects of going back to work in the Treasury".

3   Mr Lenaghan also testified that Eastman had not wanted a telescopic sight.

ammunition, both in a gunbag, in a drain under the Old Federal Highway. These were found by a member of the public on 1 May and handed to police.

In June 1988, Eastman negotiated to buy another Ruger. He later asked the owner, Scott Thompson, to sell him the gun in Queanbeyan. In November, he made further inquiries about the same gun, but did not buy it.

Eastman asserted that he had only bought guns in early 1988 because he had been in fear of the neighbour, Russo. He went to great lengths to portray Russo as a "maniac". Russo owned a shotgun and a truncheon and may have acquired a pistol, he said. Once Russo had moved out of Jerilderie Court his fears subsided and he disposed of his gun. He dumped it in a drain so it would rust and become unserviceable.

However, other incidents involving Russo later in the year rekindled Eastman's concerns and he made further inquiries about buying a weapon. But he did not actually purchase one.

The prosecution said this explanation was a lie. It said Eastman had never been in fear of Russo, and had not voiced his concerns to anyone. With one exception, he had been unable to recall the later incidents that had ostensibly caused him to renew his hunt for a weapon. He had no legitimate purpose for owning a gun other than to kill someone.

The Sightings

On the morning of 31 December 1988, Ray Webb went to the Klarenbeek residence to inspect rifles. As he was leaving, he passed a man he later identified as Eastman in the yard. He did not see Eastman's car. A blue Japanese vehicle, similar in some respects to Eastman's, was seen in a nearby street that afternoon.[4] A few days later, Klarenbeek apparently told Webb that the purchaser of the Ruger had not wanted the telescopic sight.

Webb took until October 1992 to come forward with his evidence that it was Eastman he had seen. His credibility came under strong attack from Eastman's counsel, both because of the delay in coming forward and because of his friendships with police and the deceased's brother.

Eastman denied ever going to Klarenbeek's or buying his gun. There was no direct evidence of Eastman actually purchasing the Klarenbeek weapon. Before he died,

---

4   This evidence was given by a Mrs Mercia Kaczmarowski. She lived in the street behind Mr Klarenbeek's house. Mrs Kaczmarowski recalled Saturday, 31 December 1988. She had a friend staying with her and was about to go away on holidays. She noticed a motor vehicle parked outside her home and was attracted to it because it had "a very interesting bumper bar" as well as "a new style of number plate for the ACT". At the request of the police she looked through a book of photographs of different motor vehicles and picked one that she considered to be similar to the car that she had seen. The photograph happened to be one of Eastman's car, a blue Mazda 626 sedan.

Klarenbeek was shown photos of 12 men, including Eastman, but was unable to recognise any of them.

On 1 January 1989, Eastman withdrew $200 from an ATM in Canberra. This was the same amount he had offered for the Thompson Ruger. Because Klarenbeek had died, no evidence was presented of the day on which he actually sold his Ruger and there was nothing to tie the ATM withdrawal to the gun sale.

On 4 or 5 January, Eastman allegedly tried to sell a Ruger threaded for a silencer to a Queanbeyan sports store proprietor, Dennis Reid. He declined to give Reid his phone number. Reid's son saw a blue car leaving the car park behind the store; Eastman denied this incident.

On the night of Sunday, 8 January, Anne Newcombe saw a car parked near the Winchester home. The occupant, a male, apparently attempted to conceal his face as she passed. She later recalled the number plate as YPQ 038. The car with that plate was not in Lawley Street that night. The registration of Eastman's car was YMP 028.[5]

The Scientific Evidence

The experts were agreed that the Klarenbeek gun was the murder weapon. Impressions left on the cartridge cases found at the scene, recovered by Klarenbeek from a quarry, and recovered from a reserve in Victoria where a previous owner had fired the same gun, all matched.

Propellant residue from PMC ammunition was found in the boot of Eastman's car.[6] Ammunition residues found in his car were said to be indistinguishable from those at the murder scene.

The prosecution said Klarenbeek had previously fired CCI and Stirling ammunition through his Ruger. Propellant residue consistent with CCI and Stirling were found

---

5   Mrs Newcombe gave evidence that in the evening of Sunday, 8 January 1989, she had been walking in Lawley Street with her mother and daughter at about 8.30 pm or 9 pm. She said that she observed a car that was parked outside the house next door to the Winchester's. At that stage, Eastman was represented by counsel and Mrs Newcombe was allowed to say, without objection, that as she passed the car, the person seated in the driver's seat "moved to position himself so that he would not be seen". Earlier, Mrs Newcombe had explained that she "felt uncomfortable about the car being positioned there". As she returned home from her walk, she retraced her route and she noticed that the car was in the same position. She had intended to make a note of the registration number when she returned home but was distracted by a telephone call. Later, Mrs Newcombe was able to identify the car as a Mazda 626 sedan. As to its colour, she thought that it was "sort of a turquoisey-bluey-green". Eastman's car was a metallic blue Mazda 626. Mrs Newcombe's recollection of the registration number was YPQ 038; the registration number of Eastman's car was YMP 028. YPQ 038 was the registration number of a cream Mazda 323 hatchback owned by a Ms Betty Fitzgerald. During the weekend of 7 and 8 January 1989 that car was parked in a locked garage in Yarralumla.

6   Propellant residue from PMC ammunition was also found at the crime scene.

on Winchester's body, in his car and in Eastman's Mazda 626 sedan. Distinctive particles found at the scene and in the Mazda were said to be the result of the use of a silencer.

During the trial, Eastman said that if this material was in fact found in his car, he did not know where it came from.

However, the inference to be drawn from the defence case was that it probably came from the Bradshaw or Lenaghan rifles which Eastman said had been placed unprotected in the boot of his car after firing, or from a hitchhiker who had been on a shooting trip. The Crown did not quarrel with the suggestion that primer residue found in Eastman's car, which was consistent with PMC, may have come from the Bradshaw or Lenaghan rifles. What the Crown did rely on was the presence in the car, and at the murder scene, of PMC propellant material and the charred, chopped-disc particle which, it was said, could only have come from the use of a silencer.

The Threats

The prosecution produced evidence that in early 1988 Eastman told a member of the staff of then Australian Democrats leader Senator Janine Haines that he would have to kill someone so people would see the injustice which had been done to him. A former neighbour, Donna Heritage, said that Eastman had spoken to her in mid 1988 about the pending Russo assault case. He had been unhappy that police had charged him and had said it had been Russo's fault, that the police were corrupt and that if it was the last thing he did "he'd get back at them" and clear his name. She said remarks to this effect had also been made after Winchester's murder.

A former Eastman lawyer, Dennis Barbara, said that in late 1988 Eastman had told him, "I'll kill Winchester and I'll get the Ombudsman, too." Eastman denied saying this. He said Barbara's evidence showed that the name Winchester had meant nothing to him at the time and he had only recalled the incident one or two months after the event.

A week after a consultation on January 6, 1989, Eastman's doctor, Dennis Roantree, recorded his patient as saying, "I should shoot the bastard."

This was in the context of a conversation in which Eastman had, according to Dr Roantree, referred to his interview the previous month with the "Commissioner", that he had been virtually thrown out of his office, and that he had felt like pushing the Commissioner off his chair. The references to the Commissioner were assumed to mean Winchester, the Assistant Commissioner.

Eastman disputed this evidence, pointing out that Dr Roantree had crossed the words out after writing them because of his uncertainty. Neither Barbara nor Roantree were cross-examined about their evidence.

The Tapes

The prosecution asserted that, while being taped by police, Eastman had used language which amounted to an assertion that he had killed Winchester. Eastman had said he knew he was being taped and said certain things to make a fool of police. The prosecution suggested that Eastman had been so distressed by what he had done that he had needed to repeat the allegations made against him and "adopt" them.

Eastman was legally bugged between September 1989 and January 1993. Everything he said or did was recorded. Of the many thousands and thousands of hours of tape recordings, a mere five hours were used by the Crown to support its case.

Before the trial was over, the jury had heard, or heard about, six different versions: those of the police, prosecution expert Dr Peter French, the three defence experts, Christopher Mills, Professor Butcher and Dr Elizabeth McClelland, and, finally, Eastman's own interpretation. The only version that really mattered was that heard through headphones by the jurors themselves.

One of the most crucial passages contained, according to police, the words, "I killed Winchester". Dr French initially accepted this but later changed his opinion and thought the words had probably been, "I kept watching her".

But two passages were largely agreed upon by most of the experts. One contained the words along the lines of, "He was the first man, the first man I ever killed. It was a beautiful feeling, one of the most beautiful feelings you have ever know."

However, the word "killed" was not accepted as definite by Dr French. Without "killed", the passage lost its significance. The explanation put forward by Eastman was that the passage – with no reference to killing – had sexual connotations.

The prosecution concentrated much more on a longer passage which read:

"You drove more slow. I cannot miss him. You drove more slowly to give me a better chance. In fact, the situation is I ran out of sight. It's pathetic".

"And even when he called the first night and he missed you. That was a very frustrating night. And I had to go back again the next night to kill him, poor bugger. Then all of a sudden you're dead.

"And you go back the next night, same car, same registration, same driver, and your film crew is the same, and try to set it up again.

"Finally, on the second night, you succeed. Honestly, it's like trying to shoot miracles . . . It required about 50 takes before you get what you want. I mean, about the only thing you didn't do, you didn't provide me with a bag full of stones."

Justice Carruthers explained to the jury that the material contained in the tapes – and not this passage specifically – was very important because, if the jury accepted that it contained an admission that Eastman had killed Winchester, this was direct evidence pointing to his guilt.

Eastman's explanation for the "bag full of stones" passage was that it related to an incident where surveillance police, armed with a video camera, had driven repeatedly and increasingly more slowly, round the block. He had thrown pebbles at them but missed. The incident had been repeated the following night, with the same car and occupants, and finally he had hit the car. The reference to running "out of sight" was, in fact a reference to running "out of stones".

The prosecution had a starkly different explanation. Mr Adams put it that Eastman saw himself as the biblical David, and Winchester as Goliath. The passage, he said, was a reference to the Winchester murder.

The relevant verses in the Book of Samuel contained references to "five smooth pebbles", a slingshot and a bag of stones. Eastman had referred to these objects in his evidence. The rest was a description of the murder, and Eastman's stalking of his victim.

Other Evidence

Two police officers spoke to Eastman the day after the murder. In the presence of his lawyer, he said he had been out driving on the evening of January 10, as he regularly did, but could not remember where he had gone. He agreed that it was an important issue and thought he might have gone out at about 8pm for a take-away meal and returned to his flat in Reid at 10pm.

The following day he told two other officers that the murder had been "a terrible thing" and that he would like to assist police but could not. He had already told police all he knew.

During his trial, Eastman maintained the line that he could not remember where he had driven on the night of the murder. He did, however, remember that he visited a brothel in Fyshwick and had sex with a prostitute. Her evidence suggested that the visit took place some time between 11pm and 2am. This did not provide Eastman with an alibi.

Eastman did not tell the police on January 11 about his visit to the brothel. His explanation at the trial was that he had thought the prostitute, Felicity, to be an impressive sort of person, quite possibly a university student.

Concerned for her position, he did not want police to turn up on her doorstep to verify his visit, and "spill the beans" about Felicity's employment to an unsuspecting parent, boyfriend, husband or child. Eastman rejected the notion that he had been embarrassed on his own account.

The prosecution, on the other hand, suggested that Eastman had not mentioned Felicity because he knew she could not provide him with an alibi. The only reason he could not recall his movements on January 10 was that he was "a guilty man who needed a convenient memory loss".

The closing address: "The Coincidences"

[11.50] Following is the final section of the *Canberra Times* article:

During his final address, Mr Adams put it to the jury that if the theory were propounded that Eastman was innocent, there were a remarkable number of coincidences to contend with. He sought to illustrate the point by discussing a hypothetical murder and a hypothetical suspect.

In the hypothetical murder, the first person police would look at was someone who had threatened to kill the victim. Their suspect had done this twice, once a few months before the murder and then a few days beforehand. He had threatened to use the method actually adopted by the killer, namely, shooting.

Coincidentally, a description of a suspicious car near the victim's home two days before the murder was similar to that of the suspect's. Even the registration number was similar.

In a striking coincidence, leaving aside the Y on the ACT registration plate, three of the remaining five numbers or letters matched, and in a similar order.

The victim's name was not in the ordinary electoral roll, having recently been living away from Canberra for some time. It was, however, on the "additional roll" of newly enrolled voters. Coincidentally, some time before the murder, the suspect had visited the electoral office and inspected that roll.

When questioned by police the day after the murder, the suspect could not recall his movements the previous evening. Assuming his failure of recollection was genuine, one might expect it to be only temporary and that as soon as police had gone, he would rack his brains and reconstruct his movements.

One might expect that he would discuss the matter with his solicitor – who had been present when police had called – because, quite unjustifiably, he might be a suspect. But the following day, he again told police he could not recall his movements.

Then it emerged that the suspect had been trying to buy a rifle without a licence and in circumstances where he had tried to hide his identity. He had started the search shortly after expressing a desire to "kill the bastard police".

A further, most unfortunate coincidence, was that of all the brands of weapons he might buy, he ended up with the type used in the murder.

The suspect had sought to explain his interest in weapons on the basis that he had needed one to defend himself against a neighbour with a shotgun who had assaulted him and was a maniac. He said he had expressed his fears to officialdom but could produce no evidence of this.

The suspect said he had thrown the gun he bought away after the neighbour moved out but later events had caused him to make further inquiries about firearms.

Unfortunately, his poor memory led him to forget all but one of the incidents.

Police had then searched the suspect's car. To his misfortune, it was found to contain a substantial amount of PMC-brand propellant, the very type used in the murder. Worse still, there were a few particles of non-PMC residue found in his car. By a singular coincidence, the same residue had been found at the murder scene.

The evidence suggested that a silencer had been used in the murder.

In another unfortunate coincidence, residues which could only be explained by the use of a silencer were found in the suspect's car.

In a remarkable coincidence, when the murder weapon had been sold, the buyer had not wanted the telescopic sight, either because he already had one or had not needed one, because the gun was to be fired at close range.

The suspect had purchased a rifle and a sight some months earlier, but had not returned the sight when he took the malfunctioning rifle back for a refund.

In an unfortunate coincidence, a car similar to the suspect's had been seen parked in a nearby street, out of sight of the home of the man who sold the murder weapon, and on the day he had advertised the weapon. It was the suspect's dreadful misfortune that another person who had gone to the house had wrongly identified him as being there too.

Shortly before the murder, a man who looked very much like the suspect, and who had been wearing an Akubra hat like his, had tried to sell the same type of weapon as used in the murder.

Coincidentally, a blue car had been seen leaving the area shortly afterwards. The suspect had a blue car. And this man had not wanted to leave a phone number to identify him, just as the suspect had done on earlier occasions.

To make matters look even worse, the suspect had been to see the victim to get a criminal charge dropped but had been refused any assistance. He had appealed to the victim's superior but had been told on the day of the murder that his representations had failed.

And finally, the suspect had been taped describing the murder and himself as a murderer.

Could this accumulation of facts merely be "an unhappy coincidence?" Mr Adams asked. There could only be one answer – and that was in the negative.

"This, of course, is the case against the accused," he said.

ANALYSING THE EVIDENCE

First steps

[11.60] In this analysis we will be adopting the standpoint of the prosecution, and will be doing so on the basis of the evidence presented at trial, not including the additional evidence that emerged during the course of the Martin Inquiry. The aim of the prosecution, of course, was to prove that Eastman murdered Winchester. Had we been analysing the actual brief of evidence in this case, then, given the large number of witnesses, a "who's who" is likely to have been essential. We would also have needed to prepare a detailed chronology. Among other things, such a chronology would have revealed some interesting anomalies in the evidence relating to Eastman's "campaign" to rejoin the public service; his inquiries about, purchases of, and attempts to sell, the various firearms; and his attempts to have the "Russo" charges dropped. For example:

- Eastman first purchased a firearm (the Bradshaw rifle) on 10 February 1988 (which he returned), and then purchased another (the Lenaghan rifle) on 13 February 1988, which he disposed of sometime prior to 1 May 1988.
- Eastman made inquiries about a further firearm (the Thompson rifle) in June 1988, and made further inquiries about the same firearm in November 1988.
- Eastman apparently purchased the Klarenbeek rifle on or about 31 December 1988, but then attempted to sell it again on 4 or 5 January 1989.
- Eastman met with Winchester on 16 December 1988, was informed that he had been turned down by him on 21 December 1988, was apparently scouting out Winchester's home on 8 January 1989, and was informed that he had been turned down by Commissioner McAulay on 10 January 1989.
- However, on 21 December 1988, Eastman was also informed that he had succeeded in overcoming the second major obstacle to his rejoining the public service (albeit subject to a condition about the nature of the work for which he was deemed to be medically fit).

The sequence of these events would need to be accounted for in any theory of the case, and would have particular implications for any argument we might wish to make about Eastman's motive for killing Winchester. For example, the sequence of events is at odds with any argument that Eastman had killed Winchester as part of a rational (albeit extreme) plan to remove an obstacle to his return to the public service, such as that he killed Winchester in order to have his request that the Russo charges be dropped, heard and determined by another (hopefully more sympathetic) decision-maker. The sequence of events – in particular, the attempted sale of the Klarenbeek rifle on 4 or 5 January 1989 – is also inconsistent with Eastman having formed a fixed plan to kill Winchester sometime after 21 December 1988.

What the sequence of events suggests, in other words, is that if Eastman killed Winchester, then his motive must have been more emotional, and perhaps vengeful – with Winchester, for example, perhaps having come to represent an outlet for all of Eastman's accumulated frustrations and anger – than rational. The sequence of events also suggests a degree of volatility and vacillation on the part of Eastman and any plans he may have had. Similarly, the fact that Eastman was apparently scouting out Winchester's home on 8 January 1989, two days before the murder, suggests that Eastman may have been planning (or at least contemplating) the murder of Winchester prior to his receipt of Commissioner McAulay's letter on 10 January 1989. This suggests that the receipt of the letter can only have played a relatively minor role in motivating Eastman to murder Winchester.

The case map

[11.70] In preparing the case map, our first step should, as always, be to identify the **real issues** in the case. Eastman was charged with murder. There was no issue that Winchester was dead, nor that the act of someone (the "gunman") caused his death. The circumstances of the shooting also suggest that whoever the gunman was, he or she intended to kill Winchester: this is on the basis of the obvious generalisation that a person who shoots another person twice in the head at close range usually intends to kill that person. So in the circumstances of this case, proof of the actus reus would tend to carry with it, as a matter of almost irresistible inference, proof of the mens rea. This was particularly so given that Eastman's defence was that he was not the gunman, rather than that he was the gunman, but that the shooting had been accidental. This is an example of the way in which the factual theory advanced by an opponent limits the issues that need to be considered. For the same reason, the question of whether Eastman was acting in self-defence or under provocation could safely be disregarded. The only real issue, then, was one of **identity**: was Eastman the gunman?

There are a number of important differences between a case map prepared for the purposes of litigation (whether it takes the form of visual charts, prose or an outline) and the *Canberra Times* article we are using as the basis for our analysis. First, and most fundamentally, the standpoint is different: we are engaged in the process of constructing an argument, whereas the journalist who wrote the article was attempting to inform his readers about the evidence and arguments that had been used against Eastman. These are very different purposes.

Second, the article uses **headings** that are really just "tags" or "labels" – for example "Motive" and "The Threats". These are shorthand for **factual propositions**, such as that "Eastman had a motive to kill Winchester" and that "Eastman had threatened to kill Winchester (and others)". In constructing a case map it is always preferable to use factual propositions rather than tags, and this is true whether our case map takes the form of a visual chart, prose or an outline. The reasons for this are that the use of factual propositions reminds us that we are constructing an argument and that the "fact" in question is actually a proposition that must be proved if our argument is to succeed. The use of tags will also often obscure, rather than clarify, the nature of the argument we are making. For example, while we can readily understand that the tag "Motive" is shorthand for the proposition that "Eastman had a motive to kill Winchester", it is far more difficult to know what arguments the tags "Firearms", "The Sightings", "The Scientific Evidence" and "The Tapes" are shorthand for, and simply impossible to tell from the tag "Other Evidence" anything about either the nature of the evidence being referred to or the arguments that were made from that evidence.

Third, the evidence referred to in the article is mainly **organised** according to the **subject-matter** or **type** of evidence, rather than the **arguments** that were, or could have been, made from it. For example, some of the evidence referred to under the heading "The Sightings" forms part of an argument that Eastman was the purchaser of the Klarenbeek rifle; whereas the evidence of Anne Newcombe appears to form part of an argument that Eastman was checking out the area around Winchester's home as part of his preparations for killing him. Similarly, while some of "The Scientific Evidence" is relevant to prove that the Klarenbeek rifle was the murder weapon, other parts of that evidence are being used to prove that Eastman was the gunman on the basis that particles found at the crime scene matched particles that could be connected to Eastman. These are completely separate arguments.

[11.80] We can, nevertheless, use the article to identify what must (or could) have been the prosecution's main arguments in the case. There are many possible ways of drafting these, and what follows is merely one of those possibilities:

- Eastman had a **motive** to kill Winchester: there may be some question about precisely what that motive was (see the discussion at [11.60], for example), but this was undoubtedly part of the prosecution case.
- Eastman **owned the weapon** used to kill Winchester: it was clearly part of the prosecution case that the Klarenbeek rifle was the murder weapon and that Eastman was the owner of this weapon at the time of Winchester's murder.
- Eastman had been **in possession** of the murder weapon **after it had been used to shoot** Winchester: the ballistics evidence seems to do more than just show that Eastman owned the Klarenbeek rifle, it also shows that he was in possession of it after it had been fired, from which it can be inferred that he was the person who fired it.
- Eastman **threatened** to kill Winchester.
- Eastman was **planning** to kill Winchester: this argument could encompass both the fact that Eastman purchased a weapon on or about 31 December 1988, and that he was seen in the vicinity of Winchester's home on 8 January 1988.

- Eastman **admitted** killing Winchester: this is the argument being built upon the evidence from "The Tapes".

What about the "Other Evidence"? At its most basic level, this evidence is being used to prove that Eastman did not have an alibi for the murder: this is evidence of opportunity, and even though it is fairly weak evidence of opportunity, it is an argument that we should make because we can make it. But it is not necessarily the most powerful use of that evidence. Remember that Eastman was asked about his movements on the evening of 10 January 1989 the very next day, and failed to provide any details whatsoever. One might suggest that people can usually remember what they did the night before (assuming that they were not incapacitated in some way, such as through excessive alcohol consumption). If this generalisation applies to Eastman, then he did remember what he had done, but chose not to say. We might infer from this that he had something to hide, and this might provide the foundation for a consciousness of guilt inference. So this one piece of evidence can be used as the basis for two separate arguments:

- Eastman had the **opportunity** to kill Winchester.
- Eastman **believed** that he had killed Winchester.

The evidence in the article and in the court report also suggests a further argument: that Eastman had a **tendency** towards violence. The support for such an argument could be found in the evidence of Eastman stating his desire to kill various people (as, for example, in his letter to Ms Finke); in the evidence of Eastman having threatened violence against persons other than Winchester; and in the evidence of his history of violent and threatening behaviour as set out in the AAT's reasons for decision, and relied on by the AAT as a reason for finding that Eastman was not medically fit for a return to the public service. But although arguably relevant to prove Eastman's tendency towards violence, the evidence is unlikely to have been admissible for that purpose (because of the strict exclusionary rules that apply to such evidence) and, no doubt because of this, the prosecution did not seek to rely on it in this way. Instead, the evidence was put forward as relevant to motive, both to show the depth of Eastman's anger and to show why he might have thought that the Russo charges were a serious obstacle to his proposed return to the public service. For this reason, I have not charted the possible tendency argument.

This leaves us with **eight main arguments**, and you will remember that it was suggested in Chapter 6 that we should generally avoid having more than seven main arguments. If we wished to adhere to this principle we could combine some of the arguments above: for example, the two arguments relating to the murder weapon could be combined into one (very large and complex) argument; and, more readily, the admissions argument could be subsumed under the consciousness of guilt argument. In the present case, however, for the sake of conformity with how the case actually appears to have been argued, I am going to choose to breach the "rule of seven", and map each of the eight arguments above. In order to fit the various charts comprising the case map into the confines of the pages of this text, some relatively unimportant aspects of them – such as the angle or originating point of some of the connecting arrows – have had to be modified or compromised; but their essential structure remains unaltered.

[11.90]   Having identified our main arguments, the next stage of our analysis will be to create a map of the case that charts each of the arguments, starting with the case as a whole, in **Figure 11.1**. Each of our eight main arguments is a separate, independent reason for finding Eastman guilty. In this chart, I have left out the generalisations that justify the drawing of an inference from, for example, the proposition that Eastman had a motive to kill Winchester, on the basis that the relevance of each one of the propositions is self-evident and beyond question. When this is so, the inclusion of a generalisation often serves no useful purpose. This chart, and those that follow, devote relatively little attention to the defence case: this is largely because Eastman's defence mainly consisted of a simple denial of the various circumstances relied on by the prosecution, rather than an attempt to provide innocent explanations for them. In other words, there was very little defence case to map.

Some of the arguments are clearly stronger than others: for example, the admissions argument is fairly weak because there is significant doubt both about the words actually spoken by Eastman, and the meaning that should be attributed to them. Both the arguments relating to the murder weapon, on the other hand, are extremely strong, and might have provided sufficient basis for conviction regardless of what the jury thought of the other arguments. For that reason, I will begin with the two murder weapon arguments. It will also be apparent as you look at the various charts, that some of the arguments are much more complex than others. The opportunity argument, for example, is as simple as an argument can be: a single inference. Other arguments involve long chains of inferences, or several separate but convergent strands of proof.

[11.100]   The first of the arguments about the murder weapon aims to prove that Eastman **owned the weapon** used to murder Winchester. This argument has two main elements, both of which must be proved: first, that the Klarenbeek rifle was the murder weapon; and second, that Eastman was the purchaser of the Klarenbeek rifle. There are separate charts for each of these elements. In terms of proving that the Klarenbeek rifle was the murder weapon, an argument mapped in **Figure 11.2**, a difficulty faced by the prosecution was that the Klarenbeek rifle was not available for testing. However, cartridges recovered from separate and distant locations at which the Klarenbeek rifle had been fired matched cartridges found at the crime scene. Ultimately, the conclusion that the Klarenbeek rifle was the murder weapon therefore depends on both the reliability of the experts' opinions (which were not challenged) and on the inherent implausibility of a different Ruger (this one being the actual murder weapon) having been fired, by coincidence, at the very same locations at which the Klarenbeek rifle had also been fired. If the defence had had available to it the material that emerged during the Martin Inquiry, then the credibility and reliability of Mr Barnes would undoubtedly have been challenged. Indeed, mapping the material relevant to Mr Barnes's credibility would require a large and complex chart of its own.

The chart in Figure 11.2 also demonstrates the way in which the universe of alternative explanations that we might conceivably have to eliminate is limited by the explanations actually advanced by our opponent. In the Eastman case, for example, Eastman claimed that he never purchased the Klarenbeek rifle, not that he had purchased it but had subsequently sold or otherwise disposed of it. This makes it unnecessary to lead any evidence to prove that Eastman did not sell the Klarenbeek rifle prior to 10 January 1989. For this reason, I have included the evidence of Eastman's being in possession of a rifle threaded with a silencer on 4 or 5 January in Figure 11.3 as part of the argument to prove that he had purchased the Klarenbeek rifle a few days earlier, rather than as an argument to show that he had not sold it by that date.

Ideally in a case map, we will be able to include the source – usually a witness or a document – for every item of evidence on which we are relying. This has not been possible in these charts, however, simply because the reports relied on did not always identify the source of the evidence.

With the second element of the first argument, mapped in **Figure 11.3** – that Eastman was **the purchaser of the Klarenbeek rifle** – it is obvious that some of the subsidiary arguments are stronger than others. For example, the argument based on the sighting of a car "similar" to Eastman's is weak, but it does nevertheless provide some independent support for Webb's evidence that he saw Eastman at Klarenbeek's house. That said, I have deliberately mapped the evidence in such a way as to bring out the fact that there is quite a jump from the proposition that a car similar to Eastman's was parked near Klarenbeek's house and the conclusion that it was Eastman's car. Such subtleties would be lost if we had simply included a proposition to the effect that Eastman's car was seen near Klarenbeek's house. The argument based on the withdrawal of $200 is also weak, given that it is not unusual for a person to withdraw such an amount, and that the prosecution was unable to prove that the Klarenbeek rifle was purchased for $200; but again, the evidence still provides some small degree of additional support to the prosecution case.

[11.110] The second firearms argument, mapped in **Figure 11.4**, is aimed at proving that Eastman had been **in possession** of the murder weapon **after it had been used to shoot Winchester**, from which it can easily be inferred that he was the gunman. The argument is based on the matching of residue and other particles found at the crime scene and in the boot of Eastman's car. Many witnesses would have been used to prove these facts, not all of whom were identified in the reports, so for the sake of simplicity I have chosen not to include any sources for the evidence in this chart. Indeed, this chart clearly fails to capture all the complexity and detail of the expert evidence needed to prove the various factual propositions relied on. It does, nevertheless, point to the fact that the strength of the argument really derives from Eastman's inability or failure to advance any explanation at all for some of the particles found in his car and, in particular, the chopped-disc particles that the expert evidence showed could only have come from the use of a silencer. The weakness of the argument (which did not emerge until the Martin Inquiry) was that there was no proper scientific foundation for the opinion of the prosecution expert Mr Barnes that the particles from the boot were from PMC ammunition.

[11.120] As persuasive as the firearms evidence may have appeared at trial, a jury would still want to know *why* Eastman might have chosen to murder Winchester: this brings us to the motive argument. There is a common misconception that because evidence of motive is concerned with a person's mental state, it is only ever relevant to proof of the mens rea, and not to proof of the actus reus. This case shows why this is a misconception: the evidence of Eastman's motive is not being used to prove that Eastman intended to kill Winchester when he shot him because this is not a real issue in the case. Rather, the fact that Eastman had a motive to kill Winchester is being used to identify him as the gunman, the perpetrator of the actus reus. It does this by placing him in a fairly limited class of persons (persons with a motive to kill Winchester, albeit that in the case of a high-ranking police officer this class might be more numerous than in relation to a member of the general public) to which the actual gunman is likely to have belonged.

Nevertheless, in this case the motive argument is perhaps the hardest of all the arguments to chart. This is due to the difficulty in formulating, with any clarity, precisely what Eastman's motive to kill Winchester might have been. The particular argument that I have chosen to map in **Figure 11.5** places relatively little emphasis on the details of Eastman's campaign to rejoin the public service, or on the question of whether the Russo charges really were an obstacle to Eastman rejoining the public service. Instead, I have sought to show why Winchester might have been perceived by Eastman as an appropriate target for his anger at, and his desire for revenge for, the injustices he believed he had suffered. The reasons for this choice were explained earlier at [11.60] under the heading "First steps". But I do not claim that this motive argument accounts for all the evidence, or that it could not be improved. For example, the bald proposition that "Eastman had been campaigning for several years to rejoin the public service, with only limited success" clearly summarises the effect of a vast body of evidence, sourced from numerous different witnesses and documents, and which was contested by Eastman in many different ways. If we were really preparing the case for trial, then all this evidence would need to be mapped.

[11.130] The next chart, in **Figure 11.6**, maps the argument that Eastman had **threatened** to kill Winchester. It is a very simple, and powerful, argument that in the end depends entirely on the credibility of the two witnesses giving evidence in respect of the conversations in which they say Eastman made the threats. You may notice that I have not included in this chart the evidence of Eastman making more general threats; we could do so, however, by broadening the argument to something along the lines that Eastman threatened to kill someone, and to kill Winchester specifically, as in **Figure 11.7**. The chart does not include a fact that was unknown to the defence at the time of the trial but that emerged during the Martin Inquiry, namely that Dr Roantree had told the prosecution that he had "a niggling doubt" as to whether Eastman had ever uttered the words "I should shoot the bastard".

If we were instead preparing our case map in the form of an **outline**, then the outline for the argument in Figure 11.7 might look something like the outline below, which uses indentation to differentiate between different levels of the argument:

Argument: Eastman had threatened to kill someone, and to kill Winchester specifically

- *Eastman had threatened to kill someone*
    - *Eastman said he would have to kill someone so that people would see the injustice that had been done to him*
        o *Testimony of Senator Haines' staff member*
    - *Eastman had said the police were corrupt and that if it was the last thing he did "he'd get back at them"*
        o *Testimony of former neighbour, Donna Heritage*
- *Eastman had threatened to kill Winchester*
    - *Eastman said "I'll kill Winchester and I'll get the Ombudsman too"*
        o *Testimony of Eastman's lawyer, Dennis Barbara*
    - *Eastman said "I should shoot the bastard" in the context of a conversation about his interview with Winchester*
        o *Testimony of Dr Dennis Roantree*

[11.140] The next argument is that Eastman was **planning** to kill Winchester. This depends in part on proof of Eastman's purchase of a firearm after his meeting with Winchester. However, this argument has already been fully mapped in Figure 11.3, so rather than duplicating the argument, the chart in **Figure 11.8** simply cross-refers to Figure 11.3. The weakness in this argument is the leap from Eastman purchasing a firearm, or being parked near Winchester's home, to the conclusion that he was planning to kill Winchester. If, however, the jury was satisfied that Eastman had purchased the Klarenbeek rifle, and that he was parked near Winchester's home, then his failure to offer any innocent explanation for these facts (he denied them instead) might well have provided a basis for them to draw the inferences sought.

If we were preparing our case map in **prose**, then it might be written in a much more discursive and narrative-based style, and with the use of rhetorical devices (such as the asking of questions) that might be adopted in a closing address. For example, a prose version of the case map in Figure 11.8 might look something like this (as with any case map, the use of headings will help to clarify the structure of the argument; in this map, I have assumed that this is the fifth argument):

5.   Eastman was planning to kill Winchester

5.1   Eastman purchased the Klarenbeek rifle in order to kill Winchester

Eastman met with Winchester on 16 December 1988 in order to seek his assistance in having the Russo charges dropped. On 21 December 1988 he found out that Winchester had refused to help him. Ten or so days later, as has clearly been proved, Eastman purchased the Klarenbeek rifle. Eastman has failed to provide any innocent explanation for this purchase; indeed he simply denies that he was the purchaser. In these circumstances, we can infer that Eastman had no legitimate reason for the purchase. Moreover, the closeness in time of the purchase to his unsuccessful meeting with Winchester suggests that the purchase was prompted by the outcome of that meeting, and was a step in a plan that Eastman was then forming to kill Winchester as an outlet for his sense of anger and his desire for revenge.

5.2   Eastman was scouting Winchester's home in order to plan his murder of him

On the evening of 8 January 1989 Anne Newcombe was walking in Lawley Street with her mother and daughter when she saw a car parked outside the house next door to Winchester's home. There was a man in the car, who sought to conceal his face as she passed. Mrs Newcombe was suspicious about the car, and returned home via the same route. The car was still there. She got a good look at it, and later identified it as a Mazda 626 sedan, "sort of a turquoisey-bluey-green" in colour. Mrs Newcombe also made a note of the registration number, intending to write it down on her return home, but she was distracted by a phone call; she eventually remembered it as YPQ 038. But the car with that registration number, which was owned by a Mrs Betty Fitzgerald, was cream in colour, and it was locked in its garage in Yarralumla all weekend. So if it wasn't Mrs Fitzgerald's car parked next door to Mr Winchester's home, whose car was it? The mystery car shared a remarkable number of similarities with Eastman's car: like his, it was a Mazda 626 sedan; like his, it was blue in colour; and like his, the first letter of its registration number was Y, the last digit was 8, and it had a P and an 0 in between. On the basis of these similarities, it can

be inferred that the car was Eastman's, and that it was Eastman who was inside it. And what
was Eastman doing there? In circumstances where Eastman has failed to provide any innocent
explanation for his presence, we can only infer that he had found out where Winchester lived, and
was there to scout the location at which he was planning to murder him.

As with the argument about Eastman's threats, the planning argument could be broadened to include an argument that Eastman was planning to kill someone, as in **Figure 11.9**. We can see that this chart also uses evidence that was used in Figure 11.3 – namely the evidence of the other firearms purchases in 1988 – but it uses that evidence for a different purpose. This merely reinforces the point that the same evidence will often be relevant for more than one purpose.

[11.150] Arguments based on **admissions** are often very powerful on the basis that a person would not usually admit to doing something unless they actually did it. In this case, too, if the evidence had clearly established that Eastman had admitted killing Winchester, this would be one of the strongest arguments against him. The weakness of the argument in this case arises from the fact that the alleged admissions are so equivocal and ambiguous, as is reflected in **Figure 11.10**. In the Martin Inquiry, Eastman also argued that the recordings should have been excluded because they were the product of improper police conduct, namely the harassment of Eastman by the police during the period 1989-1991. Martin AJ agreed that during that period "police conduct was deliberately aimed at harassing [Eastman] with a view to upsetting him and provoking him into reacting", and that the conduct was for that reason improper. However, Martin AJ did not accept that the alleged admissions were made as a result of that conduct.

[11.160] The final two charts map the arguments we can make out of the fact that Eastman failed to account for his whereabouts at the time of the murder. Because *lack* of **opportunity** (that is, an unbroken alibi) is necessarily fatal to a case, it is always worth attempting to prove opportunity, even when the particular opportunity argument is a weak one, such as in the present case: see **Figure 11.11**. The **consciousness of guilt** argument is much stronger: see **Figure 11.12**. In Australia, such an argument would need to be accompanied by a direction about lies, of the kind mandated by the High Court in cases such as *Edwards v The Queen* (1993) 197 CLR 316 and *Zoneff v The Queen* (2000) 200 CLR 234; [2000] HCA 28.

[11.170] The case map provides a ready draft for a **closing address**. In this case, for example, the address could simply follow the structure of the case map, enumerating and explaining each of the main reasons the jury should find that Eastman had killed Winchester. However, the logical structure provided by the case map will not necessarily be the most persuasive form for the closing address to take. In the *Eastman* case itself, for example, the prosecutor adopted the theme of "The Coincidences". One can imagine that this might have had a particularly strong impact in a case where Eastman's sense of persecution and injustice would no doubt have been communicated to the jury time and time again: the prosecutor was effectively saying that if Eastman is being wrongly prosecuted, as he claims, then this is due to the most extraordinary series of coincidences that one could possibly imagine.

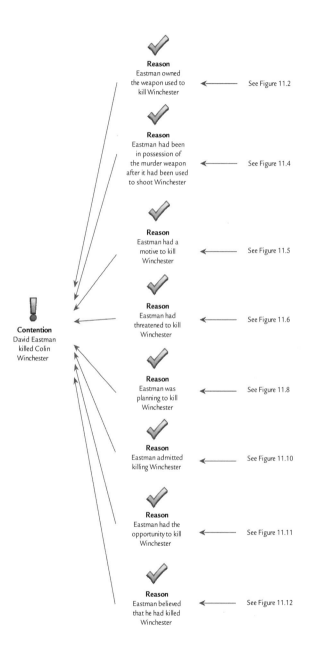

Figure 11.1: The main arguments

Figure 11.2: Eastman owned the murder weapon –
the Klarenbeek rifle was the murder weapon

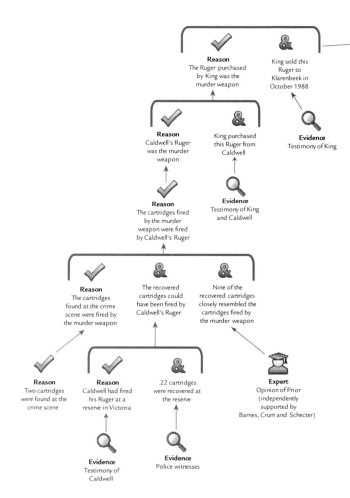

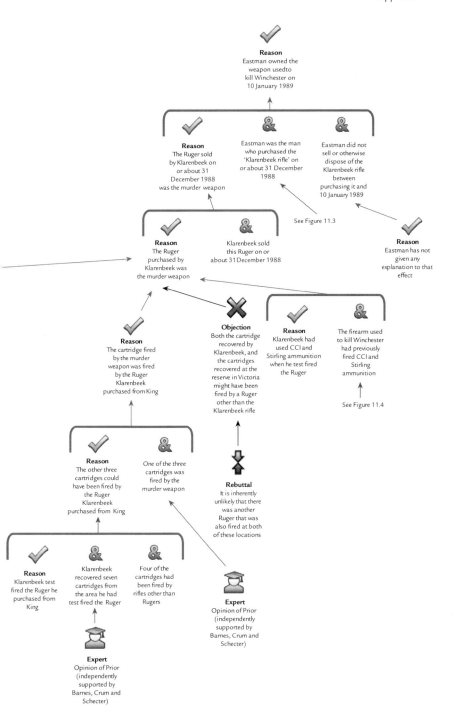

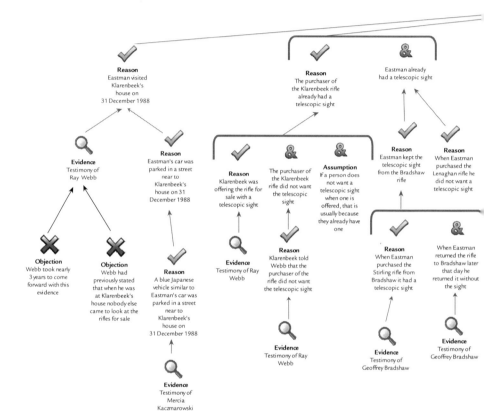

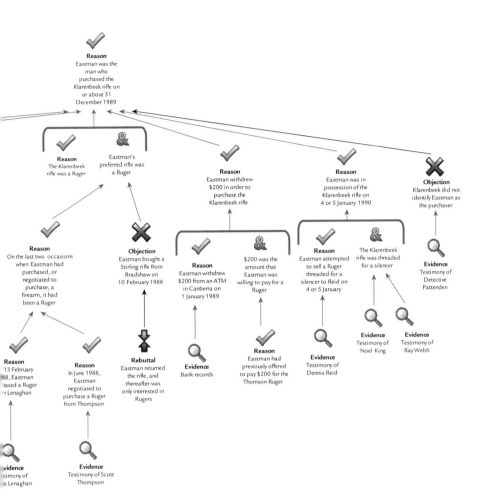

Figure 11.3: Eastman owned the murder weapon – Eastman purchased the Klarenbeek rifle

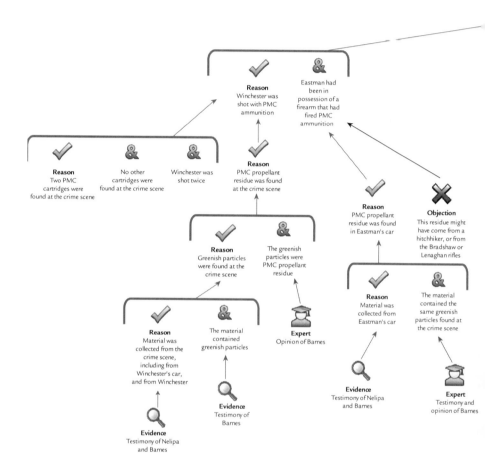

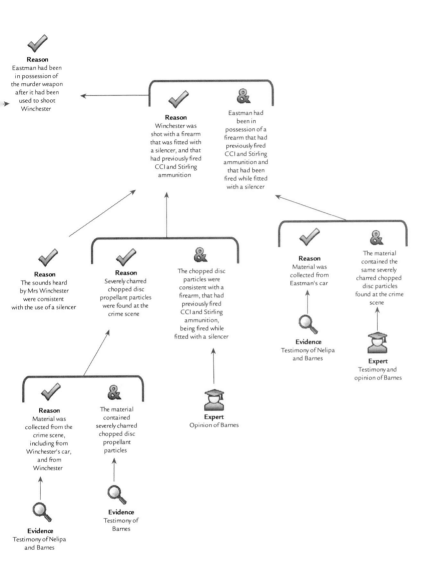

Figure 11.4: Eastman had been in possession of the murder weapon after it had been used to shoot Winchester

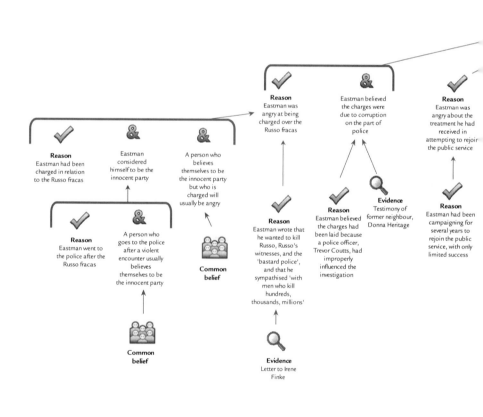

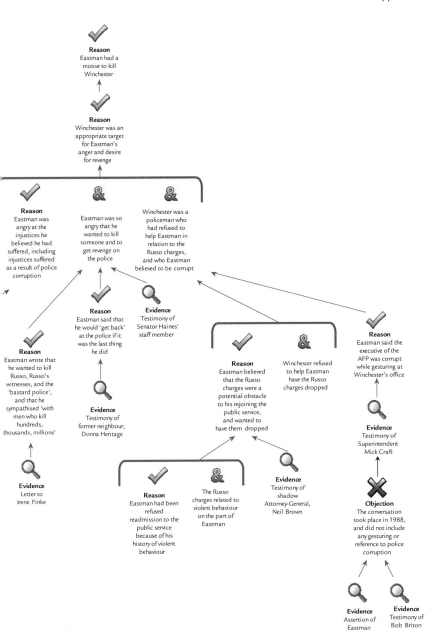

Figure 11.5: Eastman had a motive to kill Winchester

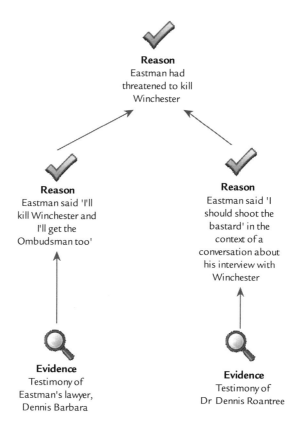

Figure 11.6: Eastman had threatened to kill Winchester

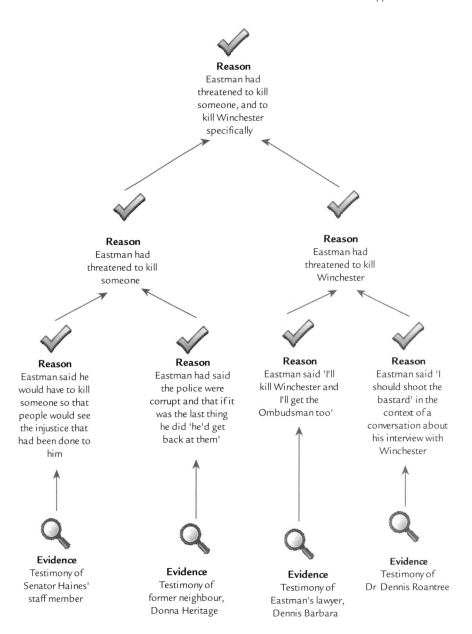

Figure 11.7: Eastman had threatened to kill someone, and to kill Winchester specifically

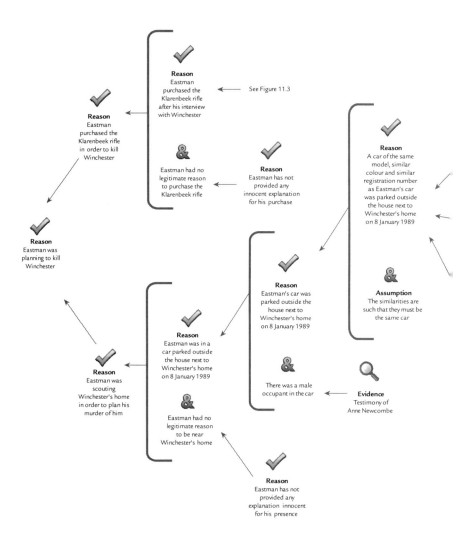

Figure 11.8: Eastman was planning to kill Winchester

Reason
A Mazda 626
sedan was parked
outside the house
next to Winchester's
home on 8 January 1989

Evidence
Testimony of
Anne Newcombe

Eastman's car
was a Mazda 626 sedan

Reason
The car parked outside
the house next to
Winchester's home on
8 January 1989 was
'turquoisey-bluey-green'

Evidence
Testimony of
Anne Newcombe

Eastman's car
was blue

Reason
A car with a
registration number
that a witness
mistakenly recalled
as YPQ 038 was
parked outside the
house next to
Winchester's home
on 8 January 1989

Assumption
When someone
makes a mistake in
recalling a registration
number the actual
number is likely to be
similar to the number
they recalled

Reason
A car with a
registration number
that a witness
recalled as
YPQ 038 was
parked outside the
house next to
Winchester's home
on 8 January 1989

Evidence
Testimony of
Anne Newcombe

The car with
registration
number YPQ 038
was not parked
outside the house
next to
Winchester's
home on
8 January 1989

Evidence
Testimony of
Betty Fitzgerald

Reason
A car with a
registration number
similar to YPQ 038
(but not YPQ 038)
was parked outside
the house next to
Winchester's home
on 8 January 1989

The registration
number of
Eastman's car
was YMP 028

Assumption
YPQ 038 and
YMP 028 are
similar

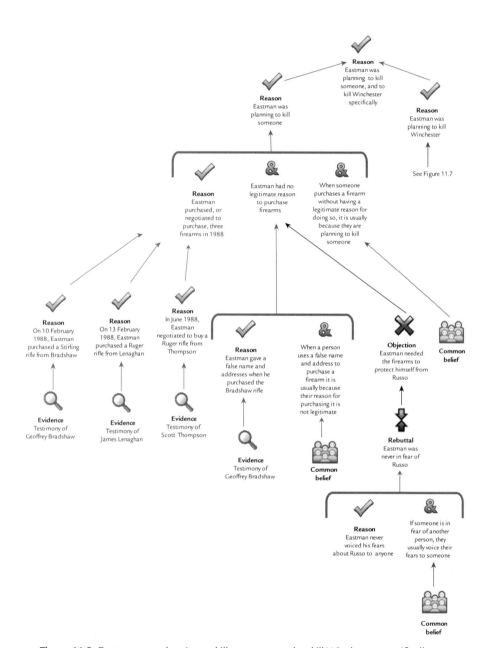

Figure 11.9: Eastman was planning to kill someone, and to kill Winchester specifically

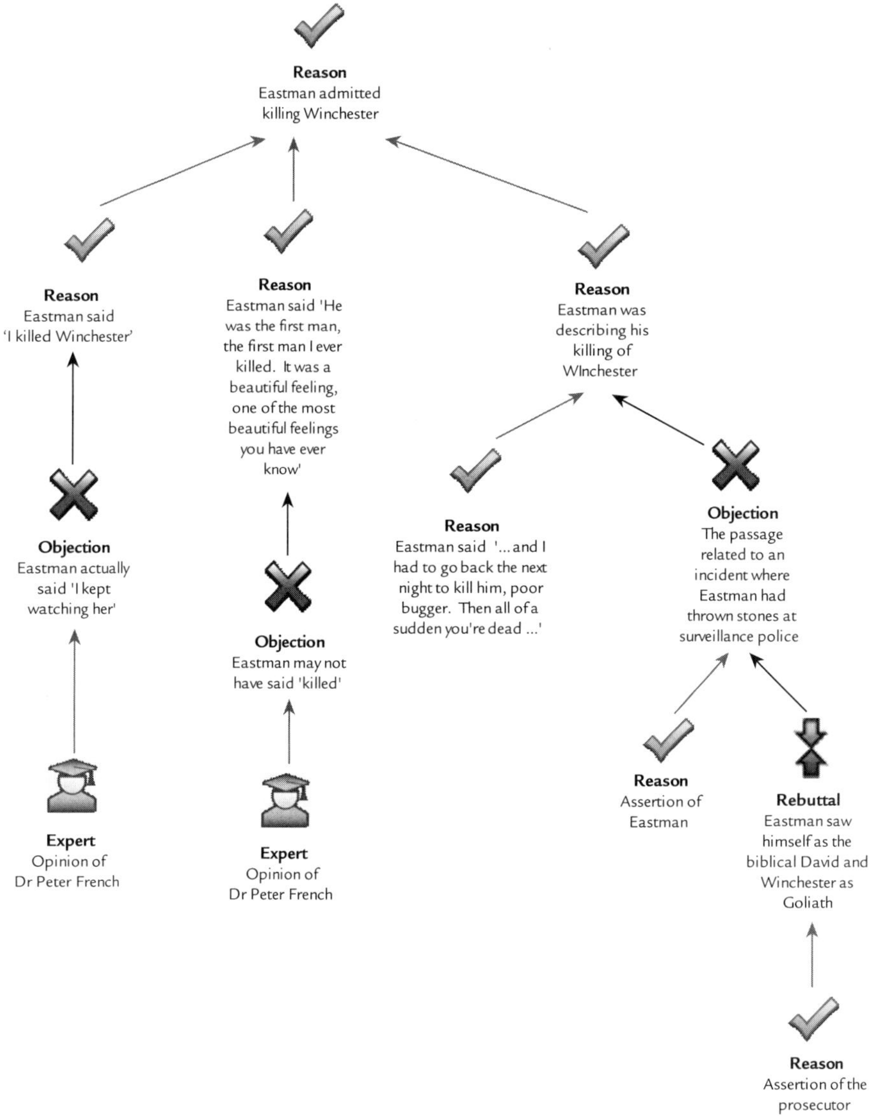

Figure 11.10: Eastman admitted killing Winchester

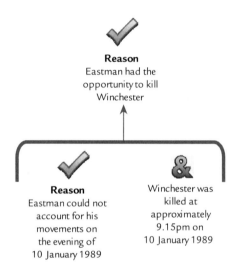

Figure 11.11: Eastman had the opportunity to kill Winchester

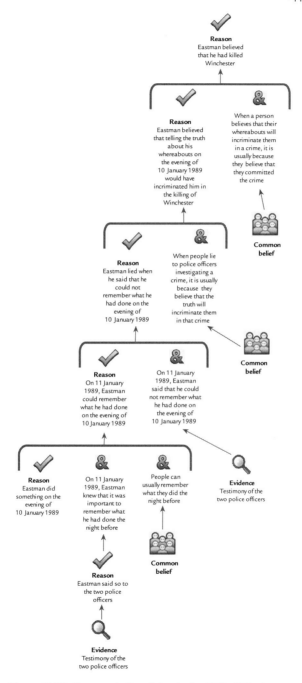

Figure 11.12: Eastman believed that he had killed Winchester

SIX COMMON CHARTING MISTAKES

[11.180] In my experience of teaching charting, there at least six mistakes that are commonly made in the preparation of charts:

1. leaps in logic;
2. reasoning in the wrong direction;
3. reasoning in the box;
4. treating co-premises as a series of inferences;
5. treating co-premises as independent arguments; and
6. treating independent arguments as co-premises.

The first two mistakes concern the relationships between factual propositions at different levels of a chart; in a chart where the reasoning goes from bottom to top, as in most of the charts in this text, they are about the vertical relationships. The final three mistakes all concern the horizontal relationships in the chart – that is, the relationship between factual propositions at the same level of the chart. The third mistake can relate to either the vertical or the horizontal relationships, or both.

[11.190] Whether something constitutes a **leap in logic** will often be a question of degree and judgment. In Figure 11.3, for example, the proposition that "Eastman visited Klarenbeek's house on 31 December 1988" is shown as being inferred, in part, from the proposition that "Eastman's car was in a street near to Klarenbeek's house on 31 December 1988". If we were being really precise, however, then there are at least two intermediate inferences that need to be drawn between these two propositions, such as that it was Eastman who parked his car in the street near to Klarenbeek's house and that he did so for the purpose of visiting someone in a nearby house. But when we look at the chart we can, hopefully, intuitively understand why the fact of Eastman's car being in the street near Klarenbeek's house makes it more likely that he visited Klarenbeek, without needing to have the intermediate inferences spelt out.

Similarly, in Figure 11.5, there is something of a leap from the propositions that "Eastman had been refused readmission to the public service because of his history of violent behaviour" and "The Russo charges related to violent behaviour on the part of Eastman" to the proposition that "Eastman believed that the unjust charges were a potential obstacle to his rejoining the public service, and wanted to have them dropped". Nevertheless, we can again probably intuitively understand the connection between the propositions without having to have the reasoning spelt out in all its detail. When this is the case, it may not be worth the extra effort required to tease out every single step in the inferential process.

A leap in logic does become problematic, however, when it is *not* possible to understand why a particular inference should be drawn. So with the example of Eastman's car, if the relevant section of Figure 11.3 had instead looked like the chart on the left of **Figure 11.13** or, even more obviously, like the chart on the right of Figure 11.13, the argument would have been much harder, if not impossible, to follow. With these two versions of the chart, someone unfamiliar with the case might well wonder why it is that the factual proposition about a car similar to Eastman's renders more probable the inference apparently being drawn from that fact. The test is really this: would someone else be able to understand why this inference should be drawn from that fact? Unlike magicians, we can't just pull a rabbit out of the hat: our audience needs to be able to understand exactly how the rabbit got there.

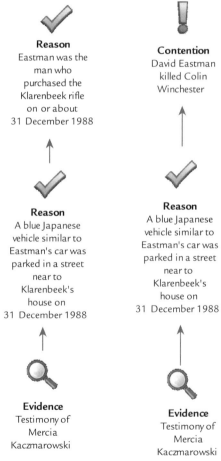

Figure 11.13: Leaps in logic

In the example we are working with, the leap in logic can, as it happens, be remedied by spelling out the intermediate inferences. At other times, however, it may not be possible to remedy the leap: some sort of leap may be unavoidable. This is usually a sign that the argument is fairly weak. This was the case, for example, with some of the inferences in Schum's analysis of the Sacco and Vanzetti case depicted in Figure 7.7. It is also probably the case with the inference being drawn in Figure 11.3 from Eastman's withdrawal of $200 from an ATM in Canberra: without any evidence to eliminate the many other possible explanations for this withdrawal, we are unable to avoid leaping from the fact of his withdrawal to its inferred purpose.

[11.200] The second common mistake is to **reason in the wrong direction**. This typically involves placing the item of evidence relatively high in the chart, and then reasoning down (or both down and up) from that, rather than in a single direction from the evidence up to the material facts or facts in issue. **Figure 11.14** shows some examples of this mistake, based on three of the arguments in Figure 11.3. Although the arrows suggest that the reasoning is going in a single direction from top to bottom, in fact the reasoning goes both up from the evidence to the main argument being proved, and down from the evidence to the inferences that are needed to connect the evidence to the main argument. This is confusing!

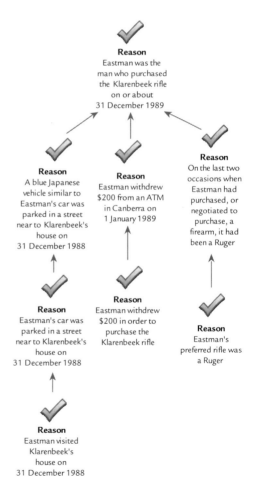

Figure 11.14: Reasoning in the wrong direction

[11.210] The third common mistake is to **reason in the box**. **Figure 11.15** shows three examples of this based on the arguments in Figure 11.3. All of the examples are problematic in two ways: first, because they contain two distinct co-premises, which might need to be proved by distinct items of evidence from different sources, and each of which could be the subject of independent attack; and second, because they not only contain the propositions from which an inference is to be drawn, but also the inference itself. In other words, all the reasoning is within the "box", rather than proceeding from one "box" to another.

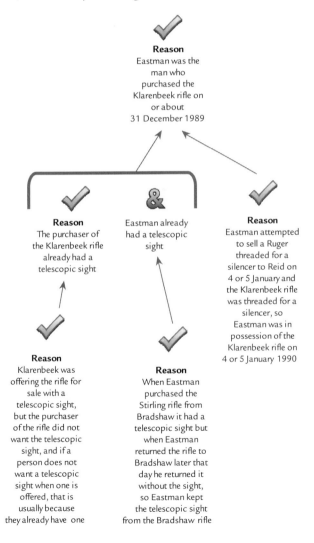

Figure 11.15: Reasoning in the box

Sometimes, however, treating two or more co-premises as a single proposition can be convenient and time-saving. In Figure 11.6, for example, there is a proposition that "Eastman said 'I should shoot the bastard' in the context of a conversation about his interview with Winchester". This could have been broken down into two separate propositions: that Eastman said "I should shoot the bastard", and that he did so in the context of a conversation about his interview with Winchester. Although I chose not to do so, there would have been some advantage in "unpacking" the box in this way, in that it would have highlighted the fact that Eastman could have dealt with this evidence in two ways: either by denying that he spoke the words, or by denying that the words referred to Winchester.

By contrast, I did choose to unpack the proposition in Figure 11.8 that "A car of the same model, similar colour and similar registration number as Eastman's car was parked outside the house next to Winchester's home on 8 January 1989" into three separate elements relating to the model, colour and registration number of the car. This was to highlight the fact that there were three distinct similarities between the car seen by Anne Newcombe and the car owned by Eastman. As with leaps of logic, the extent to which we should "unpack" compound factual propositions into their constituent elements really depends on the extent to which there are advantages to be gained from doing so.

[11.220] The fourth common mistake is to include **co-premises** in a chart as if they were **a series of inferences**. This involves placing in a vertical relationship propositions that actually have a horizontal relationship. **Figure 11.16** rearranges part of the argument about the telescopic sight from Figure 11.3. In this version of the argument, the proposition that "When Eastman returned the

Figure 11.16: Co-premises as a series of inferences

Reason
Eastman was the man who purchased the Klarenbeek rifle on or about 31 December 1989

↑

Reason
The purchaser of the Klarenbeek rifle already had a telescopic sight

↑

Reason
Eastman already had a telescopic sight

↑

Reason
Eastman kept the telescopic sight from the Bradshaw rifle

↑

Reason
When Eastman returned the rifle to Bradshaw later that day he returned it without the sight

↑

Reason
When Eastman purchased the Stirling rifle from Bradshaw it had a telescopic sight

rifle to Bradshaw later that day he returned it without the sight" is shown as being inferred from the proposition below it, that "When Eastman purchased the Stirling rifle from Bradshaw it had a telescopic sight". Similarly, the proposition that "Eastman already had a telescopic sight" is shown as a reason for inferring that "The purchaser of the Klarenbeek rifle already had a telescopic sight". Of course, it is not. This category of mistake is easily uncovered: we can just look at a factual proposition at any level of the chart and ask ourselves: how can we know that this proposition is true? If the factual proposition below it does not provide the answer, then there is a problem with the way in which we have structured our argument.

[11.230] The fifth common mistake is to show **co-premises as independent arguments**; or, to put it another way, to treat conjunctive propositions as if they were convergent. **Figure 11.17** rearranges the argument about the telescopic sight and Eastman's preference for Rugers from Figure 11.3. In this version of the arguments, the proposition that "The purchaser of the Klarenbeek rifle already had a telescopic sight" is shown as being independent of the proposition that "Eastman already had a telescopic sight", whereas it is clear that the relevance of each proposition is entirely dependent on proof of the other. On its own, the fact that Eastman may have had a telescopic sight means nothing. Similarly, Eastman's apparent preference for Rugers is meaningless without the evidence that the Klarenbeek rifle was a Ruger.

[11.240] The sixth common mistake is the reverse of the third – namely to show **independent arguments as co-premises**; or, to put it another way, to treat convergent propositions as if they were conjunctive. **Figure 11.18** shows the top level of factual propositions in Figure 11.3 as a series of co-premises. Depicting them in this way suggests that in order for the argument to succeed, each of the propositions must be accepted as proved: in fact, of course, the jury would be entitled to reject some and still find that Eastman was the purchaser of the Klarenbeek rifle on the basis of those that remained.

In the end, of course, we should be pragmatic about "mistakes": a case map is not an end in itself, and the construction of a chart that has some logical imperfections is still likely to assist us in preparing our matter for trial.

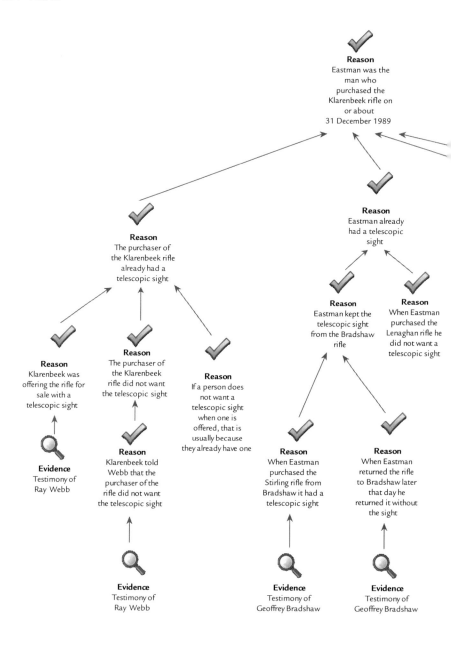

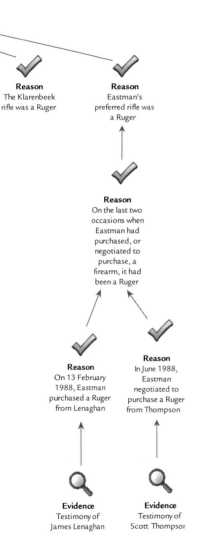

Reason
The Klarenbeek
rifle was a Ruger

Reason
Eastman's
preferred rifle was
a Ruger

Reason
On the last two
occasions when
Eastman had
purchased, or
negotiated to
purchase, a
firearm, it had
been a Ruger

Reason
On 13 February
1988, Eastman
purchased a Ruger
from Lenaghan

Reason
In June 1988,
Eastman
negotiated to
purchase a Ruger
from Thompson

Evidence
Testimony of
James Lenaghan

Evidence
Testimony of
Scott Thompson

Figure 11.17: Co-premises as independent arguments

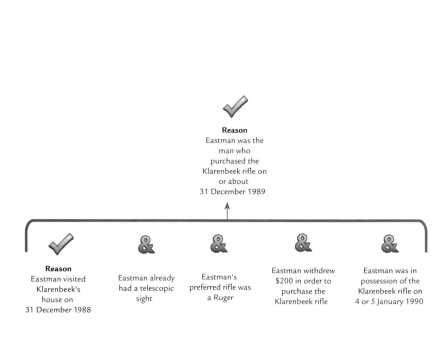

Figure 11.18: Independent arguments as co-premises

Bibliography

Abimbola K, "Questions and Answers: The Logic of Preliminary Fact Investigation" (2002) 29 *Journal of Law and Society* 533.

Adamson T, *Criminal Pretrial Advocacy* (Vandeplas Publishing, 2013).

Allen R, "The Nature of Juridical Proof" (1991) 13 *Cardozo Law Review* 373 (1991a).

Allen R, "The State of Mind Necessary for a Juridical Verdict" (1991) 13 *Cardozo Law Review* 485 (1991b).

Anderson J, Williams N and Clegg L, *The New Law of Evidence: Annotation and Commentary on the Uniform Evidence Acts* (2nd ed, LexisNexis Butterworths, Sydney, 2009).

Anderson T, "Refocusing the New Evidence Scholarship" (1991) 13 *Cardozo Law Review* 783.

Anderson T, "On Generalizations I: A Preliminary Exploration" (1999) 40 *South Texas Law Review* 455.

Anderson T, Schum D and Twining W, *Analysis of Evidence* (2nd ed, Cambridge University Press, Cambridge, 2005).

Anderson T J, "Visualization Tools and Argument Schemes Revisited" (2007) 6 *Law, Probability and Risk* 141.

Anderson T and Twining W, *Analysis of Evidence: How to do Things with Facts* (Weidenfeld and Nicholson, London, 1991).

Bench-Capon T J M, "Persuasion in Practical Argument Using Value-based Argumentation Frameworks" (2003) 13 *Journal of Logic and Computation* 429.

Bennett P, "An English Point of View" in Rumsey D (ed), *Master Advocates' Handbook* (2nd ed, National Institute for Trial Advocacy, Notre Dame, 1988).

Berger M, Mitchell J and Clark R, *Pretrial Advocacy: Planning, Analysis and Strategy* (4th ed, Wolters Kluwer Law & Business, New York, 2013).

Bex F J, *Arguments, Stories and Criminal Evidence: A Formal Hybrid Theory* (Springer, New York, c2011).

Bex F, Prakken H, Reed C and Walton D, "Towards a Formal Account of Reasoning About Evidence: Argumentation Schemes and Generalisations" (2003) 11 *Artificial Intelligence and Law* 125.

Bex F, van den Braak S, van Oostendorp H, Prakken H and Vreeswijk G, "Sense-making Software for Crime Investigation: How to Combine Stories and Arguments?" 6 *Law, Probability and Risk* 145.

Bex F J, van Koppen P J, Prakken H, and Verheij B, "A Hybrid Formal Theory of Arguments, Stories and Criminal Evidence" (2010) 18 *Artificial Intelligence and Law* 123.

Bex F and Verheij B, "Legal Stories and the Process of Proof" (2013) 21 *Artificial Intelligence and Law* 253.

Bex F and Walton D, "Burdens and Standards of Proof for Inference to the Best Explanation: Three Case Studies" (2012) 11 *Law, Probability and Risk* 113.

Binder D and Bergman P, *Fact Investigation: From Hypothesis to Proof* (West Publishing, St Paul, 1984).

Borgelt C and Kruse R, "Probabilistic Networks and Inferred Causation" (1997) 18 *Cardozo Law Review* 2001.

Boyle C, "A Principled Approach to Relevance: The Cheshire Cat in Canada", Chapter 3 in Roberts and Redmayne (2007).

Brewer S, "Logocratic Method and the Analysis of Arguments in Evidence" (2011) 10 *Law, Probability and Risk* 175.

Cohen L J, *The Probable and the Provable* (Clarendon Press, Oxford, 1977).

Cohen L J, "Should a Jury Say What It Believes or What It Accepts?" (1991) 13 *Cardozo Law Review* 465.

Cottrell S, *Critical Thinking Skills: Developing Effective Analysis and Argument* (2nd ed, Palgrave Macmillan, Basingstoke, 2011).

Curthoys J and Kendall C, *Advocacy: An Introduction* (LexisNexis Butterworths, Sydney, 2006).

Davies G L, "Common Pitfalls in Decision Making" (2002) 11 *Journal of Judicial Administration* 130.

Dawid P, Twining W and Vasilaki M (eds), *Evidence, Inference and Enquiry* (Oxford University Press, Oxford, 2011).

Eco U and Sebeok T (eds), *The Sign of Three: Dupin, Holmes, Peirce* (Indiana University Press, Bloomington, 1983).

Eggleston R, *Evidence, Proof and Probability* (2nd ed, Weidenfeld and Nicholson, London, 1983).

Friedman R, "Infinite Strands, Infinitesimally Thin: Storytelling, Bayesianism, Hearsay and Other Evidence" (1992) 14 *Cardozo Law Review* 79.

Gabby D M et al (eds), *Approaches to Legal Rationality* (Springer, New York, c2010).

Gans J and Palmer A, *Uniform Evidence* (2nd ed, Oxford University Press, Melbourne, 2014).

Glissan J, *Advocacy in Practice* (5th ed, LexisNexis Butterworths, Sydney, 2011).

Goldman A, *Knowledge in a Social World* (Clarendon Press, Oxford, 1999).

Goldman A, "Quasi-objective Bayesianism and Legal Evidence" (2002) 42 *Jurimetrics* 237.

Hamer D, "The Civil Standard of Proof Uncertainty: Probability, Belief and Justice" (1994) 16 *Sydney Law Journal* 506.

Hamer D, "The Continuing Saga of the Chamberlain Direction: Untangling the Cables and Chains of Criminal Proof" (1997) 23 *Monash Law Review* 43.

Hamer D, "'Chance Would be a Fine Thing': Proof of Causation and Quantum in an Unpredictable World" (1999) 23 *Melbourne University Law Review* 557.

Hamer D, "'Hoist with His Own Petard'? Guilty Lies and Ironic Inferences in Criminal Proof" (2001) 54 *Current Legal Problems* 377.

Hamer D, "The Structure and Strength of the Propensity Inference: Singularity, Linkage and the Other Evidence" (2003) 29 *Monash University Law Review* 137.

Hampel G, Brimer E and Kune R, *Advocacy Manual: The Complete Guide to Persuasive Advocacy* (Australian Advocacy Institute, Melbourne, 2008).

Hay B L, "Les Demoiselles d'Evanston: On the Aesthetics of the Wigmore Chart" (2008) 7 *Law, Probability and Risk* 211.

Heydon J D, *Cross on Evidence* (9th Australian ed, LexisNexis Butterworths, Sydney, 2013).

Hodgson D, "The Scales of Justice: Probability and Proof in Legal Fact-finding" (1995) 69 *Australian Law Journal* 731.

Hunter J, Cameron C and Henning T, *Litigation II: Evidence and Criminal Process* (7th ed, LexisNexis Butterworths, Sydney, 2005).

Hunter J and Cronin K, *Evidence, Advocacy and Ethical Practice: A Criminal Trial Commentary* (Butterworths, Sydney, 1995).

Imwinkelried E, "The Development of Professional Judgment in Law School Litigation Courses: The Concepts of Trial Theory and Theme" (1986) 39 *Vanderbilt Law Review* 59.

Jackson J, "Analysing the New Evidence Scholarship: Towards a New Conception of the Law of Evidence" (1996) 16 *Oxford Journal of Legal Studies* 309.

Kadane J and Schum D, *A Probabilistic Analysis of the Sacco and Vanzetti Evidence* (John Wiley & Sons, New York, 1996).

Kaptein H, Prakken H, and Verheij B (eds), *Legal Evidence and Proof: Statistics, Stories, Logic* (Ashgate, Farnham, c2009).

Keppens J, "Argument Diagram Extraction from Evidential Bayesian Networks" (2012) 20 *Artificial Intelligence and Law* 109.

Krehel G, "Chronology Best Practices" (article available at www.casesoft.com).

Lempert R, "The New Evidence Scholarship: Analyzing the Process of Proof" (1986) 66 *Boston University Law Review* 439.

Lempert R, "Telling Tales in Court: Trial Procedure and the Story Model" (1991) 13 *Cardozo Law Review* 559.

Leubsdorf J, "Presuppositions of Evidence Law" (2006) 91 *Iowa Law Review* 1209.

Ligertwood A and Edmond, G, *Australian Evidence: A Principled Approach to the Common Law and the Uniform Acts* (5th ed, LexisNexis Butterworths, Sydney, 2010).

Ligertwood A, "Evidence and the Practical Process of Proof", Chapter 9 in Roberts and Redmayne (2007).

Lowrance J D, "Graphical Manipulation of Evidence in Structured Arguments" (2007) 6 *Law, Probability and Risk* 225.

Lubet S, "The Trial as a Persuasive Story" (1990) 14 *American Journal of Trial Advocacy* 77.

Lubet S, *Modern Trial Advocacy: Analysis and Practice* (4th rev ed, National Institute for Trial Advocacy, Boulder, 2013).

Lupacchini R and Corsi G (eds), *Deduction, Computation, Experiment: Exploring the Effectiveness of Proof* (Springer, Berlin, c2008).

Macagno F and Walton D, "Common Knowledge in Legal Reasoning About Evidence" (2005) 3 *International Commentary on Evidence* 1035.

Macagno F and Walton D, "Presumptions in Legal Argumentation" (2012) 25 *Ratio Juris* 271.

Mack K, "Teaching Evidence: Inference, Proof and Diversity" (2000) 11 *Legal Education Review* 57.

Malsch M and Nijboer J, *Complex Cases. Perspectives on the Netherlands Criminal Justice System* (Thela Thesis, Amsterdam, 1999).

Mason S, *Electronic Evidence* (3rd ed, LexisNexis Butterworths, London, 2012).

Mauet T and McCrimmon L, *Fundamentals of Trial Techniques* (3rd Australian ed, Thomson Reuters, Sydney, 2011).

McLellan P, "Who is Telling the Truth: Psychology, Common Sense and the Law" (2006) 80 *Australian Law Journal* 655.

Minto B, *The Pyramid Principle: Logic in Writing and Thinking* (3rd ed, Financial Times Prentice Hall, London, 2002).

Morris A, "Preparing Briefs Made Simple" (1991) 21 *Queensland Law Society Journal* 261.

Nesson C, "The Evidence or the Event? On Judicial Proof and the Acceptability of Verdicts" (1985) 98 *Harvard Law Review* 1357.

Nesson C, "Agent Orange Meets the Blue Bus: Factfinding at the Frontier of Knowledge" (1986) 66 *Boston University Law Review* 521.

Odgers S, *Uniform Evidence Law* (11th ed, Thomson Reuters, Sydney, 2014).

Ohlbaum E, "Basic Instinct: Case Theory and Courtroom Performance" (1993) 66 *Temple Law Review* 1.

Palmer A, "The Scope of the Similar Fact Rule" (1994) 16 *Adelaide Law Review* 161.

Palmer A, "Hearsay: A Definition that Works" (1995) 14 *University of Tasmania Law Review* 29 (1995a).

Palmer A, "*Pfennig v R*: Two Versions of the Similar Fact Rule" (1995) 20 *Melbourne University Law Review* 600 (1995b).

Palmer A, "Guilt and the Consciousness of Guilt: The Use of Lies, Flight and Other 'Guilty' Behaviour in the Investigation and Prosecution of Crime" (1997) 21 *Melbourne University Law Review* 95 (1997a).

Palmer A, "*R v Elliott*" (1997) 21 *Melbourne University Law Review* 331 (1997b).

Palmer A, "Propensity, Coincidence and Context: The Use and Admissibility of Extraneous Misconduct Evidence in Child Sexual Abuse Cases" (1999) 4 *Newcastle Law Review* 46.

Palmer A, "A Proof-Oriented Model of Evidence Teaching" (2002) 13 *Legal Education Review* 109.

Palmer, A, "Why and How to Teach Proof" (2011) 33 *Sydney Law Review* 563.

Pennington N and Hastie R, "A Cognitive Theory of Juror Decision Making: The Story Model" (1991) 13 *Cardozo Law Review* 519.

Pollock J, "Defeasible Reasoning" (1987) 11 *Cognitive Science* 481.

Pollock J, *Cognitive Carpentry: A Blueprint for How to Build a Person* (MIT Press, Cambridge, Massachusetts, 1995).

Pollock J, "Perceiving and Reasoning about a Changing World" (1998) 14 *Computational Intelligence* 498.

Prakken H, Reed C and Walton D, "Argumentation Schemes and Generalisations in Reasoning about Evidence" in *Proceedings of the 9th International Conference on Artificial Intelligence and Law* (ACM Press, New York, 2003).

Prakken H, "Analysing Reasoning about Evidence with Formal Models of Argumentation" (2004) 3 *Law, Probability and Risk* 33.

Redmayne M, "Objective Probability and the Assessment of Evidence" (2003) 2 *Law, Probability and Risk* 275.

Redmayne M, "Analysing Evidence Case Law", Chapter 4 in Roberts and Redmayne (2007).

Roberts G, *Evidence: Proof and Practice* (LBC Information Services, Sydney, 1998).

Roberts P, "Rethinking the Law of Evidence: A Twenty-first Century Agenda for Teaching and Research", Chapter 1   in Roberts and Redmayne (2007) (first published in (2002) 55 *Current Legal Problems* 297).

Roberts P and Redmayne M (eds), *Innovations in Evidence and Proof: Integrating Theory, Research and Teaching* (Hart Publishing, Oxford, 2007).

Robertson B, "John Henry Wigmore and Arthur Allan Thomas: An Example of Wigmorian Analysis" (1990) 20 *Victoria University of Wellington Law Review* 181.

Rose III, C H and Underwood J M, *Fundamental Pretrial Advocacy: A Strategic Guide to Effective Litigation* (2nd ed, Thomson/West, St Paul, c2012).

Ross D, *Advocacy* (2nd ed, Cambridge University Press, Melbourne, 2007).

Ruggiero V R, *Beyond Feelings: A Guide to Critical Thinking* (8th ed, McGraw-Hill Higher Education, Boston, c2008).

Schum D, *Evidence and Inference for the Intelligence Analyst* (2 volumes, University Press of America, Lanham, 1987).

Schum D, "Hearsay from a Layperson" (1992) 14 *Cardozo Law Review* 1.

Schum D, *Evidential Foundations of Probabilistic Reasoning* (John Wiley & Sons, New York, 1994).

Schum D and Tillers P, "Marshalling Evidence for Adversary Litigation" (1991) 13 *Cardozo Law Review* 657.

Scragg R and Cull C, "The Introduction of the Professional Legal Studies Course in New Zealand" (1988) 6 *Journal of Professional Legal Education* 117.

Selby H, *Winning Advocacy: Preparation, Questions, Argument* (2nd ed, Oxford University Press, Melbourne, 2004).

Selby H, *Advocacy: Preparation and Performance* (Federation Press, Sydney, 2009).

Stanfield A, *Computer Forensics, Electronic Discovery and Electronic Evidence* (LexisNexis Butterworths, Sydney, 2009).

Stuesser L, *An Introduction to Advocacy* (2nd ed, Thomson Reuters, Sydney, 2011).

Thomson J J, "Liability and Individualized Evidence" (1986) 49 *Law and Contemporary Problems* 199.

Tillers P and Schum D, "A Theory of Preliminary Fact Investigation" (1991) 24 *University of California, Davis Law Review* 931.

Tillers P, "Discussion Paper: The Structure and the Logic of Proof in Trials" (2011) 10 *Law, Probability and Risk* 1.

Tillers P and Schum D, "Hearsay Logic" (1992) 76 *Minnesota Law Review* 813.

Toulmin S, *The Uses of Argument* (Updated ed, Cambridge University Press, Cambridge, 2003).

Toulmin S, Reike R and Janik A, *An Introduction to Reasoning* (2nd ed, Macmillan, New York, 1984).

Twining W, "Taking Facts Seriously" (1984) 34 *Journal of Legal Education* 22 (reprinted as Chapter 2 in Twining (1990)).

Twining W, *Theories of Evidence: Bentham and Wigmore* (Weidenfeld and Nicholson, London, 1985).

Twining W, *Rethinking Evidence: Exploratory Essays* (Basil Blackwell, Oxford, 1990).

Twining W, "Necessary But Dangerous? Generalizations and Narrative in Argumentation about 'Facts' in Criminal Process" in Malsch and Nijboer (1999) (reprinted as Chapter 11 in Twining (2006)).

Twining W, *Rethinking Evidence: Exploratory Essays* (2nd ed, Cambridge University Press, Cambridge, 2006).

Twining W, "Taking Facts Seriously – Again", Chapter 2 in Roberts and Redmayne (2007) (earlier versions of the paper were published in (2005) 55 *Journal of Legal Education* 360, and as Chapter 14 in Twining (2006)).

van Gelder T, "The rationale for Rationale™" (2007) 6 *Law, Probability and Risk* 23.

Verheij B, "Evaluating Arguments Based on Toulmin's Scheme" (2005) 19 *Argumentation* 347.

Vincent F, "Preparation of a Criminal Trial" in Eames G (ed), *Criminal Law Advocacy* (Legal Services Commission of South Australia, Adelaide, 1984).

Walton D, *Argument Structure: A Pragmatic Theory* (University of Toronto Press, Toronto, 1996) (1996a).

Walton D, *Argumentation Schemes for Presumptive Reasoning* (Erlbaum, Mahwah, New Jersey, 1996) (1996b).

Walton D, *Appeal to Expert Opinion: Arguments from Authority* (Pennsylvania State University Press, University Park, Pennsylvania, 1997).

Walton D, *Legal Argumentation and Evidence* (Pennsylvania State University Press, University Park, Pennsylvania, 2002).

Walton D, "Argument from Analogy in Legal Rhetoric" (2013) 21 *Artificial Intelligence and Law* 279.

Walton D, Reed C and Macagno F, *Argumentation Schemes* (Cambridge University Press, Cambridge, 2008).

Wigmore J, "The Problem of Proof" (1913) 8 *Illinois Law Review* 77.

Wigmore J, *The Science of Judicial Proof, as Given by Logic, Psychology, and General Experience and Illustrated in Judicial Trials* (3rd ed, Little, Brown, Boston, 1937).

Wigmore J, *Wigmore on Evidence* (Tillers revision, Little, Brown, Boston, 1983), Vols IA and II.

Index

Hearsay rule – *continued*
foundational facts, [8.50]
generalisations, [8.140]
implied assertions, [8.130]
overview, [8.120], [8.180]
rationale, [8.120]
state of mind, [8.140]
structure of hearsay, [8.120]
uniform evidence legislation, [8.120]

Imaginative reasoning *see* **Abduction**

Inferences
alternative explanations, [7.150],
　[7.160], [7.300]
charting, [7.210]
elimination, [7.190], [7.200], [7.230]
identification, [7.170]
missing evidence, [7.240]
negative evidence, [7.230]
substantiation, [7.180]
arguments about, [7.10], [7.160],
　[7.300]
alternative explanations,
　[7.170]-[7.210]
chains of inferences, [7.140], [7.150],
　[7.160]
kinds of arguments, [7.160]
chains of inferences, [6.170], [7.140],
　[7.150], [7.270]
alternative explanations, [7.150],
　[7.160], [7.170]-[7.210]
standard of proof, [7.280]
conjecture, distinction, [7.290], [7.300]
expert opinions, [7.130]
generalisations, [7.110], [7.170], [7.300]
alternative explanations, [7.210]
basis, [7.130]
charting, [7.120]
hearsay, [8.130], [8.140]
implied assertions, [8.130]
missing evidence, [7.240]
overview, [6.50], [6.170], [7.100],
　[8.130]
relevancy authorisation, [7.110]
res ipsa loquitur, [7.290]
standard of proof, [7.280], [7.290]
state of mind, [8.140]
warrants, [7.110]

Inferential force
overview, [7.270], [7.300]
probative value, [7.260], [7.300]

Interlocutory proceedings
chronologies, [2.110], [3.20], [3.110]

Interrogatories, [2.90], [2.100]

Investigation
abduction, [4.20], [4.30], [4.40],
　[4.50], [4.140]
marshalling, and, [4.60]
example of process, [4.50]
marshalling, and, [4.60], [4.140]
overview, [2.90], [4.10], [4.20], [5.10]
reference materials, [10.50]
retroduction, [4.20], [4.40], [4.50],
　[4.140]
summary of process, [4.40], [4.140]

Items of evidence
circumstantial evidence, [6.40]
direct evidence, [6.40], [6.150]
grouping, [6.40]
overview, [6.40], [6.90], [6.270]
sources of items, [6.90], [6.150]

Jones v Dunkel, rule in, [7.240]

Judicial warnings
corroboration, [8.90]

Law of evidence *see also* **Admissibility of evidence**
application, [2.140], [6.100], [7.10]
exclusionary rules, [6.100]
overview, [8.10]
uniform evidence legislation, [8.10]

Legal case *see also* **Factual theory**
alternative legal cases, [5.160]
defence theories, [5.40]
facts in issue, [5.30], [5.60], [5.200],
　[5.230], [5.250]
alternative elements, [5.210]
causation, [5.230]
defences, and, [5.40], [5.210],
　[6.70]
identification, [5.200], [6.20]
material facts, distinction, [5.220]
objects of proof, [5.230], [5.240],
　[5.250]

Witness statements
  case theories, [5.10]
  marshalling, [4.70], [4.80]
  overview, [4.80]

Witnesses *see also* **Hearsay rule**
  admissibility of evidence, [7.70]
  competence, [7.70]
  contradictory testimony, [6.130],
    [6.200]
  corroboration, [6.190], [6.200],
    [7.40]
  cross-examination, [5.20], [9.70]

  documentary evidence, [6.100]
  examination-in-chief, [9.60]
  expert witnesses *see* **Expert witnesses**
  failure to call, [7.240]
  marshalling, [4.80], [4.90]
  ordering, [9.30]
  planning cross-examination, [9.70]
  planning examination, [9.60]
  real evidence, [6.100]
  selection, [9.30]
  source of evidence, [7.30]